Body and Mind

Past, Present, and Future

Body and Mind
Past, Present, and Future

Edited by

R. W. RIEBER

John Jay College
City University of New York
New York, New York
and
College of Physicians and Surgeons
Columbia University
New York, New York

1980

ACADEMIC PRESS

A Subsidiary of Harcourt Brace Jovanovich, Publishers

New York   London   Toronto   Sydney   San Francisco

ACADEMIC PRESS, INC.
111 Fifth Avenue, New York, New York 10003

United Kingdom Edition published by
ACADEMIC PRESS, INC. (LONDON) LTD.
24/28 Oval Road, London NW1 7DX

Library of Congress Cataloging in Publication Data

Main entry under title:

Body and mind.

Includes bibliographies and index.
1. Mind and body. I. Rieber, Robert W.
BF161.B56   128'.2   79-6777
ISBN 0-12-588260-2

PRINTED IN THE UNITED STATES OF AMERICA

80 81 82 83   9 8 7 6 5 4 3 2 1

To Daniel and Ann

Contents

PART I
THE GROUNDWORK

Chapter 1

**Body–Mind Concepts in the Ancient Near East: A Comparison
of Egypt and Israel in the Second Millennium B.C.**   **3**

    L. D. HANKOFF

Chapter 6

Mind as Life and Form   131

MILDRED BAKAN

Chapter 7

Brain-Based Limitations on Mind   155

MARCEL KINSBOURNE

Chapter 8

Genetic Metaphysics: The Developmental Psychology of Mind–Body Concepts   177

JOHN M. BROUGHTON

Chapter 9

Contemporary Research and the Mind–Body Problem   **223**

HERBERT WEINER

Chapter 10

Mind and Body: A Dialogue   **241**

GREGORY BATESON AND ROBERT W. RIEBER

Appendix

The Allan McLane Hamilton Seminars   **253**

ERIC T. CARLSON AND JACQUES M. QUEN

List of Contributors

Numbers in parentheses indicate the pages on which the authors' contributions begin.

DAVID BAKAN (117), York University, Downsview, Ontario, M3J 1P3 Canada

MILDRED BAKAN (131), Division of Social Science and Department of Philosophy, York University, Downsview, Ontario, M3J 1P3 Canada

GREGORY BATESON (241), Esalen Institute, Big Sur, California 93920

JOHN M. BROUGHTON (177), Teachers College, Columbia University, New York, New York 10027

ERIC T. CARLSON (253), New York Hospital, Cornell University Medical Center, New York, New York 10021

HOWARD E. GRUBER (79), Institute for Cognitive Studies, Rutgers University, Newark, New Jersey 07102

L. D. HANKOFF (3), Department of Psychiatry, State University of New York at Stony Brook, Stony Brook, New York 11794

K. D. IRANI (57), Department of Philosophy, The City College, City University of New York, New York, New York 10031

MARCEL KINSBOURNE (155), Neuropsychology Research Unit, Hospital for Sick Children, Toronto, Ontario, M5G 1X8 Canada

JACQUES M. QUEN (253), New York Hospital, Cornell University Medical Center, New York, New York 10021

ROBERT W. RIEBER (241), John Jay College, City University of New York, New York, New York 10019; and College of Physicians and Surgeons, Columbia University, New York, New York 10032

HERBERT WEINER (223), Department of Psychiatry, Montefiore Hospital and Medical Center, Bronx, New York 10467

MARGARET D. WILSON (35), Department of Philosophy, Princeton University, Princeton, New Jersey 08540

Preface

The objective of this volume is to elucidate the relationship between the human body and mind. Each chapter approaches the subject from a different perspective: historical, philosophical, psychological, or biomedical. Each point of view is essential, although none is sufficient alone to explain adequately all aspects and issues elicited by a consideration of the relationship between body and mind.

L. D. Hankoff compares the concepts of mind, soul, and body in Egypt and Israel during the second millenium B.C., approaching history as a cyclic recurrence of standards and concepts through which modern man may study himself. Margaret Wilson discusses the historical roots of the Cartesian mind–body dualism in the context of pre- and post-Cartesian developments. In the third chapter, K. D. Irani deals with the conceptual problems contained in the body–mind relationship, centering his discussion on the logical positivism and behaviorism of the Vienna circle. Howard Gruber in Chapter 4 discusses Darwin's belief that the mind is a product of materialism and that consciousness is achieved only after the organization of bodily structure has been perfected. In the fifth chapter, David Bakan explores the intellectual territory of the effect of mind on matter and cogently argues his case for nonmaterial causation. Mildred Bakan draws upon Kant, Marx, and Hegel in the sixth chapter to develop a concept of mind as emergence of integrating orders that serve as forms or ends, organizing matter by unifying their constituent elements. In the next chapter, Marcel Kinsbourne's theme is the mind as an emergent property of the brain, which he examines through specific instances of damage to the physical brain and corresponding changes in mental states. John M. Broughton naturalizes the mind–body problem in the eighth chapter, converting it into a set of self-generating cognitive structures, where the present does not supplant the past, but develops it. The ninth chapter is a review by Herbert Weiner of recent research findings that deal with psychosomatic medicine, relating social experiences and/or psychological conflicts and induced emotions to the predisposition and initiation of changes in the structure and function of the body. The final chapter brings together many of the issues raised, in the form of a dialogue between Gregory Bateson and Robert W. Rieber.

I would like to take this opportunity to thank each of the authors for their contributions.

Body and Mind

Past, Present, and Future

PART I

THE GROUNDWORK

Chapter 1

Body-Mind Concepts in the Ancient Near East: A Comparison of Egypt and Israel in the Second Millennium B.C.

L. D. HANKOFF

Introduction

Around the year 1000 B.C. a young tribal leader named David, fearing the jealous and insane rage of his king, sought refuge with the enemy Philistines. Although fleeing for his life, this handsome, gifted youth entered the town of Gath and the king's court wearing the sword taken from a Philistine champion, Goliath, whose head he had recently cut off. The Philistines murmured for revenge against this swaggering youth, and David was desperate for survival. He feigned madness and with such successful and repulsive verisimilitude that the Philistiine king ordered him driven from the court (I Samuel 21:10–16).

This incident recounted in one of the oldest books of the Bible illustrates in six brief sentences ancient man's already fully developed grasp of the working of the mind. It portrays the meaning of losing one's mind, the stark difference between madness and sanity recognized by all, and the possibility that states of mind could be consciously simulated. It is important for us to note that it was written in authoritative form before the fall of Samaria in 722 B.C. in reference to the outstanding king of the Israelite monarchy who reigned about 1000 B.C. David's malingering was deliberate, his motive clearly demonstrated, and, as I have discussed elsewhere (Hankoff, 1975b), these few

3

BODY AND MIND
Past, Present, and Future

lines in the Book of Samuel imply a concept of mind in the ancient Israelite that would be understood by most modern men.

The relationship of body and mind has preoccupied philosophers and thinkers for many centuries. Regardless of the era, background, or need, the question of how the world of the mind and soul related to the world of matter and body has provided a fascinating area of inquiry. Schopenhauer, impressed with the extensions and ramifications of the problem, called it *Weltknoten* ("the world knot") (Schopenhauer, 1813/1974, p. 211). An inquiry into the question of the concept of body and mind in the ancient Near East will entangle us in its own particular knot, drawing together as it does the strands of so many different disciplines (anthropology, ethnology, archaeology, comparative religion, comparative psychology, etc.).

A few basic considerations are important in viewing the mental life of man in the ancient Near East. To begin with, the ancient cultures did not exist in isolation. There was a highly interrelated cultural mix between the three points of the triangle at the eastern end of the Mediterranean Sea, namely, Greece, Egypt, and Canaan. Linguistic and cultural features have been shown to be common to all three as well as linked to Mesopotamia. We find similar themes in the mythology and religion, for example, those demonstrated between the works of Homer and the Old Testament (Astour, 1967; Welles, 1955). The Ugaritic remains of Ras Shamra show elements in common with the other three cultures (Gordon, 1965, pp. 128–205). It is possible that these cultures might also have concepts of mind, soul, and body which were not developed in isolation and which have important similarities. The present study will not attempt a total view of the ancient concepts of body and mind but will be limited to a comparison of ancient Egypt and Israel only.

The medicine of the ancient Egyptians was fairly elaborate in its development by the time of the Old Kingdom, c. 3400–2490 B.C. (Ranke, 1933). The flowering of Hippocratic medicine in ancient Greece came much later, well into the first millennium (Edelstein, 1967), and its debt to Egyptian medicine is clearly demonstrable (Saunders, 1963). On the surface, the ancient Hebrews appear to have had a most rudimentary medicine and physiology. The Bible, which is our major source of information, presents meager clues as to the medical knowledge of the ancient Israelites. Investigation, however, suggests that Egyptian and Hebrew exchanges were common and that the references to physiology and medicine in the Bible are fragments of a rich heritage of Egyptian medicine which the Hebrews acquired, probably during their few hundred years stay in Egypt (Yahuda, 1947). For example, one of the 10 plagues befalling the Egyptians was a skin eruption or boils, in Hebrew *shechin* (Exodus 9:9). Reference to the same disease is to be found in Egyptian medical papyrus, with a nearly identical label. Anatomical terms were shared as in one of the two Egyptian words for heart, *chaaty*, which is reflected in the Hebrew for breast, *chaze*. Not only did the Hebrews acquire many of the significant elements of Egyptian medicine, but the Egyptians in turn appear to have borrowed from the Hebrew language in relation to medical subjects. For example, the Hebrew word for the madness feigned by David, *meshugga*, is borrowed by the Egyptians to designate imbecility or stupefaction. It is probable, therefore, that basic concepts of the body and its physiology were shared by the Egyptian and Hebrew cultures. A.S. Yahuda (1947) argues that Egyptian medicine conspicuously influenced the content of the Pentateuch in contrast to the total absence of any Mesopotamian medical influence.

The focus of the present study will be a comparison of the body–mind concepts in the cultures of ancient Egypt and Israel at the close of the second millennium B.C. I have chosen this point in time for several reasons. It is, to begin with, before the extraordinary changes in thought and culture which occurred throughout the known world and, as will be discussed, presented a basically different mentality. It is a time of two contrasting cultures which changed dramatically, the period before the final long decline of Egypt and the more dramatic Israelite catastrophes of the falls of Samaria, 722 B.C., and of Jerusalem, 587 B.C.

In a positive sense, the end of the second millennium B.C. allows for a valuable comparison of Egypt and Israel. The sojourn of the Hebrews in Egypt for some three centuries in the second millennium is well supported historically (Albright, 1957, p. 243; Montet, 1968; Petrie, 1931). It gave the two cultures an intimate exchange—the effects of which endured. The emerging Israelite nation and religion which followed the Exodus, c. 1280 B.C., and occupation of Palestine provides a vivid comparison with the established culture of ancient Egypt. By way of this contrast, I hope to demonstrate the main features of body–mind concepts in the ancient Near East of the second millennium B.C.

Cognitive Aspects

As mentioned, the historical era which is the focus of the present study may be set apart from that which follows in a fundamental way. The middle of the first millennium B.C., or more specifically the period between the eighth and fifth centuries, is marked by momentous cultural changes throughout the known world. It was the single extraordinary historical period which witnessed the thought of Confucius, Buddha, Zoroaster, and the Jewish prophets. It saw the emergence of classical Greece in an era characterized by Gouldner (1965, p. 79) as "the greatest social revolution that Europe has yet experienced." It has been labeled an "age of transcendence" (Schwartz, 1975), in which man in many different cultural settings (but not all) strained to look beyond his existing intellectual and spiritual vision. The burst of intellectual and cultural activity of Greece in the fifth century B.C., which led to a unified Greco-Roman world civilization, was marked also by the development of a formal logic which has characterized Western thought since that time (Albright, 1957, p. 121).

Albright (1957, pp. 122, 168, 176) has schematized the evolution of men-

tality in the Near East into three historical phases according to the predominant form of thought or cognitive functioning of the period: (1) a protological
stage of prehistoric man, ending around the third millennium B.C.; (2) a stage
of empirical logic of a prephilosophical nature, from 3000 to 500 B.C.; and (3)
the emergence of formal logic with the Greeks in the fifth century B.C. This
contrast of mentalities is pertinent to the present inquiry, since it is the concept of body and mind prior to "the age of transcendence" and the development of the formal logic of the Greeks which we wish to understand. It is the
second phase of empirical logic which encompasses our focus, the Egyptian
and Israelite mentalities of the second millennium B.C.

Nonliterate Mentality and Culture

In order to understand more clearly the mentality of the Near Eastern man
of the second millennium and his concept of body and mind, it is necessary to
give some consideration to the earlier phases of mental and cultural development and their residual influences in the phase which followed. It is generally
agreed that there is, apart from the mentality of modern literate societies, a
nonliterate or "primitive" mentality, whether existing in prehistoric man or in
modern day traditional or preliterate societies, which has its own distinctive
characteristics. The term "primitive" has been and continues to be used by
leading scholars (Eliade, 1965; Lévi-Strauss, 1967; Radin, 1957) to refer to ancient and modern cultures which do not share in the mainstream of literate urban society. There is, of course, full awareness in contemporary science that
the term need not be pejorative and that primitive cultures are neither
primitive nor illogical nor inferior in any consistent manner by comparison
with modern society. As an alternative to "primitive," the term "nonliterate"
has been selected for use in the present paper with the same full awareness of
the imperfection of any term for so complex a group.

The nonliterate mentality has been explained in a variety of formulations.
In 1922 Lévy-Bruhl (1922/1926) proposed "prelogical" thinking as a useful
descriptive label for a mentality which is neither antilogical nor alogical. The
formulations of Lévy-Bruhl acted as a focus for much activity in the field and
have since been the subject of considerable controversy and revision
(Albright, 1968, p. 223; Eliade, 1969, p. 189). Lévy-Bruhl's observations and
store of data remain, however, as invaluable foundations in the understanding of the nonliterate mentality, despite the fact that many criticized his term
"prelogical." Albright (1968, p. 26) acknowledges James Mark Baldwin as the
earliest to use the term "prelogical." Frankfort (1955) and others describe
"mythopoeic thinking," Schubert (1955, pp. 311–355) speaks of "mythological
thinking," Albright suggests "protological" in preference to "prelogical" (1968,
p. 27), and Lévi-Strauss (1966) speaks of "mythical thinking."

"Syncretic mental functioning," a term used by H. Werner (1957, p. 59),
refers to a lack of differentiation in perceptions and meanings, a limited
separation of object and subject, and a perceptual style of a motor-affective

type. Lévy-Bruhl described a "law of participation," according to which the primitive sees immediate connections between all of the representations in his mind. This "law" is a useful description of how, for example, the ancient Egyptians sculptured and substituted a statue for the dead king, relating to it fully as the king's actual being (Frankfort, 1955, pp. 194–162; Ranke, 1935).

Werner has described the "primitive world" as having a perceptual quality based on fused motor and affective elements, the perception being a "thing-of-action" or a "signal-thing." The highly developed sign language of the nonliterate epitomizes this fusion, since he actually uses his motor function to communicate percepts and meaning. The nonliterate's perception is physiognomic in quality, inanimate objects having for him expressive or affective qualities (Werner, 1957, p. 69). Werner makes an interesting distinction between physiognomic perception and the anthropomorphic concept of nature in nonliterate man. He sees the latter as based on the former. Furthermore, he sees the specific culture as determining "whether the original physiognomic experience of nature develops into a purely magical, or an animistic daemonic, or a religious-theistic view of the world" (Werner, 1957, p. 80). The world of the nonliterate is "near at hand" (p. 404); there is less distinction between subject and object than in the modern mind. The "nearness" of the nonliterate to the world around him applies as well to his gods and his dead ancestors. Thus, his descriptions of the world of the dead, the living, and the gods are identical. As will be discussed later in this chapter, the Egyptian concept of the afterlife was very much an extension of the earthly condition. In his thoughts the primitive exhibits this same syncretic style, fusing spatially or temporally related subjects into totalities. He utilizes holophrastic forms in communication, a single sign representing an entire group of related ideas (p. 275).

From an ethnological point of view, Ackerknecht (1971) has demonstrated that rational and supernatural elements are regularly combined in primitive medicine, an admixture which may appear to us as inconsistent and incongruous. The distinction between rational and supernatural, Ackerknecht (1971, p. 155) argues, does not exist in the primitive's mind. In terms of body and mind, for example, the primitive perceives and experiences no separate entities. Mental and physical functions are not distinct categories for him and are all attributed to a psychophysical unity. The working of this same type of unity may perhaps be seen in the use by the ancient Israelites of cleansing lustrations for various states of impurity or defilement. The lustrations used to dispel the impurity were a simultaneous physical and spiritual (mental) ritual cleansing (Kaufmann, 1966, p. 102).

The Second Millennium B.C.

Empiricological thought is that form of reasoning based on experience of a practical and logically implicit nature, without recourse to the formal syllogistic and explicit logic, that followed the intellectual advances of Greece in the fifth century B.C. Empirical thinking characterizes the everyday activity of modern man as well as ancient (Albright, 1968, p. 35). Like protological or mythopoeic thinking, empiricological thinking is as old as man (Albright, 1968, p. 28). The Near East in the third and second millennium B.C. witnessed great achievements under the influence of the empiricological mentality (Albright, 1964, pp. 30–53). Didactic literature, codified law, science, and monotheism flourished, some unsurpassed since this era. Albright (1968, pp. 31–33) cites Old Testament ethics and wisdom, for example, Proverbs and Job, as achievements of the empiricological world which are unrivaled by those of logical deduction. It is in the New Testament that logical deduction is found fused with protological and empiricological thinking. Protological thinking, however, operated to a considerable extent, particularly in the area of religion and belief systems.

Evidences of the persistence of protological thought abound in the Egyptian religion and its concept of body and mind. Accounts of the creation were numerous and conflicting. The fate of the dead, as will be discussed later, was described in half a dozen different forms. These ostensibly conflicting accounts stood side by side in the Egyptian consciousness, and their peaceful coexistence has been explained by Frankfort (1948, p. 4) as a mythopoeic attitude of a "multiplicity of approaches," in which all of the various formulations, for example, the afterlife, serve as partial and coexisting explanations which do justice to truly complex problems.

Nonspeculative Thinking

Pedersen (1926–1940, vol. 1, pp. 106, 128) has described the mentality of the ancient Israelite as devoid of theoretical, objective, or non-action-oriented thinking but rather involved in an immediate way with the rising thought, its action, and its accomplishment. Boman (1960, p. 27) describes Israelite thinking as "dynamic, vigorous, passionate," even explosive. The Old Testament contains neither a systematic theology nor the speculation or explicit logic which might be a basis for dogma or doctrine (Albright, 1957, p. 329; 1964, p. 84). This aspect of Israelite thinking resembles to some degree the processes of explanation in nonliterate thinking. The nonliterate does not search for or ruminate about causes. The nonliterate sees connections as existing between all of the parts of his perceived external reality.

Lévy-Bruhl (1922/1926, p. 76) has called this the "law of participation." The nonliterate perceives events and uses their temporal sequence as a *post hoc, ergo propter hoc* explanation (Lévy-Bruhl, 1922/1926, p. 73).

Similarly, the ancient Egyptians did not speculate about the basic origins and causes of events but viewed them often as completed realities. In the many conflicting and convoluted Egyptian myths of creation, original causes and contradictions were not questioned (Larue, 1975, p. 26). The Egyptians asked simply what occurred first, not how or where (Albright, 1957, p. 181).

It did not occur to the ancient Egyptians, for example, to inquire into the nature of their state and government. It was foreordained, complete, and provoked no curiosity. The quality of Egyptian thinking was traditionalistic, conservative, nonspeculative, and reflective of the stable culture and society of ancient Egypt (Fairservis, 1961; Frankfort, 1956; Frankfort, Frankfort, Wilson, Jacobsen, & Irwin, 1946).

Eliade's (1969, pp. 201–211) view of religious symbolism provides another insight into the same issue. Eliade has lucidly described the enormous meaningfulness of religious symbols, pointing out their transcending and unifying expression of human experience and the world condition. Religious symbolism in the "archaic levels of culture" (Eliade, 1969, p. 202) is in the nature of "pre-systematic thinking" (p. 122), not formulated conceptually and not always able to be translated into concepts.[1]

This lack of expression of theoretical or speculative thinking is not to be considered as a limitation on the ability to reason or use abstractions. Ancient man was quite capable of abstract thinking, and ethnographic studies have pointed up the complexity of cognition embedded in nonliterate folk cultures and language (Wallace, 1962). Language before 5000 B.C. among Near Eastern nations contains abstractions and generalizations (Albright, 1957, pp. 175–177), but what is not seen in second millennium writings are explicit logical speculations or philosophical abstractions.

Ancient Israelite Mentality

We must look to Israelite literature in order to grasp the Israelite view of body and mind. From an analysis of the Hebrew language from the Biblical and other early remains, one can infer certain formal aspects of the thinking of the ancient Israelite. Johnson (1964) characterizes ancient Israelite thinking as synthetic (as opposed to analytic) and in this respect similar to that of the nonliterate. Thought was oriented toward the grasping of totalities, phenomena being seen in terms of their relationships and their participation in wholes.[2] Body and mind could only be grasped as a unity (Johnson, 1964,

---

[1] In this same vein, the title of the present paper is anachronistic since the "body–mind concepts" of the ancient Near East that are being considered are our modern formulations built around the traces of ancient thought and bound by our concept of body–mind. In the views of Albright (1957, 1966, 1968) and Eliade (1969) no body–mind concept could have existed as such in the thinking of second millennium man.

[2] Boman (1960, pp. 202–203) has commented on Johnson's terminology. Boman states that Johnson's term "synthetic" might be used instead as "holistic" or "in totality," describing the characteristic Israelite grasping of phenomena or participating in a totality. Boman prefers to use the term "synthetic thinking" to describe that form of thinking which gathers together or arranges a set of points into a harmonious whole. Boman regards such synthetic thinking as characteristic of the ancient Greeks, while a contrasting mode of thinking which seeks to separate out and express the most essential aspect of a group of points is characteristic of Israelite thinking. This latter form of thinking Boman (1960, p. 203) prefers to designate as "analytic thinking."

pp. 1–4) and all of the individual's psychical and physical functions taken as a synthetic whole (Johnson, 1942, p. 5, 1964, p. 3).

A related characteristic of ancient Israelite thinking is seen in the basic grammatical form of the noun as a class term (Boman, 1960, p. 70) or collective (Pedersen, 1926–1940, vol. 1, p. 171). The orientation of the ancient Israelite was toward a general or denotational definition of a species or group, with the individual secondarily being regarded as a member of a group. The individual existed as part of a "corporate personality" (Robinson, 1925), which extended over his kinship relationships as well as over time into past and future generations. The simplest form of a noun in Hebrew was usually the collective form. The individual was designated by a modification of the simplest form, indicating that he had the characteristics of the group of which he was but one member (Pedersen, 1926–1940, vol. 1, p. 110). As will be seen the word for "soul" had a basically collective meaning.

The vividness of Old Testament language has often been noted. The perceptual orientation of the Israelite was in the outstanding characteristic of a situation or object (Pedersen, 1926–1940, vol. 1, p. 112), a quality similar to nonliterate perception in its sense of nearness and immediacy to the outer world and arresting participation.

The nature of an Israelite psychophysical unity may be further grasped from the relationship of thought and action in the Israelite mind. In Hebrew grammar, the particles or conjunctions serve to connect ideas or phrases rather than establish logical relationships, and subordinate conjunctions are nearly absent in biblical Hebrew. For example, the basic coordinate conjunction in biblical Hebrew is *vav*, meaning "and." It is, however, used with many nuances and has such various translations in the Authorized Version as "but," "therefore," "when," and "since." The more specific Hebrew particles equivalent to these words are in actuality used very little (Brown, Driver, & Briggs, 1972, pp. 251–255). Pedersen (1926–1940, vol. 1, p. 118) is of the opinion that the connections provide an instant fusion. The movement in an argument is toward the formation of a totality, and the particles are used simply to link together the ideas. In this respect it is significant that biblical Hebrew lacks a verb specifically meaning "to think." The word usually translated as "to think" (*choshev*) is, in Pederson's opinion (p. 127), more of the meaning of "to initiate, seek, or investigate." Thought in the mind of the Israelite was always linked to action. The mind does not think and then act, according to the Israelite, but does both in a single related process.

The nature of perception and image formation in the ancient Israelite is further illustrated in the apposition of a noun and its descriptive term in the present tense. There is no connecting present tense of the verb "to be," and the predicate is identical or of equal value with its subject, forming a noun clause (Boman, 1960, p. 35). Most primitive languages lack the verb "to be" (Lévy-Bruhl, 1922/1926, p. 148). Driver (1969, p. 247) has interpreted Hebrew usage as indicating that subject and predicate are taken together as a single concept.

For example, the sentence "the soul of all the flesh is the blood" (Leviticus 17:14) is understood to mean that blood and soul are identical and aspects of the same object. The verb "is" is necessary for a grammatical English translation but is not present in the Hebrew. Driver (1925) summarizes classical Hebrew writing as having the quality of a row of beads, a "speech strung together." As a correlate, language, thought, and image formation are undistinguished and complementary views of body and mind, a single psychophysical entity existing.

The Hebrew language use of tense is important in understanding ancient Israelite mentality. The Indo-Germanic time frame (past, present, future) differs basically from that found in the tense structure of Semitic languages. Tense in Hebrew verbs pertains more to the mood, aspect, or character of an action than to time (Boman, 1960, p. 144; Driver, 1969, p. 3). The Hebrew verb has only two forms: (a) that of an action completed, the perfect form, and (b) that of an action incipient or incomplete, the imperfect or subsequent form (Burney, 1919). Pedersen points out that the specific time of an action is relatively unimportant, but rather what is more important is whether the action is complete and independent of other activity as opposed to preparatory or supplementary, corresponding to the perfect and imperfect Hebrew verb forms, respectively (Pedersen, 1926–1940, vol. 1, p. 114). As we shall see, the soul in Israelite thinking was not bound by time but fitted to verb forms which conveyed only whether a matter was momentary or eternal (Driver, 1925, p. 120).

Philology

The historical phase of empiricological thinking yielded a distinguished didactic literature in the ancient Near East. Egyptian, Sumerian, and Hebrew texts all show impressive literary specimens which have left their mark on our language and thought to this day and can still be read with enjoyment. These writings are our basic source of direct material for analyzing the implicit concept of body and mind of ancient man. The known terminology in the extant Egyptian literature and the Old Testament will be briefly compared in relation to the body–mind concept.

Egyptian Terminology

The highly developed medical and embalming practices of ancient Egypt would be expected to yield a rich vocabulary of anatomical terms. The existence of Egyptian words for the brain is itself significant, since none exists in biblical Hebrew. There were two possible terms for brain, and both suggest the more general meaning of viscus, or internal, organ joined with a term for head (Iversen, 1947). The earliest reference to the brain subserving neurophysiological function may be that of a case in the Edwin Smith papyrus, c. 1600 B.C., describing a head injury with contralateral paralysis (Laver, 1972). The brain was removed in the more elaborate mummifications, a scoop being inserted via the nostril puncturing the ethmoid sinus. The removed material was not regarded with any particular reverence and perhaps even discarded.

The Egyptian words for the heart, as well as the Hebrew, appear to have been used in the sense of a seat of emotional and mental activity. This usage appears repeatedly through every era of Egyptian history, beginning with the most ancient Egyptian religious work, the great Memphite theology traceable to the First Dynasty, c. 3100 B.C. (Frankfort, 1955, pp. 24, 352; Pritchard, 1955, pp. 4-5). Here one reads that Ptah, the creator, brought into being all of the gods, the universe, and its contents by the action of his heart and tongue, that is, his thought and words. In a work attributed to the reign of King Sesostris, c. 1900 B.C., an individual asks his heart for guidance and support in his time of suffering, much as one addresses a dutiful servant or true friend (Erman, 1927, pp. 108-110).

Breasted (1933, p. 41) has described an evolution in the meaning of "heart" in Egyptian awareness. He views the earliest usages, such as in the Memphite theology, as the most abstract, "heart" originally meaning "intelligence" or "understanding." The further development of "moral discernment" in Egyptian history, according to Breasted, is seen in the Pyramid Age, approximately the Third Dynasty, c. 2600 B.C., with the emergence of a sense of righteousness, justice, and truth, personified in the Egyptian god Ma'at. The disorder and decline of the First Intermediate Period (c. 2181-2040 B.C.) (Breasted, 1959, p. 165) and the subsequent emergence of the Empire, c. 1600 B.C., evolved a new sense of heart as "conscience" along with the older meaning of "understanding" (p. 253). Breasted's view is not accepted uncritically, and Frankfort (1948, p. 73) has described the Egyptians as having little or no concept of sin upon which to develop a conscience. The ancient Egyptian simply regarded the man who fails to live by Ma'at as a fool or an aberration rather than a sinner.

The manner in which the heart was handled after death is highly significant in terms of the body-mind view of the ancient Egyptian. Convinced as he was of the afterlife and continuity of the nonanatomical aspects of man after death, the ancient Egyptian could not conceive of such a continuity without its physical substratum (Frankfort, 1948, p. 93). From this certainty regarding continuation of an existence after bodily death came the elaborate practices of mummification and entombment and the various funerary practices. In preparing the body for embalming, the abdomen was slit open and the viscera removed except for the kidneys and heart (Diodorus, 1962, vol. 1, p. 311). By contrast, the brain as we have seen was extracted and discarded or handled most casually.

The afterworld existence of the deceased had much to do with the condition of his heart. In the great judgment ceremony, the heart was weighed against the feather of truth. The ancient Egyptian viewed the heart whether in life or death as the embodiment of intelligence and psychic functioning. The continued good condition of this heart was therefore central in relation to the dead individual. The deceased needed his heart to be restored to its former powers in order to function properly and have all of the intellectual faculties which were housed in the heart (Laver, 1972; Zandee, 1960, p. 63). Spells for the enlivening of the heart were necessary along with mummification for its physical preservation. The concern with the physical remains was apparently greater than for the spiritual or what we might regard as the psychical aspects of the individual. Thus, while the nonanatomical parts of the individual, the Ba and the Ka, might be maintained in other ways, the heart, a palpable and enduring evidence of the individual, required very direct attention.

The Ka is an entity which is central to the ancient Egyptian view of body and mind and perhaps the most difficult to comprehend in modern terms. The Ka was conceived of as a guiding or protecting genius of the individual that lived the life of the individual as an invisible duplicate (Frankfort, 1955, pp. 61–78). At death the Ka went to the hereafter to act as a protector and provider for the deceased. The Ka spoke to the gods on behalf of the newly dead, obtained food, and joined him in eating. While originally the Ka was the possession of a king, in later times everyone was thought to have a Ka (Breasted, 1959, p. 55). In life the Ka was of such a nature that it could not be seen by ordinary people, but only particular classes of priests or seers with special gifts were able to see these doubles (Frazer, 1951, vol. 3, p. 29).

In the Temple of Luxor, the Ka is depicted at the birth of King Amenophis Ill as one of the two newborn children, one being the newly born king and the other his Ka (Breasted, 1959, p. 52; Frazer, 1951, vol. 3, p. 28). The theme of a double or a twin of a god or mortal is a common one in folklore and mythology. The Egyptian gods for the Sun and the Moon were addressed as twins, Re and Thoth. Furthermore, the Egyptian moon-god, Khons, had the epithet "placenta of the king" (Van Der Leeuw, 1918). Thus, the king and his placenta mirrored the twin gods in the sky. Frazer (1951, vol. 1, p. 195, vol. 11, p. 162) gives considerable evidence for the belief, in the vitality of the afterbirth or placenta. Among the traditional societies in which the afterbirth is identified as a double or twin of the child are the Baganda of Central Africa, the natives of Southern Celebes (vol. 1, p. 189), the natives of Timor (vol. 1, p. 190), the Balinese (vol. 1, p. 191), the Aborigines of Queensland, the Kooboos (vol. 13, p. 55) and Battas of Sumatra, and the Icelandic Norseman (vol. 1, p. 200). The afterbirth provides us with a remarkable model for an external soul, since it is attached to the individual and appears as a material substance at a vital time in his existence. It is understandable, as Frazer has explained, that the afterbirth provides a physical basis for the beliefs in relation to the primitive idea of an external soul. It is consistent also with the protological belief among the ancient peoples that anything connected with an individual might contain his vital spirit. The likelihood that the relationship of the *Ka* to the placenta was more than a casual or forgotten mythological one is demonstrated by the fact that the navel cord of the king was preserved in a symbolic decorative container and appears in many artistic representations in ancient Egypt (Seligman & Murray, 1911). The container of the naval cord had a distinctive shape, an inverted cone attached to an elaborate handle, and occupied a position in various pictures immediately in front of the Pharoah. It is to be found in pictures of the First Dynasty King Narmer and Fifth Dynasty King Neuserre, Old Kingdom rulers, 3100–2340 B.C. It continues to appear on royal monuments until the end of ancient Egyptian history (Frankfort, 1948, p. 71). The cult of the royal placenta is also to be found among Ugandan and Bagandan African tribes, who may have derived their belief from the Egyptians or a source common to all (Frankfort, 1955, pp. 70–71).

The widespread significance of a human being's symbolic double in primitive folklore may be related to the mythology of dioscurism, the association of twin gods or brothers with the healing arts. The physicians of the gods in Vedic medicine were the Ashvins, twin brothers riding chariots in the sky and announcing dawn and twilight (Hankoff, 1977). The Greek Dioscuri were healers as were their successors, the medieval saints, Comas and Damian, famous for their miraculous amputation and transplant of a leg. As noted, Egyptian belief had made a connection of the placenta and the newborn with the twin gods representing the sun and moon. The placenta is obviously a link to the health of man and may well be the common symbol of birth and nature's great twins—the sun, with its healing qualities, and the moon, with its rhythmical life pulse.

The Egyptian *Ba*, or *Bi*, is usually translated in the literature as the "soul" or "self" and depicted in art as a falcon or storklike bird with a human head (Cooney, 1968). Later representations, the Middle Kingdom portrayals, are more stylized and decorative than the earlier. The *Ba* found its most important role serving the individual in death. The *Ba* is pictured as fluttering about the tomb and via a special shaft was enabled to pass upward to the sunlight and make contact with the outside world (Frankfort, 1955).

The *Ba* of the living in the Egyptian literary portrayals is a kind of reflective ego or voice for mental and spiritual matters. By contrast, the *Ka* was a vital spirit or force which guided and protected the individual and was his invisible duplicate. In the famous dialogue of the man weary with life, the *Ba* appears as a spiritual or mental "self" in conversation with his conscious personality (Faulkner, 1956; Goedicke, 1970). The resemblance of the ancient *Ba* to the much later Greek winged representation of Psyche, or the soul, is apparent. There is no evidence, however, that their meaning in the two cultures was analogous. The *Ba* in ancient Egypt did not represent an abstract or personified psyche or soul. On the other hand, Cooney has suggested that the *Ba* being a funerary adornment may have become the basis for the winged sirens depicted in Greek art of the sixth and fifth centuries B.C.

An individual's name, *ren* in Egyptian, was associated with considerable magical significance as an extension of its bearer, a source of his power, and a possible route to the inner being. There is no evidence, however, that the magical powers of an individual's name involved a conception of the name as a functional unit or specific incorporeal aspect of body or mind. As will be discussed further, almost every aspect of the individual which could be concretized or represented served as an extension or surrogate of the dead person. As such, the name engraved on a statue or tomb was viewed as a very real part of the dead person and participant in all of his needs and procedures.

Israelite Terminology

The Old Testament is, of course, our richest source of references and the most minutely studied for Hebrew terms referring to mental, emotional, and psychical matters. While providing us with an extraordinary verbatim record going back to 1000 B.C. and with oral traditions from much before, the Old Testament must be clearly viewed in context. As the reflection of the development of a nation and a religion, it is not a systematic theology (*Encyclopaedia Judaica*, 1973, vol. 4, p. 429, vol. 15, p. 1103). The old Testament does not provide a total explicit statement of the religion of the ancient Israelites nor does it systematically eradicate all archaic elements of nonmonotheistic periods.

By far the most important and significant Hebrew word in the present inquiry is *nefesh*. *Nefesh* occurs 754 times in the Old Testament, is usually translated as "soul," and has three main usages: (*a*) Most commonly it indicates the vital or life principle, that is, the existence of the quality of life in an individual. (*b*) A second usage corresponds approximately to our "psyche" or "mind" and touches a variety of emotional and cognitive functions. (*c*) Another major usage of *nefesh* is as a linguistic form to indicate the self or to function as a personal pronoun; this usage accounts for about one-third of the 754 Old Testament occurrences (Briggs, 1897b; Johnson, 1942; Murtonen, 1958). *Nefesh* is almost always used to refer to the soul or psyche of man, with a very small number of the usages referring to animals (32 times = 5%) or to God (21 times = 3%).

The etymology of *nefesh* has been much discussed and debated. While formerly considered to have its origin in a verbal root, such as to rest, pant, or breathe, recent thinking has related it to nonverbal forms, such as bodily parts, for example the Akkadian "throat" or "neck" or the Ugaritic "appetite." Murtonen (1958) notes that all the Semitic languages contain the word *nefesh* and invariably with a meaning of "soul" or "vital principal." He concludes that it is a very old word and of a substantive rather than verbal origin. The etymology of the word in no way suggests a "mysterious potency" but rather points to a bodily site where the action of the being is concentrated.

The original Old Testament usage of *nefesh* is characteristically collective and signifies a comprehensive and unified manifestation of man as a psychophysical totality. In the collective sense of the word, the soul is common to the group and not sharply delimited in terms of space or time. A soul may be united or expanded with other souls (Pedersen, 1926–1940, vol. 1, p. 164). The soul may extend back in time to other members of the family. This collective sense of nefesh occurs clearly in 180 out of the 754 Old Testament usages.

Murtonen (1958) argues that this collective sense gives way in later books of the Old Testament. The plural form of the word which indicates a more individualistic concept, occurs altogether only 50 times and usually in the later writings. Its earliest appearance is in Jeremiah 24:19 and Ezekiel 13:18. The use of a plural form of the noun points to individuals acting as individuals and not in the prelogical corporate or collective sense. The more archaic collective concept of the soul embodied a "mental functional community" (Brown et al., 1972, pp. 523–524; Cohen, 1967). When the members of such a community followed their leader and worked together in orderly fashion, the collective soul experienced peace and harmony.

The vital unity of nefesh is illustrated by a contrast with the familiar Old Testament term "son of man." The parallel expression "son of a soul" does not exist in the Old Testament, such a fractionating of the psychophysical unity of man being incomprehensible to the Old Testament author.

The Hebrew words for heart, laev and laevav, occur 850 times in the Old Testament. The origin is obscure and has been related to an Assyrian root meaning an organ of activity and life (Cohen, 1967). There is no essential difference between the two forms laev or laevav, although laev occurs more frequently in the earlier books of the Old Testament (Briggs, 1897a). The usual sense of laev and laevav is a seat of emotion, will, or self; the word never occurs in a purely anatomical sense. When used abstractly 166 times for emotions, the term covers the widest range of emotions. The only usage of laev or laevav other than a psychological one is the occasional meaning of "in the midst of." The psychological meaning of laev and laevav is considerably broader than the English "heart" and includes the sense of an instrument of the entire intellectual and affective functions.

"Heart" is always used in Old Testament Hebrew in the abstract sense of a psychical function, yet it clearly retains its anatomical identification for metaphorical purposes. In contrast to nefesh, laev and laevav occur with a wide number of adjectives exploiting the sense of an organ of the body serving the mind. Thus, we have the vivid expressions for the vicissitudes of the heart familiar in English, for example, the hard heart (Exodus 4:21), the stolen heart (Genesis 31:26), the broken heart (Psalms 34:19), the clean heart (Psalms 51:12), the stone heart (Ezekiel 11:19), the melting heart (Deuteronomy 20:8). The use of the physical properties of the anatomical organ points up the concepts of psychophysical unity basic to the ancient Israelite view of man. The heart in its state of constant agitation in the living was the ideal representation of man as a vital unit (Cohen, 1967).

A particularly interesting use of *laev* is the occurrence four times of the meaning of a "new heart" in relation to a powerful emotional and spiritual experience. In connection with this usage, Albright (1968, p. 24) notes that Hebrew writings provide the first mention in history of religious conversion. Furthermore, the personal crisis or transforming experience is an aspect of the consciousness of most Old Testament prophets. Might this signal the emergence of the personal crisis as a mode of personal experience in the context of a changing mentality?

The word *ruach* meaning "wind" or "breath" occurs 378 times in the Old Testament. The origin of the word is traced to the Akkadian meaning "to be wide" and is related to the Arabic terms for "wind" (Johnson, 1964, p. 23). The literal meaning of "wind" accounts for about one-third of the usages of the word *ruach*. A second usage of *ruach* is in reference to a spirit or perhaps inspiration coming from God. Robinson gives 134 such usages, although other authorities have a lesser number (Brown *et al.*, 1972, pp. 924–926). A third meaning, closely related to the second, is that of an indwelling principle of life derived from God. The postexilic writings of the Old Testament contain a fourth usage which occurs 74 times, that of human temper or mental qualities, resembling very much the other important terms for mental functions, *nefesh* and *laev* or *laevav*. This fourth usage points to an evolving or emerging meaning of the word.

It is important to note that *ruach* in all of its usages supports the concept of psychophysical unity and is never used as spiritual reality apart from the rest of man.

A fourth expression related to the mind or soul is *neshama*. It occurs but 26 times in the Old Testament. Mitchell (1961) has demonstrated that 18 of these have a fairly specific meaning in terms of the breath of life imparted by God to man and making him unique from animals. The first usage of *neshama* is the vivid creation account: "and breathed into his nostrils the *neshama* of life and the man was a living soul" (Genesis 2:7).

A possible relationship to the concept of *neshama* as the vitalizing breath of God entering the nostrils may be found in a description of anatomy in the Papyrus Ebers, c. 2200–1800 B.C., where the right ear is described as containing the vessel into which the breath of life enters (Ebbell, 1937). Another Egyptian reference of possible relevance is the extraordinary ritual of "opening the mouth" at the climax of a lengthy mystery play of royal succession in which the dead king's mummy or statue was ritually fed and prepared for an active existence in the afterlife (Frankfort, 1948, p. 93, 1955, pp. 112, 134, 377).

The word for blood, *dahm*, occurs frequently in the Old Testament, being used in an anatomical as well as symbolic sense of lifeblood or life element. Blood as the vital substance that carried with it the life of man or animal as it gushed out of the wound was considered the ultimate life humor. The blood of both man and animals was regarded as containing the soul and in both re-

quired respect. Laws were specific regarding the spilling of both human and animal blood. The ancient practices of drinking or eating blood were vigorously prohibited (Smith, 1956). The blood was treated as a taboo object, hedged about with ritual, and capable of producing both ritual uncleaness and a state of special grace. The careful avoidance of the consuming of blood affirmed the biblical belief that the life principle came from the Creator and was not to be taken from another by man.

The unity of body and soul in the Israelite is demonstrated in the manner in which blood was regarded. The flowing out of blood and the concomitant physical ebbing of life resembles very much the metaphoric usages of *nefesh* (soul) and *laev* (heart). Thus, the heart is described as cold or passing away in a state of weakness (Pedersen, 1926–1940, vol. 1, p. 150); the soul is emptied out in the individual who is miserable (Johnson, 1964, p. 9; Pedersen, 1926–1940, vol. 1, p. 149).

Psychophysical Unity

Is it possible to derive an organized concept of the mind or psyche from these various terms? The various combinations of *nefesh, ruach,* and *laev,* their interchangeability, and the Old Testament totalistic view of man indicate that we are dealing not with structures or organisms but rather with aspects of a psychophysical unity (Johnson, 1964).

While these psychical terms are used in contradistinction to terms for such physical portions of the body as blood, flesh, or bones, the distinctions are functional ones and in no way point to separate existences. Terms for blood or flesh are used to refer to the individual in his weaker, more vulnerable, or temporal qualities as opposed to the vital and potentially powerful aspect of the individual in his *nefesh, ruach,* or *laev.* As an aspect of the living, the soul experiences changing vitality and extent. The soul, usually *nefesh,* is described as drained away or poured out at certain times and at other times strengthened, but it never exists beyond the corporeal existence of the individual and leaves with life.

The totalistic approach to the individual is seen in the usage of *nefesh.* While referring to the vital or life principle of man, it also frequently refers to an individual proper; the Israelites in a group are spoken of as a number of souls, using *nefesh* in the sense of an individual. Thus, *nefesh* did not separate body from mind; in other words, "man does not have a soul, he is a soul" (Pedersen, 1926–1940, vol. 1, p. 99).

C. A. Van Peursen (1966) has argued that the body–mind concept of the ancient Hebrew corresponded with the primitive and archaic view, a prephilosophical one, of psychophysical unity. There is, however, a very significant area of difference, namely, the lack of the belief by the ancient Israelite in an external soul. The belief of many nonliterates very clearly envi-

sioned an external soul capable of a separate existence and vicissitudes apart from the body and the individual. Whereas an afterlife of the soul was a commonly accepted belief of the nonliterate, in the view of the ancient Israelite, no such separation was conceivable and a dead soul could not exist (Murtonen, 1958).

Anatomical Terms

The various parts of the body were used in the poetic and metaphorical language of the Bible to express the emotions commonly associated with these parts of the body. Anatomical terms are frequent in biblical Hebrew and are of a very ancient origin, as indicated by the fact that they are usually formed from two rather than three consonants, the later form of Hebrew roots. There are Hebrew names for all of the external bodily parts as well as for most internal organs. There is no biblical term for brain.

The word for hand was used widely to indicate the power and activity which is demonstrated or portrayed by the hand. The hand symbolized strength or, when outstretched in blessing, benevolence. The word for arm was similarly used as symbolic of strength; nostril, as an expression of anger; forehead, for obstinacy; belly, for greed.

Some terms provide interesting insights into the associations of the ancient Israelite. The term for mercy or compassion, *rachamim*, is derived from the word for womb, *rechem*. The association appears to be one of maternal feelings in relation to the womb. Another interpretation is that compassion is the brotherly feelings of those born from the same womb (Brown *et al.*, 1972, p. 933). The word for stupidity, *kasal*, is derived from the word for loins, *kasalim* (Brown *et al.*, 1972, p. 492).

A distinction in the terminology for concepts of body and soul in ancient Hebrew may be made between the inner and outer parts. The deeper bodily parts or processes are used to refer to the soul or mental life. This includes the various terms for breath, heart, blood, liver, and bowels. On the other hand, the bodily parts pertaining to the outside, such as flesh, are used to designate the body proper in contrast to the soul.

These various derived terms for emotional aspects of the individual's functioning as well as the range of terms pertaining to soul do not suggest a division of the individual into a mental and physical reality but rather serve as designations for various functions of the psychophysical unity.

Indeed the existence of these specific terms and elaborated concepts pertaining to emotional functioning supports our view of the ancient Israelite as possessing a unified concept of the individual. The ancient Israelites possessed the awareness of a highly literate people regarding emotional functioning and utilized it freely in their language and metaphor. Nowhere do we find the concept of the external soul or a body without a soul after death.

Belief Systems

The third area in relation to the body–mind concept of the ancient Egyptians and Israelites is that of their systems of belief and religion. My inquiry into the mentality of the two peoples and the specific language usages for body and mind has brought us repeatedly to matters of belief. It is apparent that the three areas are complementary in the total understanding of the body–mind concept. In turning now to belief systems, I will necessarily limit myself to areas of particular relevance to body–mind concepts: (a) mythology and personification; (b) death and afterlife beliefs; (c) creation beliefs; and (d) representational aspects.

Paganism and the Bible

The biblical attitude toward pagan mythology helps to explain the divergence of Israelite and Egyptian views of body and mind. In general, the Bible minimizes mythological themes and makes no references to natural qualities of the polytheistic gods (Encyclopaedia Judaica, 1973, vol. 4, p. 430; Kaufmann, 1966, pp. 7–127). The God of Israel is never pictured in battle with foreign gods (Kaufmann, 1966, p. 62). There are, however, numerous references to idols, a biblical preoccupation which might very well be misinterpreted as a concern with other gods. The idols of the Canaanites and Egyptians were not neutral objects for the Hebrews. They were a source of impurity and, more important, were associated in the popular mind with magic and sorcery. Thus, while the Bible does not view idols as representations of gods, it does attribute to them occult powers and potential dangers.

The biblical conception of ancient polytheism was simply the worship of idols and other inanimate objects. The Pentateuch viewed paganism as mere fetishism (Kaufmann, 1966, p. 17), hence the prohibition on image making is among the most basic of laws. The biblical commandment is explicit in referring to the actual making of the idol (pesel) or the likeness (tmunah) as the forbidden acts (Exodus 20:4, Deuteronomy 5:8). It is likely that the Israelite prohibition on graven images extended to Egyptian hieroglyphics. The law would have served to separate the Israelites in both religious practices and style of thinking from the people surrounding them. This nongraphic, nonrepresentational approach is bound to have had great impact on Israelite mentality, reducing the scope of protological thinking which was stimulated by idol making and the worship of replicated objects.

The obliviousness to mythology of the Israelite Bible has other implications for the concept of mind and soul. In particular, ideas about an external soul and concretized external influences on mental functioning were facilitated by paganism and inhibited by Israelite attitudes and biblical law.

Kaufmann (1966, p. 21) has formulated the basic difference between the biblical view of God and the pagan view of gods. Paganism was, in essence, a two-tier system of divine forces, maintaining a basic belief that a divine realm exists outside of, and prior to, the more familiar pagan pantheon. Paganism accepted a transcendent order or realm above the pantheon. It saw its gods as limited by universal laws of a transcending primordial or what Kaufmann (1966, p. 23) has termed "metadivine" realm. The gods of the pagans are decidedly constrained and have emotional and physical needs, sexual differentiation, and an interdependence with their human worshippers. Pagan magic, and therefore pagan idols, was directed at the transcendent realm which superceded the pantheon.

The existence of a primordial realm and a pantheon of derived divine beings sets the stage for the elaboration of paganism. The dramatic presentations in primitive religious festivals, initiatory rituals (Eliade, 1965), and such rites of kingly succession as the Egyptian rite after the death of the Pharoah (Frankfort, 1948, p. 134) are enactments of the history of the gods and their cosmos. The Egyptians regarded the history of the gods as the only important history and that of human events as inconsequential. History for the Egyptians was a fixed matter, all important events being part of a preordained order (Fairservis, 1961; Frankfort, 1956, p. 91). The universe for the Egyptian was created in a complete, permanent form. Historical events and accidents were trivial matters in the face of the permanence and absolutely predictable rhythm of nature as witnessed by the yearly cycle of the Nile (Frankfort, 1948, p. 88, 1955, pp. 4–5). The ahistorical view of the ancient Egyptian facilitated a view of man's soul and body existing eternally, since the noncorporeal aspects of man were similarly part of the eternal reality of the metadivine.

By contrast, the Bible recognizes no evolution of its God or primordial realm. No events precede biblical creation. The history which is detailed in the Bible and that pertaining to the festivals is not the history of a god or cosmos but rather of a tribe or people in relation to their God. The orientation to mythology is thus inseparable from the ancient Israelite's evolving view of (a) the reality of human history and (b) the inevitability of change in the life of man, both psychical and physical portions.

Mythological Personification

Ancient man's attitude toward his emotional life and his means of communicating about it are reflected in his mythological personifications pertaining to psychological functions. For example, the personified figure of death or god of the afterlife is prominent in the mythology of Egypt (Anubis), Phoenicia (Met), and, of course, classical mythology. In the Memphite theology are found justice personified in the divine form of Ma'at; authoritative utterance, as Hu; and understanding, as Sia (Frankfort, 1955, pp. 51–362). The elimination or nearly total expurgation of all mythological figures in the Old Testament included such personifications.

An interesting and unresolved question is how an emotion became personified in mythology. Was it preceded by an abstraction? Does it represent an earlier or later development in relation to an understanding of emotion? Dietrich (1967, pp. 358–360) speculates that personification in Greek mythology stemmed from an early belief in animalistic or demonic existences. Subsequently personality and emotional qualities of humans were attributed to demonic forces. Still later demons were seen as the actual actors in relation to human events (Dietrich, 1967, p. 358). Some earlier personifications of abstract qualities, were absorbed into personal gods of broader powers and representation; for example, Hygieia (goddess of health) was absorbed into Apollo. The deities in later times absorbed a number of specific qualities, which appeared as their various epithets.

Roman religion shows a late proliferation of mythological personification in the post-Augustan period. The process is not dependent on protological mental processes but occurred in a polytheism with its habitual use of representational forms despite advancing logical mentality and monotheistic concepts (Hastings, 1955, vol. 9, pp. 781–803). It is likely that no simple progression occurred but rather a cyclical process related to such factors as advances and declines in general social conditions.

Personifications may assist the culture and the individual in defining or delineating emotions and motivations. It is, however, a concrete and externalizing approach to psychological truths. The Israelite's rejection of mythology and its representations may have led him to a more conceptual and metaphorical approach. The ancient Israelite may have, in the absence of such personifications, turned to a more consciously descriptive approach to his emotional life and toward an awareness of the emotional content of his experiences without benefit of retreat or detour into mythology and externalization.

In summary, from the psychological point of view, the development of biblical monotheism had intense repercussions on Israelite mentality; the meaningfulness of everyday events as history, the finite limitations of the soul and body, the denial of ritual dramatizations and all forms of graphic and plastic representational art, and an increased awareness of one's own emotional reactions were all concomitants of the Israelite acceptance of the pentateuchal law and history.

Egyptian Death Beliefs

The beliefs of the Egyptians, Israelites, and Mesopotamians are distinctly different with regard to death and afterlife. As is well known, the Egyptians had a highly specific and detailed understanding of the afterworld and its occupants, a preoccupation which was the greatest of any ancient people (Albright, 1957, p. 181; Breasted, 1933, p. 45). By contrast, for the Mesopotamian death was final and hateful, and the existence of an afterlife in their thinking and mythology was vague (Frankfort *et al.*, 1946, p. 208).

The Egyptian view of life and death was rooted in an absolute belief in the eternal coexistence of living, dead, and divine beings. The archaeological evidence for this firm belief is to be found in the earliest Egyptian dynasty remains and in earlier remains (Emery, 1961, pp. 128–164). Suicide was probably accepted with much the same attitude toward the afterlife existence (Hankoff, 1975a). The calm, unswerving belief of the ancient Egyptian in an external existence of one form or another is understandable as the natural extension of his basic attitude toward the preordained, ahistorical universe, as discussed earlier.

The Egyptian conception of psychophysical unity buttressed the belief in an eternal existence. Since body and soul were an indissoluble unit, any temporary lack of vitality in the corporeal portion seen in death needed only be remedied to keep pace with the incorporeal portions. With total commitment to this belief, they pursued the preservation of the earthly remains and arranged matters properly for the afterlife.

Care of the dead. From the knowledge of their own divinely ordained permanency, the Egyptians elaborated and evolved their religious beliefs concerning the afterlife with interest, exactitude, and even exuberance. In the earliest period of Egyptian history, the Archaic Period (First and Second Dynasties, fourth millennium B.C.), there are to be found elaborate burial structures as well as beginning attempts at maintaining the dead body with preservatives and wrappings (Emery, 1961, pp. 128–164). The physical attention to the dead reached its fullest complexity and elaboration during the second millennium B.C.

The body itself was prepared for the afterworld through mummification. The very dry climate favored and even may have initiated these efforts, since bodies in graves often remained undecayed for very long periods (Breasted, 1933, p. 45). Most of the population aspired to some form of preservation, the kings, of course, receiving the most elaborate preparation. The desired end was a body which would be received into the afterworld, found spiritually acceptable, and then systematically restored to full intellectual, sensorial, and physiological functioning (Zandee, 1960).

Embalming and funerals were religious practices carried out under the aegis of the priesthood. A body discovered unclaimed in the open was the particular concern of the priest and received full burial care (Herodotus, 1966, vol. 1, p. 375). The Egyptian fervor for preserving the remains extended even to their animals, the remains of hundreds of embalmed crocodiles, cats, dogs, and other animals being found in the cemeteries.

The tomb and its contents were designed to provide the dead with an abode and the support for a full and happy afterlife existence. The ancient pyramids were made of smoothly polished and fitted stones, built to last forever in a static world, and symbolized the primeval hill created when the first mount of mud was raised by the gods from watery chaos (Frankfort, 1948, p. 156) as

well as a ladder to the Sun god (Breasted, 1959, p. 153). The contents of the
tomb included replicas of objects and people to serve the deceased in the afterworld; the Egyptian assumed that replicas of objects would serve the world of
the dead through their nonmaterial counterparts.

Portrait statues of deceased kings and commoners were placed in their
tombs beginning in the Third Dynasty, 2780 B.C., down to the Christian Era.
It is noteworthy that this practice originated nowhere else in the ancient world
(Ranke, 1935). These statues were treated as if they were the dead themselves
and referred to as the "new dwelling place" or "body of the *Ka*."

Written and decorative works directly applied to the tombs and coffins
were of great importance. The Pyramid Texts, dating between 2400 and 2200
B.C., covered the interior chambers of the pyramids with carvings and paint-
ings and are the longest and oldest known religious texts (Albright, 1957, p.
160; Breasted, 1959, pp. 84–93). These were succeeded by the Coffin Texts of
the Middle Empire (c. 2000–1780 B.C.) and later by mortuary papyri and the
Book of the Dead through the remainder of the second millennium (Albright,
1957, p. 225). These various writings, which were not expected to be seen by
the living, bear further testimony to the Egyptian certainty of the active state
of the dead. Letters written to the dead by relatives attest to the same conviction (Frankfort, 1955, p. 362). Such letters, which usually express affection,
may ask the dead one to intervene with another dead one who is troubling the
writer. These letters have been found in the tombs of the Sixth through
Twelfth Dynasties, c. 2315–1786 B.C. (Gardiner, 1935, p. 18).

Afterlife concepts. In turning to the Egyptian concepts of the afterlife, we
are confronted with a confusing and massive array of facts and ideas. While
the Egyptians were extremely conservative in their view of the universe and
history, they had a highly developed culture which contained the ingredients
for continuing cultural fermentation. In viewing the belief systems of ancient
Egypt, we must weigh simultaneously the facts of historical change, the continuing evolution of concepts, and their accumulation and overlap through
3000 years of history. Albright (1957, pp. 171–172) gives evidence that
religious beliefs do not follow a single upward progression but pass through
an evolutionary process of completed cycles returning to similar starting
points. For example, afterlife beliefs can be dated back to Mousterian Nean-
derthals of the Middle Paleolithic Period of 100,000 B.C. The Neolithic Period
of 5000 B.C. saw reappearance of afterlife beliefs.

The emanations, or noncorporeal aspects of the deceased, took at least
three forms: the *Ka*, the *Ba*, and the *Akh*. All three were present in some form
during life but achieved their greatest importance and definition when death
made the corporeal part of man less imposing. All three were probably viewed
by the Egyptians in different manners simultaneously, that is, as distinct entities, as overlapping phenomena of the deceased, and as indisoluble elements
of man as a psychophysical unity. The *Ka*, as we have seen, was a vital
presence or life essence, with caution translated as "soul" or "genius" of the

deceased. The *Ba* appeared as a birdlike ghostly presence of the deceased one. The *Akh*, meaning "shining" or "glorious," also depicted as a bird, the ibis, in hieroglyphics, was another ghostly aspect of the deceased but was impersonal and transcendent, residing far off near the north star as part of a general celestial influence.

The afterworld, or the continuing abode of the dead, was variously described. The dead king existed forever as a polar star. The dead dwelt in a "Field of Rushes" or underground in a perilously upside-down position with feet against the earth's dome (Frankfort, 1955, pp. 117–120; Zandee, 1960). We are confronted with the "multiplicity of approaches," conflictual and yet somehow accepted and integrated. Frankfort (1955, pp. 119–120) has explained the profusion of afterworld sites as indicating that the dead were not static but moved in a circuit which embodied the cyclical movement of nature.

The nature of the deceased's actual existence presents another challenge to our modern dualistic language. The dead person not only fluttered near his tomb as a *Ba* but shone in the heavens as a transfigured *Akh*. The king in death was identified with the god Osiris, drowned in the Nile, now existing ruler of the dead as well as the perenially regenerating spirit in the sprouting grain of the river bed. The advance of the Osirian faith in the Middle Kingdom, c. 2000–1780 B.C., saw the spread of these beliefs to the masses, an eventual identification of all dead with Osiris and the "democratization" of the afterlife (Breasted, 1959, p. 252).

The Old Testament View of Death

The dead in ancient Israel were handled and disposed of with dignified simplicity. Burial probably took place on the day of death in a burial chamber or natural cave (DeVaux, 1961, p. 57). Public and ritual expressions of mourning were customary.

The death of the body for the ancient Israelite was equated with death of the soul, since their unity was indisoluble and it was inconceivable to the Israelite that one could survive without the other (Murtonen, 1958; Robinson, 1925; Vriezen, 1958, p. 203). Kaufmann (1966, pp. 311–316) has stated this view of death in somewhat different terms. He feels that all matters pertaining to death and the afterlife were excluded from the concern of pentateuchal monotheism. The care of the dead and mourning were kept as purely secular universal human matters in order to avoid involvement with the ancient forbidden practices surrounding the dead.

Regardless of the basis, it is clear that the ancient Israelites were stringently separated from a realm of the dead. No relation between Yahweh and the dead is mentioned; embalming was not practiced; contact with the dead was defiling; no coffin was used; necromancy was forbidden (Leviticus 19:31) as were gifts and food to the dead (Deuteronomy 26:14); and the priesthood was particularly enjoined from contact with the dead (Kaufmann, 1966, p. 304).

The contrast with Egyptian practices is so thoroughgoing that one suspects, as suggested by Kaufmann, that the pattern is specifically based on avoidance.

References to a netherworld of the dead in the Old Testament are passing ones to a place called Sheol.[3] A rather vague entity in the Old Testament, Sheol appears to have been based on an ancient Semitic common grave, the deepest place in the universe, where both good and bad dwelt (Pedersen, 1926–1940, vol. 1, p. 460). The dead in Sheol were a collectivity, consistent with the view of an individual as a member of his group in ancient Israelite thinking. The dead existed in a silent state of unconsciousness or sleep. The inhabitants of Sheol are *refaim*, a word meaning "deprived of power" or "weak" and the opposite of *nefesh* (Murtonen, 1958; Pedersen, 1926–1940, vol. 1, p. 462). A confusing aspect of Sheol lies in the fact that death was regarded as a process in which the soul underwent progressive weakness (Murtonen, 1958). The Hebrew word for "dead" may also be translated as "dying," indicating an incomplete or imperfect state. It thus implies a residuum, and a world inhabited by these weakened souls, the soul and the body remaining alive for a time despite an outward appearance of lifelessness. In some places *nefesh* is translated as "dead"; for example, Leviticus 22:4 mentions that a priest in contact with a soul, that is, a dead person, is made unclean. The word "soul" is here used metonymously to mean an individual (a body–soul) who has now died. That the individual died and his body and soul came to a radically altered state is clear from the Old Testament writings. However, the soul, that is, the individual who dies, is never referred to as a "dead soul" in the Bible (Murtonen, 1958).

Because of its collective nature, the soul existed in relation to the hereditary line and material extensions of the individual. The absence of time and space limitations meant that the individual might die but that continuity of the soul in relation to the tribe, his forefathers, and his offspring was maintained.

The nonmythological aspect of the ancient Israelite religion also had an impact in minimizing afterlife beliefs. There was no place in Israelite thinking for a god of the dead, such as is found in the religions of Egypt and Mesopotamia as well as of their Ugaritic neighbors (Obermann, 1948). Thus, the Israelite afterworld was depopulated of its usual divine leadership. This would have served to attenuate beliefs pertaining to an afterlife and a relationship to divine beings. The weakening of afterlife beliefs through their mythological underpinnings might thus have also fostered an Israelite concept of psychophysical unity. With the afterlife all the less believable and imaginable, the single entity of body and soul simply ended in toto with death and disintegration, no opportunity existing for a disembodied psychical portion to continue.

---

[3] The discussion of Sheol here is, of course, limited to the Old Testament portrayal. Later talmudic and rabbinic writings, which are not discussed here, elaborated a different concept in relation to current eschatological speculations (*Encyclopaedia Judaica*, 1973, vol. 2, pp. 335–337).

Egyptian and Israelite Contrasts

The manifest differences in beliefs and practices of the ancient Egyptians and Israelites regarding the dead is clear. The contrast is all the more interesting, since both cultures shared a syncretic, fluid monistic view of man as an indissoluble body and soul. The Israelite witnessed the disintegration of the body and therefore concluded that the soul sooner or later ended its existence as well. Separate existences for body and soul were inconceivable to him. The Egyptian, perceiving a static enduring universe, assumed that the noncorporeal aspects of man must also endure. It followed for the Egyptians that to maintain the body in some physical form was the only solution to the continuing existence of man as a psychophysical unity (Frankfort, 1948, p. 93).

Along with the striking difference in views of death and the afterworld, some interesting similarities exist. The ancient Israelite term for the dead, *refaim*, "the weak," suggests the impotent state of the Egyptian dead. In the afterworld, the Egyptians need to be revivified, are constantly dependent on the living, ask for physical sustenance, request prayers be said in their name, and need spells cast to maintain them in an adequate and felicitous condition. The underworld geography of the Hebrew Sheol and the Egyptian afterworld are somewhat similar. In at least one of their views, the ancient Egyptians regarded the afterworld as a circular disk under the earth upon which the dead walked, upside down, and were exposed to the possible reverse flow of their gastrointestinal contents.

The Biblical impression of death as a protracted process in which body and soul gradually disintegrate (DeVaux, 1961, p. 56; Murtonen, 1958) finds a counterpart in the Egyptian noting of two dates in relation to a royal death. The first date on the tomb of Queen Meresankh III is the date of her death; the second, the date of her burial following the lengthy embalming and funerary ritual (Frankfort, 1955, p. 63). Both Israelite and Egyptian conceived of a transitional period in relation to death. Israelite and Egyptian shared a horror of the unattended dead body, and both demanded immediate and reverential funerary attention to the corpse discovered in the open by the individuals in nearest proximity to the body. Finally, a similarity lay in the fact that neither had any real fear of the dead per se. The dead of the Egyptians needed the living more than vice versa; the dead of the Israelites were completely out of the sphere of the living and of no consequence in daily affairs.

Creation Accounts

The ancient accounts of man's creation also touch on the concept of body and mind. It would take us far afield to consider the entire complex of Egyptian creation accounts, their "multiplicity of approaches," and their challenging symbolism. Suffice it to say the Egyptians regarded their king as a god created by the gods, and divine powers intermingled freely with his human features. By contrast, the biblical creation account portrays a man formed from dust into whom the breath or spirit of life is breathed by God. Biblical man's qualities, his mind, will, and temperament, perish with his body. In the biblical creation account, the finiteness of man and of a psychophysical unity appears as an inescapable reality. Both Israelite and Egyptian cultures showed great achievements in empirical logic in the second millennium B.C. in such areas as didactic literature, science, and law (Albright, 1968, p. 30), but the two paths also diverged, sharply, most particularly in the area of montheism. One of the results of this fork in the road of ancient cultural evolution was that Egypt remained with its pantheon and a concept of mind which looked to the afterlife for its greatest adventures, while the monotheistic Israelites assumed that this life provided the only arena for an individual's psychophysical activity.

Idols and Images

The radical departure of the Israelites in attitudes toward representations of body and mind is demonstrated in the words of the Second Commandment:

> Thou shalt have no other Gods before My face. Thou shalt not make unto thee any graven image, or any manner of likeness, of any thing that is in the heaven above, or that is in the earth beneath, or that is in the water under the earth; thou shalt not bow down to them, nor serve them [Exodus 20:3–5].

In these few sentences the Israelites were denied all efforts to portray the divine in any aspect. The cosmic, the visible, the arcane, and the chthonic were all excluded from efforts at representation. Particularly in relation to the psychical or noncorporeal descriptions and portrayal, Egyptian and Israelite conceptions diverge sharply. The Egyptians were pushed constantly to represent or graphically depict their ideas of mind or soul. They repeatedly portrayed many of the noncorporeal aspects of man in their tombs, inside caskets, on the walls of monuments, and on the objects produced for art and utility in the daily world and in the afterlife.

In contrast, the ancient Israelites were kept from representational art in many ways. Basically, their culture did not supply them with the involvement in these forms of material representations. After the exodus from Egypt, as wanderers and invaders the Israelites were little attuned to produce permanently implanted graphic or plastic representational objects.

More important, however, was the meaning and effect of the attitude toward idols and the extraordinary lengths taken to prevent their deliberate or accidental production. The Second Commandment not only forbids idol manufacture but further explicates that the prohibition extends to copying the works of the Creator in the cosmos and heaven above, the surrounding earth, and the unseen subterranean realm. (This lack of involvement in representational art may also be reflected in the account of importing Phoenician craftsmen to complete the metalcraft needs of Solomon's temple.)

The avoidance of the representation of the divine or the works of God was even extended to dramatic arts. As mentioned earlier in relation to the non-mythological quality of the Israelite religion, there was no place in the Mosaic religion for the primitive or traditional enactments of the lives of the gods. In such pagan ritual dramas, it was usual for individuals to impersonate the divine beings or forces, an activity forbidden to the Israelites. Thus, the Israelites were further directed toward inner as opposed to outer experiences for personal transformation.

The writing of the ancient Israelites contrasts with that of the Egyptians. Egyptian writing was hieroglyphic, and with each line they exercised the faculty and interest which brought them joy and participation in the universe. Written Hebrew in the second millennium B.C. was free of any pictographic or ideographic quality and had evolved to a purely phonetic alphabet written in cursive form. Diringer (1967) has demonstrated from artifacts that the ancient Hebrew script was used extensively among the general population of Palestine in the second millennium and that a cursive rather than a monumental or formal script was preferred.

Primitive or protological mentality has been characterized by the immediacy and vividness of its perception and the sense of participation with the external environment. In the second millennium B.C., the empiricological mentality of the Near East was highly admixed with mythopoeic thinking. The two markedly different practices in relation to depicting mental representations appear to have been a critical matter in subsequent intellectual development. The Egyptians in the empiricological era freely applied their visual mindedness to the elaboration of their mythological concerns (Bleeker, 1967, p. 143). Such a route was unavailable to the Israelites, who subsequently demonstrated through their literary productions the emergence of a mentality capable of new forms of experiencing and expression and oriented to verbal and conceptual communication rather than representational and concrete forms.

With his already existing grasp of mind and body as a psychophysical unity, the ancient Israelite was achieving an orientation toward the individual which is unique in the history of ideas. His concept of mind and body as one continued as his empiricological accomplishments advanced. We know that the subsequent age of the prophets was associated with a new sense of individuality and self-awareness and experience. It is interesting to conjecture what form of mentality and concept of mind might have emerged had not the logical age of the Greeks prevailed over Western culture and eventually over Judaeo–Christian thinking as well.

Summary and Conclusion

The Egyptians and Israelites of the second millennium B.C. experienced a rich interchange of culture, language, and thought, which is reflected in similarities and contrasts in their concepts of body and mind. Both viewed man as an indissoluble psychophysical unity, whose thoughts, emotions, and actions issued from his total being. The heart was the major organ of intellectual and emotional functioning. The brain was inconsequential in the scheme of things, although other parts of the body, particularly internal organs, had important roles in emotional experiences.

The Egyptians and Israelites differed in their beliefs concerning blood. The Israelites regarded blood as particularly important to the psychophysical unity, feeling that the vital or life principle, usually called *nefesh*, was associated with the blood. Blood was regarded with particular reverence by the Israelites and of little specific concern to the Egyptians.

The psychophysical unity of man was complicated by an evolving terminology referring to psychical functions. It is in the area of noncorporeal functions that Egyptian and Israelite views diverged most sharply. Biblical language uses several different terms which give depth and nuance to man's emotional and spiritual experiences. These terms were used for the condition of the living and almost never in relation to the dead. In the language of the Old Testament, the soul ceases to exist upon the death of the individual. The term "a dead soul" does not exist in the Old Testament.

In contrast, the Egyptians maintained a complex picture of noncorporeal man. The *Ka, Ba,* and *Akh* were existential aspects of man which assumed particular importance upon death. As the complement to these noncorporeal aspects of man, the Egyptians assured the individual's continuing psychophysical integrity through a vast array of religious activities involving the dead individual's body, possessions, and survivors. The Egyptian who was able to entertain this complex set of beliefs and reconcile it effortlessly with the psychophysical unity of man displayed a characteristic mentality. It was a mentality combining empiricological thinking of the second millennium with archaic mythopoeic or protological thinking which utilized a "multiplicity of approaches" in dealing with complex questions.

The Israelite mentality, which presented the same admixture of thinking modes, was able to reconcile the idea of a vital principle or essence which was unfettered by time, space, and individuality with a view of man as a psychophysical unity. Other factors were at work, however, to yield a totally different view of noncorporeal man as held by the Israelites in contrast with the Egyptians. The impact of biblical monotheism was critical in establishing a belief system (*a*) largely free of mythological elements, (*b*) detached from cultic aspects of death, and (*c*) sternly prohibitive of all forms of external representations. The Israelite mind was set on a path of a radically different orientation toward man's inner reality. To the Israelite of 1000 B.C., an external soul or spirit was inconceivable.

In concluding, our opportunity to examine the mentality of ancient man is a most valuable one. We see that the passage of man through time and culture is not simply a straight line of upward progress with rationalism supplanting nonrationalism but rather a recurring cycle in which religions and aesthetic standards and concepts advance and decline, returning to starting points of a similar nature. And we find that in studying the mentality of ancient man we have again studied ourselves.

References

Ackerknecht, E. H. *Medicine and ethnology*. Baltimore: Johns Hopkins Press, 1971.

Albright, W. F. *History, archaeology, and Christian humanism*. New York: McGraw-Hill, 1964.

Albright, W. F. *From the stone age to Christianity: Monotheism and the historical process* (2nd ed.). Garden City, N.Y.: Doubleday and Co., 1957.

Albright, W. F. *Archaeology and the religion of Israel* (5th ed.). Baltimore: Johns Hopkins Press, 1968.

Astour, M. C. *Hellenosemitica*. Leiden: E. J. Bill, 1967.

Bleeker, C. J. *Egyptian festivals: Enactments of religious renewal*. Leiden: E. J. Brill, 1967.

Boman, T. *Hebrew thought compared with Greek* (J. L. Moreau, trans.). London: SCM Press, 1960.

Breasted, J. H. *The dawn of conscience*. New York: Charles Scribner's Sons, 1933.

Breasted, J. H. *Development of religion and thought in ancient Egypt*. New York, Harper and Brothers Publishers, 1959.

Briggs, C. A. A study of the use of (laev) and (laevav) in the Old Testament. In G. A. Kohut (Ed.), *Semitic studies in memory of Dr. Alexander Kohut*. Berlin: S. Calvary and Co., 1897 (a).

Briggs, C. A. The use of Nefesh in the Old Testament. *Journal of Biblical Literature*, 1897, *16*, 17–29. (b)

Brown, F., Driver, S. R., & Briggs, C. A. (Eds.) *A Hebrew and English lexicon of the Old Testament*. Oxford: Clarendon Press, 1972.

Burney, C. F. A fresh Examination of the current theory of the Hebrew tenses. *The Journal of Theological Studies*, April 1919, *20*, 200–214.

Cohen, I. The heart in biblical psychology. In H. V. Zimmels, J. Rabbinowitz, & I. Finestein (Eds.), *Essays presented to Chief Rabbi Israel Brodie on the occasion of his seventieth birthday*. London: Soncino Press, 1967. Pp. 41–57.

Cooney, J. D. Siren and ba, birds of a feather. *The Bulletin of the Cleveland Museum of Art*, October 1968, *55*, 262–271.

DeVaux, R. *Ancient Israel: Its life and institutions*. New York: McGraw-Hill, 1961.

Dietrich, B. C., *Death, fate and the gods*. Glasgow: Athlone Press, 1967.

[*Diodorus of Sicily*] (12 vols.). (C. H. Oldfather, C. L. Sherman, R. M. Geer, & F. R. Walton, Trans.). Cambridge: Harvard University Press, 1962 (Loeb Classical Library).

Diringer, D. A millenium of early Hebrew culture as based on biblical archaeology and epigraphy. In H. J. Zimmels, J. Rabbinowitz, & I. Finestein (Eds.), *Essays presented to Chief Rabbi Israel Brodie on the occasion of his seventieth birthday*. London: Soncino Press, 1967. Pp. 67–80.

Driver, S. R. The modern study of the Hebrew language. In A. S. Peake (Ed.), *The people and the book: Essays on the Old Testament.* Oxford: Clarendon Press, 1925. Pp. 73–120.

Driver, S. R. *A treatise on the use of the tenses in Hebrew* (3rd ed.). Oxford: Clarendon Press, 1969.

Ebbell, B. (Trans.). [*The Papyrus Ebers.*] Copenhagen: Levin and Munksgaard, 1937.

Edelstein, L. *Ancient medicine.* Baltimore: Johns Hopkins Press, 1967.

Eliade, M. *Rites and symbols of initiation: the mysteries of birth and rebirth.* (W. R. Trask, Trans.). New York: Harper and Row, 1965.

Eliade, M. *The two and the one.* (J. M. Cohen, Trans.). New York: Harper and Row, 1969.

Emery, W. B. *Archaic Egypt.* Middlesex, Eng.: Penguin, 1961.

Encyclopaedia Judaica (16 vols.) Jerusalem: Keter, 1973.

Erman, A. *The literature of the ancient Egyptians.* London: Methuen and Co., 1927.

Fairservis, W. A. Problems in the origins of the civilizations of India and China. *Transactions of the New York Academy of Sciences,* April 1961, 23:6 (Series No. 2), 531–539.

Faulkner, R. O. The man who was tired of life. *Journal of Egyptian Archaeology,* 1956, 42, 21–40.

Frankfort, H. *Ancient Egyptian religion: An interpretation.* New York: Columbia University Press, 1948.

Frankfort, H. *Kingship and the gods.* Chicago: University of Chicago Press, 1955.

Frankfort, H. *The birth of civilization in the Near East.* Garden City, N.Y.: Doubleday and Co., 1956.

Frankfort, H., Frankfort, H. A., Wilson, A., Jacobsen, T., & Irwin, W. A. *The intellectual adventure of ancient man.* Chicago: University of Chicago Press, 1946.

Frazer, J. G. *The golden bough* (3rd ed.) (13 vols.). New York: Macmillan, 1951.

Gardiner, A. H. *The attitude of the ancient Egyptians to death and the dead.* Cambridge: Cambridge University Press, 1935.

Goedicke, H. *The report about the dispute of a man with his "Ba."* Baltimore: Johns Hopkins Press, 1970.

Gordon, D. H. *The common background of Greek and Hebrew civilizations.* New York: W. W. Norton and Co., 1965.

Gouldner, A. W. *Enter Plato.* New York: Basic Books, 1965.

Hankoff, L. D. Ancient Egyptian attitudes toward death and suicide. *The Pharos of Alpha Omega Alpha,* April 1975, 38, 60–64; 75. (a)

Hankoff, L. D. The hero as madman. *Journal of the History of the Behavioral Sciences,* 1975, 11, 315–333. (b)

Hankoff, L. D. Why the healing gods are twins. *Yale Journal of Biology and Medicine,* 1977, 50, 307–319.

Hastings, J. (Ed.). *Encyclopedia of religion and ethnics* (13 vols.). New York: Charles Scribner's Son, 1955.

[*Herodotus*] (4 vols.). (A. D. Godley, Trans.). Cambridge: Harvard University Press, 1966 (Loeb Classical Library).

Iversen, E. Some remarks on the terms (amem) and (a'ys). *The Journal of Egyptian Archaeology,* 1947, 33, 47–51.

Johnson, A. R. *The one and the many in the Israelite conception of God.* Cardiff: University of Wales Press, 1942.

Johnson, A. R. *The vitality of the individual in the thought of ancient Israel.* Cardiff: University of Wales Press, 1964.

Kaufmann, Y. *The religion of Israel: From the beginnings to the Babylonian exile* (M. Greenberg, Trans.). Chicago: University of Chicago Press, 1966.

Larue, G. A. *Ancient myth and modern man.* Englewood Cliffs, N.J.: Prentice-Hall, 1975.

Laver, A. R. Precursors of psychology in ancient Egypt. *Journal of the History of the Behavioral Sciences,* 1972, 8, 181–195.

Lévy-Bruhl, L. *How natives think.* (L. A. Clare, Trans.). London: George Allen and Unwin, 1926. (Originally published, 1922.)

Lévi-Strauss, C. *The savage mind.* Chicago: University of Chicago Press, 1966.

Lévi-Strauss, C. *Structural anthropology.* (C. Jacobson and B. G. Schoepf, Trans.). Garden City, N.Y.: Doubleday and Co., 1967.

Mitchell, T. C. The Old Testament usage of Nesama. *Vetus Testamentum,* 1961, *11,* 177–187.

Montet, P. *Egypt and the Bible.* Philadelphia: Fortress Press, 1968.

Murtonen, A. The living soul: A study of the meaning of the word Naefaes in the Old Testament Hebrew language. *Studia Orientalia,* 1958, *23,* 1–105.

Obermann, J. *Ugaritic mythology: A study of its leading motifs.* New Haven: Yale University Press, 1948.

Pedersen, J. *Israel: Its life and culture* (2 vols.). London: Oxford University Press, 1926–1940.

Petrie, W. M. Flinders. *Egypt and Israel.* New York: Macmillan, 1931.

Pritchard, J. B. (Ed.). *Ancient near eastern texts relating to the Old Testament.* Princeton, New Jersey: Princeton University Press, 1955.

Radin, P. *Primitive religion: Its nature and origin.* New York: Dover, 1957.

Ranke, H. Medicine and surgery in ancient Egypt. *Bulletin of the Institute of the History of Medicine,* 1933, *1,* 237–257.

Ranke, H. The origin of the Egyptian tomb statue. *Harvard Theological Review,* 1935, *28,* 45–53.

Robinson, H. W. Hebrew psychology. In A. S. Peake (Ed.), *The people and the book: Essays on the Old Testament.* Oxford: Clarendon Press, 1925.

Saunders, J. B. de C. M. *The transition from ancient Egyptian to Greek medicine.* Lawrence: University of Kansas Press, 1963.

Schopenhauer, A. *On the fourfold root of the principle of sufficient reason* (E. F. J. Payne, Trans.). LaSalle, Ill.: Open Court, 1974. (Originally published, 1813.)

Schubert, P. The twentieth century West and the ancient Near East. In R. C. Dentan (Ed.), *The idea of history in the ancient Near East.* New Haven: Yale University Press, 1955. Pp. 311–355.

Schwartz, B. I. The age of transcendence. *Daedalus,* 1975, *104,* 1–7.

Seligman, C. G., & Murray, M. A. Note upon an early Egyptian standard. *Man,* 1911, *11,* 165–171.

Smith, W. Robertson. *The religion of the Semites: The fundamental institutions.* New York: Meridian Books, 1956.

Van Der Leeuw, G. The moon-god Khons and the king's placenta. *Journal of Egyptian Archaeology,* 1918, *5,* 64.

Van Peursen, C. A. *Body, soul, spirit: A survey of the body-mind problem.* London: Oxford University Press, 1966.

Vriezen, T. C. *An outline of Old Testament Theology.* Oxford: Basil Blackwell, 1958.

Wallace, A. F. C. Culture and cognition. *Science,* 1962, *135,* 351–357.

Welles, C. B. The Hellenistic Orient. In R. C. Dentan (Ed.), *The idea of history in the ancient Near East.* New Haven: Yale University Press, 1955. Pp. 133–167.

Werner, H. *Comparative psychology of mental development* (Rev. ed.). New York: International Universities Press, 1957.

Yahuda, A. S. Medical and anatomical terms in the Pentateuch in the light of Egyptian medical papyri. *Journal of the History of Medicine,* 1947, *2,* 549–574.

Zandee, J. *Death as an enemy according to ancient Egyptian conceptions.* Leiden: E. J. Brill, 1960.

Chapter 2

Body and Mind from the Cartesian Point of View [1]

MARGARET D. WILSON

Introduction

When contemporary philosophers speak about "the mind–body problem," they usually have in mind the problem of understanding the relation between such "mental" states as conscious experiences, beliefs, desires, trains of reasoning, on the one hand, and such "physical" states as neural processes, on the other hand. Frequently the central issue is whether the relation between these sorts of states can (or must) be one of identity: whether we should hold, for example, that S's experiencing a pain just is (is nothing other than) the occurrence in S's body of a particular sort of neural energy-exchange. If it is argued that mental states are not the same thing as physical states, a further question arises. We say that neural discharges and the like are states of a particular physical entity (S's body). If, then, we suppose that mental states are different from physical states, should we further suppose that S's mental states are "had" by another particular entity, S's "mind"? Many (I think most) contemporary philosophers have wanted to avoid the latter conclusion. Not only is it "unscientific," but, many have argued, it involves demonstrable conceptual incoherencies. But we still lack a way of thinking about the relation between the "mental" and the "physical" that is generally regarded as satisfactory. Hence, "the mind–body problem" remains a live philosophical issue.

[1] Work on this paper was supported in part by a grant from the Guggenheim Foundation.

The mind–body problem in its modern philosophical form is in many ways the heritage of the seventeenth-century French philosopher and scientist René Descartes (1596–1650). This is not to say that any contemporary scholar would grant to Descartes's theories and conceptions the complete and utter novelty that he himself sometimes claimed for them. To an almost startling extent the elements of the philosophical system Descartes expounds (in the *Discourse on Method*, 1637, the *Meditations Concerning First Philosophy*, 1641, the *Principles of Philosophy*, 1644, and other works) can be traced to such antecedents as Augustine of Hippo, William of Ockham, Montaigne, and the late scholastic Spanish philosopher Suarez. But Descartes was the first thinker to develop a systematic account of mind and the mind–body relation within the context of the "modern" mechanistic–materialist theory of nature.[2] Certain implications of this scientific world view—reinforced by philosophical considerations and by aspects of traditional Christian theology—led Descartes to espouse the position now widely known as "Cartesian dualism." According to this view, mental states such as sensations and trains of reasoning are distinct from states of matter or body and do have their own distinct, immaterial subject—the "mind". (Descartes also tended to identify himself, the "I," as the immaterial mental subject that inhabited his body.)

The primary purpose of this chapter is to set forth the main aspects of Descartes's notions of the mind, and of the mind–body relation, within their historical scientific contexts. I want to show that Cartesian dualism is in many ways an intellectually comprehensible response to certain problems insistently posed by the mechanistic world view itself. To this extent I will be opposing the rather common general view that, from Descartes's time to the present, departures from reductive materialism, with respect to the human mind, must be ascribed to such motives as superstitious prejudice, religious piety, wishful thinking, or political timidity. I also oppose the more limited view that Descartes himself was influenced primarily by such motives in espousing a dualistic position on the mind–body issue, rather than embracing reductive materialism. (According to the reductive materialist, mental states are identical with physical states, and the subject or "haver" of thoughts, desires, beliefs, and sensations is nothing other than the human body.) I will suggest that Descartes's dualism is to some extent a response to deep conceptual features of the physical theory of his time. The fact that these features may still be present in the far more sophisticated scientific world view of today partly accounts for the continued influence of the Cartesian perspective, despite many contemporary philosophers' desire to reject dualism in whole or in part. At the same time, I will point out certain ways in which Descartes's position on the mind–body issue merely reflects now-obvious limitations in the physical theory of his time. I will also acknowledge in passing the importance of certain religious concerns in helping to shape Cartesian doctrine.

[2] There had been mechanistic materialists in the ancient world: most notably the atomists, such as Democritus, Epicurus, and Lucretius. But, as will be noted later, the teleological Aristotelian philosophy of nature had been dominant for centuries, up to the time of Descartes. In addition,

The next section, then, will expound in a general way some of the intellectual concerns that lie behind Descartes's acceptance of dualism—especially those deriving from his commitments as a physical scientist. In the following section, I sketch and briefly discuss three formal arguments that Descartes presented in defense (or, as he thought, proof) of the view that the human mind is an immaterial substance. The fourth section surveys certain fundamental difficulties in Descartes's dualism that have been stressed by critics from his time to our own. In the fifth and final section, I attempt to provide a somewhat fuller picture of seventeenth-century contributions to the mind–body issue by going beyond the work of Descartes himself. I will sketch there certain historically important departures from the Cartesian treatment of the mind among Descartes's contemporaries and immediate successors. These include an increased interest in the notion of unconscious mental states; development of the notion that mental phenomena, too, are subject to rigorous and systematic explanation; and some movement away from conceiving the human mind as a largely independent subject or immaterial thing.

To avoid possible misunderstanding, I should perhaps state explicitly that this chapter is not primarily intended as a contribution to the specialists' literature on seventeenth-century philosophy. It is rather an attempt to provide a readily intelligible but reasonably sophisticated account of the Cartesian viewpoint for those with general of specialized interests in the mind–body problem, but without specialized philosophical training or interests. In the course of the chapter, I draw on previous work of my own and others, as well as what must be regarded as common knowledge of the field. References are kept to a minimum. (I provide them mainly for direct quotations and for a few especially notable or relevant secondary works.) For much more detailed discussion of some of the issues considered (including defense of the more controversial claims) and for many references both to Descartes's works and the relevant philosophical literature, see Wilson (1978).[3] On the other hand, the essay is not merely a review of conclusions established or defended elsewhere. It is an attempt to present certain Cartesian ideas in a new and illuminating way. Thus, I hope it will be of some interest, even for specialists in the period.

Assumptions Motivating Descartes's Dualism

The Theory of Nature: A General Account

Descartes's account of the mind–body relation was developed against the background of a particular theory of the nature and behavior of matter or body, and certain fundamental philosophical commitments or assumptions

---

there are important differences between Cartesian physics and classical atomism—although I will not attempt to discuss these here. (Descartes himself discussed them in *Principles of Philosophy*, IV, ccii, A.T., H.R. I., 298–299.) (See reference list for full titles of works cited in text by initials.)

[3] I have also touched on some of the points developed here in my introduction to *The Essential Descartes* (E.D.).

that accompanied it. Let us begin by sketching the theory. First, Descartes's theory of matter involved an elegant, if overly optimistic, attempt vastly to simplify the conception of physical nature, with the purpose of developing a clear and certain science. Sweeping away the complex Aristotelian hierarchy of immanent "forms," which had been supposed to account for natural change (such as the growth and activity of organisms, and the movement of bodies toward earth), Descartes held that all of nature is simply *res extensa*, literally "extended thing." Its only intrinsic properties are those entailed by extension: it is indefinitely divisible into parts of different sizes and shapes, subject to movement relative to each other. Second, while matter is *intrinsically* only divi*sible*, through the addition of different relative motions to its different parts, motion has in fact been added to the world by a special act of God. In causing the parts of *res extensa* to move relative to each other, God has also laid down certain "laws of motion" that make their behavior and interactions uniform and predictable. (Descartes's statement of these laws includes an early, though erroneous, formulation of the conservation of momentum.) The actual division of *res extensa* through the addition of motion has been carried through to the level of very small particles (although Descartes denied the existence of atoms in the strict sense). The enormous variety of phenomena we perceive in the physical world are all to be explained in terms of the law-governed motions and interactions of bits of *res extensa*, most of them taking place on the subsensible level.

In the early seventeenth century, geometry was viewed as the model science because of its clarity and its alleged certainty and completeness. Descartes, especially, was impressed with these features, and took geometry as his model for physics. The conceptualization of matter as *res extensa* allowed him to suppose that physics required no concepts except those already clear and familiar from geometry (with the inclusion, obviously, of kinematics).

It did not take long for Descartes's contemporaries to see that the Cartesian simplification of the conception was an *over*simplification and that Descartes had not really succeeded in formulating the true "laws of motion." Indeed, Descartes made relatively few sound and lasting contributions to the understanding of specific phenomena. Nevertheless, discrediting the details of Cartesian physics has not been sufficient to discredit some of its more general assumptions—especially those that relate most clearly to the mind–matter dichotomy. This point should become clearer as I spell out these assumptions more fully.

Assumptions and Implications

UNIVERSALITY

One of Descartes's most important commitments as a scientist was that physics must be universal. This commitment really has two different aspects—one still alive today and the other conspicuously outdated. First,

Descartes thought that physical science is universal in the sense that the same (mechanistic) patterns of explanation apply to everything material, and every physical event is thoroughly comprehensible in principle. This view follows directly from the position that matter is the same throughout all of creation and that it is everywhere governed by the same relatively simple laws. As a result of this aspect of his position, Descartes is sometimes given credit for orginating the modern notion of the unity of science. An important corollary, which Descartes expressly drew—on which he indeed insisted—is that physiology is simply a branch of physics. In fact he maintained that all animal behavior can be accounted for through mechanistic principles: Animals are therefore nothing but relatively complex machines. Much human behavior also can be adequately explained in this way: The human body is itself a "machine." In this respect Descartes departed emphatically from the Aristotelian view, which accounted for the behavior as well as the growth and development of any organism through the specific internal teleological principle which constituted its form or "soul." Descartes himself conducted extensive physiological and behavioristic researches based entirely on the mechanistic assumption.[4]

But, second, Descartes's physics was also "universalist" in its own pretensions. For example, Descartes said of the *Principles:* "I believe I have begun to explain all Philosophy [including physics] in order, without having omitted any of the things which should precede the last of which I have written [A.T. IX-2, 16–17; H.R. I, 212–213:]." (See reference list for full titles of standard editions of Descartes's, Leibniz's, and Locke's works, which are represented by initials in text citations.) He acknowledged that his physics was not yet "complete"; it did not, for instance, include accounts of the natures of all the different animals, plants, and minerals. But he held that all that is necessary for bringing it to completion is additional experiments of the sort that he has already carried out. He even suggested that he himself might be able to complete the task in his lifetime, if sufficient public support could be provided. This outlook of course reflects rather deluded personal ambition. But Descartes probably thought it was entailed by his very conception of science and of matter. Body is by nature extremely simple; the laws governing motion are simple and few. It may have seemed to follow quite directly (especially under the influence of the model of geometry) that all phenomena must be readily accessible to the unprejudiced and methodical human mind. If his physics were incomplete, with respect to explanatory potential, this would indicate a defect in his method, or his conception of nature, or both. In any case, I will suggest later that both "universalist" aspects of Descartes's position may have had important bearing on his dualism.

---

[4] Descartes was very far from being a mere armchair theorist—even though some of his results, such as the claim that the heart is a furnace, might strongly suggest the contrary.

MECHANISM

Another assumption that must be stressed here is the commitment to mechanism itself. Here again we must distinguish the more dated from the more enduring aspects of his doctrine. Considered most concretely, Descartes's commitment to "mechanistic" explanation in physics was a commitment to the view that all physical phenomena must be explained in terms of the impact and pressure of extended particles on each other. This rather naive model was not destined to survive very long. But Cartesian mechanism can also be considered in its more general aspects, as a form of determinism and a denial of teleology in nature. Thus, Descartes was committed to the view that every purely physical event follows of necessity from preexisting states of matter, characterized fully in terms of a small set of nonteleological states (in Descartes's view, extension, figure, and motion). There are, so to speak, no options in nature and no room or need for internal "purposes." The deterministic conception of nature, while now abandoned by physicists, of course had a much longer history than the specific Cartesian impact model of causation in nature. And although the doctrine of immanent teleology has had its occasional proponents since the time of Descartes, modern physicists agree with Descartes in rejecting it.[5]

I will suggest in the following discussion that Descartes's limited conception of admissible explanation in science may have been one factor in his development of dualism, partly tying the philosophical position to limitations of seventeenth-century thought. On the other hand, it should be immediately obvious that the more general commitments to determinism and antiteleology (that have been retained in more advanced and complex theories of nature) by themselves could have provided some grounds for moving to dualism. In fact, the antiteleology alone would have been sufficient grounds. For conscious purposes and decision making can hardly be denied in human beings, even if they can be denied (as Descartes held) in animals. This fact provides at least a prima facie intellectual problem for the attempt to view any mechanistic system as the comprehensive truth about reality.

SCIENTIFIC REALISM

Finally, an extremely important part of Descartes's scientific perspective, from the point of view of the mind–body issue, is what we may call (following Sellars, 1963, and others) his "scientific realism." Descartes believed the world is really just as his physics describes it. A rose, for example, is really nothing but a small piece of *res extensa*, consisting of a congeries of particles with only "geometrical" properties. It is therefore really very different than it appears to

---

[5] It should be emphasized that determinism and denial of teleology are logically distinct doctrines. A modern physicist can deny teleology in nature and still not accept determinism because he or she believes in *chance*. Conversely, one could accept teleology in nature and still be a determinist, at least to the extent of holding that everything that happens is necessarily brought about by preexisting circumstances (some of them irreducibly teleological or desirelike).

the human senses, which seem to present it as saliently characterized by, say, a sweet smell and a lovely pinkness. Similarly, Descartes thought, thrills of pleasure and stabs of pain, which we humans may relate to the various parts of our bodies, cannot truly be attributed to the body at all. For, like the perceived color or scent of the rose, pleasure and pain cannot be counted among the actual properties of a mere bit of *res extensa*. This problematic contrast between "the world of physics" and "the world of sense" is another Cartesian assumption that is still operative today: it has not been fundamentally affected by the development of a complex and un-Cartesian theory of physical reality.

How These Lead to Dualism

These various Cartesian commitments—universalism (in two senses), mechanism, and scientific realism—all provide more or less interesting reasons for the postulation of a radical distinction between physical and mental states, and, ultimately, of an immaterial mind, *res cogitans*. For example, our experiences of purposiveness and freedom of choice, hard to reconcile with thorough-going mechanism, can be (in a sense) removed as a problem for the mechanistic theory of nature if one merely holds that we are something other than *res extensa* and hence outside of nature. (This is, of course, one point on which religious concerns may reinforce the Cartesian move. According to a tradition that Descartes seems to have accepted, human beings and not God are responsible for sin, since they make their choices between good and evil through exercise of their own free will.)[6] Similarly, we know by immediate experience that there is something real about our sensations of color, odor, and pain. But color, odor, and pain, like purpose and free choice, have been denied of the realm of *res extensa*. There must therefore be some reality apart from *res extensa*, which includes them. Further, since such things cannot exist "on their own," without some kind of substantial support (Descartes here follows philosophical tradition), they must exist in an immaterial thing. Since they certainly have some sort of existence in our consciousness (if nowhere else), it is most natural to assume that the immaterial thing in which they exist is us. (One might also turn this reasoning around and argue: We must be immaterial things, because we think, and are conscious, whereas material things have only geometrical properties and therefore cannot have a property like thought which is not among the geometrical ones. As we shall see, however, Descartes thought he could demonstrate that thought and extension must qualify different substances, without simply presupposing his own austere theory about the properties of matter.)

Descartes's stance as a scientist prevented him from embracing reductive materialism in another way, as well. We have seen that Descartes claimed his

---

[6] In the *Fourth Meditation*, Descartes used this same general approach also to absolve God from responsibility for our intellectual errors.

science was able to explain *all* the phenomena of nature through its mechanistic models and simple, general laws. Now Descartes perceived very clearly that he was unable to provide a mechanistic account of rational human behavior. In fact, he thought it possible to show that such an account was impossible in principle. It follows from this conclusion (we will consider the argument in a moment) that human behavior is governed by a nonmechanistic and hence (on Cartesian assumptions) immaterial principle. And this latter conclusion in turn protects Descartes's cherished claim to have provided a comprehensive science of nature. An immaterial principle is by definition not a part of "nature."

These various influences, then, tend to converge on the Cartesian concept of the human self as an immaterial, thinking, rational, free, purposive, consciously sensing thing, complementing the unthinking, mechanical, nonpurposive, unfree, and unconscious operations of the realm of extension. They were no doubt reinforced by additional perceived requirements of religion: for example, an unextended, immaterial self could not perish by division and would not necessarily have its fate tied to the fate of "its" body. (Descartes originally claimed to have established the immortality of the human mind in the *Meditations*, although he later retracted this claim.)

Descartes, however, presented his dualism as based on straightforward, conclusive arguments. Of the influences so far considered, only the impossibility of a mechanistic model of human reason counts among these. The next section offers brief discussion of the three Cartesian arguments for mind–body dualism. But before moving to these, let us consider a little more fully the dualistic nature of the human being according to Descartes.

The Two-Substance Human Being

We have seen that both perceptual experiences and purposive acts of free will are ascribed by Descartes to *res cogitans*, rather than to any body. All the states of *res cogitans* are called "thoughts" (*cogitationes*), and "thought" (*cogitatio*) is said to be the "principal attribute" of mind, paralleling the material attribute of extension. By a terminological oddity, Descartes thus construed sensation, perception, and volition as among our "thoughts." But of course the states of *res cogitans* include thoughts in the more normal sense as well: fantasies, judgments, trains of reasoning, and so forth. According to Descartes, what all these states have in common is that I am *conscious* of them: "There can be nothing in me, that is, in my mind, of which I am not conscious [A.T. III, 273; P.L. 90]." At least this was Descartes's official doctrine; when pressed he tended to admit that many things in our minds are not "expressly," or even "actually" conscious (Rodis-Lewis, 1950; Wilson, 1978, Chap. 4, §2). Among these are, very notably, the "innate ideas" (e.g., of God or of a triangle), whose existence Descartes consistently affirmed.

Apparently Descartes assumed there is one individual thinking thing "in" each normally functioning human body. Thus, each human being is composed of an immaterial thinking thing—a *res* or substance in its own right—and a material body. (The latter is usually conceived as a subpart or "mode" of the single extended substance that is the whole of nature.) Mind and body have entirely different natures[7] (thought and extension, respectively), and they are distinct, different things. In each of us mind and body are, however, closely or "intimately" conjoined. We become aware of this intimate mind–body union, Descartes claimed, when we become conscious of states of our body through such "sensations" as pain, hunger, or thirst. These experiences depend on the joining of mind with body and on direct causal pathways between them. Conversely, in voluntary actions the mind causes certain changes in the body: It "moves" the body through acts of free will. (Descartes's position is thus usually described as "dualistic interactionism": It posits causal interaction between two substances of different natures.) Despite this de facto union in the current circumstances of life, mind and body could exist independently of each other—indeed, this is a large part of what is meant by calling them separate substances. Presumably, however, a mind existing independently of body would have a life very different from that of a normal human being: it would not, for example, have sensations—which arise from bodily causes—and would also be free of most of the emotions of our present life. An important tenet of Descartes's dualism—and one that surely reflects seventeenth-century limitations—is that some mental processes have no dependence on the body: "The brain," he asserts, "can be of no use to pure understanding [A.T. VII, 359; H.R. II, 212]."

In the Aristotelian philosophy to which Descartes opposed himself, the human soul was understood as the form or activity of the human body, just as animal and vegetable souls were identified with the form or activity of the appropriate bodies. (Plants possessed nutritive souls; animals nutritive and sensitive souls; humans both of these plus the power of reason.) Descartes differs from the Aristotelian view in denying any continuity between what thinks and wills in us, on the one hand, and the operations of animals, plants, and nature in general, on the other hand. Similarly, the human mind or soul is not conceived by Descartes as involved in the human body's vital functions: The "life" of the human body, like that of animals and plants, is essentially a matter of clockwork. Finally, where the Aristotelian philosophy represents the rational principle in us as conceptually dependent on the body—reason is the most unique and characteristic activity or function of the human body—Descartes from the beginning conceived the mind as a distinct thing, the exclusive subject of the activity of thought. Within the Cartesian perspective, then, the mind–body problem becomes essentially the problem of the relationship of consciousness and self-awareness to matter. The other traditional functions of "souls," such as nutrition and growth, are seen as unproblematically material.

---

[7] "Nature" is used here in the sense of "essence" (compare "the nature of x"). This is different, of course, from Descartes's use of the term to signify the whole of the material world (compare "existing in nature").

Descartes's Arguments for Mind–Body Dualism

In the previous section I tried to show how the conception of an unextended thinking substance, defined in contrast with the physical world, is partially motivated by certain assumptions Descartes made about the nature of physical reality and scientific explanation. An important reason for the persistence of the mind–body problem in contemporary philosophy is that some of these assumptions seem still to be present in the scientific world view of today. In addition, at least one of Descartes's arguments for mind–body dualism retains a certain force—although I do not claim it is sound or fully persuasive. This is what I have elsewhere called the "Epistemological Argument" for mind–body distinctness (Wilson, 1976). This argument depends on the separate conceivability of mind and body. Of the other two arguments, I think it may be said that both are interesting and significant, despite the fact that one (from the indivisibility of the self) is fallacious and the other (from the "unmechanical" nature of reason) appears to depend partly on the limitations of seventeenth-century science. All the arguments raise issues about the mind–body relation that have not even yet been dealt with fully and effectively. We will consider first the argument from the nature of reason, then the Epistemological Argument, and finally (and more briefly) the argument from the indivisibility of the "I."

The Diversity of Human Behavior

The argument from the nature of reason is fully stated, I believe, only in the *Discourse on Method*.[8] It is an argument based primarily on an "external" viewpoint—on observation of human behavior—rather than on introspection. Basically, Descartes argued that human rational behavior and human language use is too "diverse"—adaptable to too wide a range of circumstances and challenges—to be regarded as in principle subsumable under the sort of "mechanistic" account that will work for animal behavior and the rest of physical nature. He wrote:

> [Machines] could never use words or other signs in composing them as we do to declare our thoughts to others. For we can easily conceive a machine's being constituted so that it utters words, and even that it utters some à propos of corporeal actions, which cause some change in its organs; for instance, if it is touched in a certain place it will ask what we wish to say to it; if in another place it will exclaim that it is being hurt, and so on; but not that it arranges words differently to reply to the sense of all that is said in its presence, as even the most moronic man can do [*Discourse*, Part V; A.T. VI, 57; H.R.I., 116].

Similarly, Descartes argues that while machines—and animals—may perform

---

[8] There are related passages in certain letters (compare, e.g., A.T. IV, 573–576; P.L., 205–208). There may also be hints of the argument in Descartes's description of our ability to apprehend the "infinite variability" of a particular body, at the end of *Meditation II*.

one or a few activities with superior proficiency, they never show the versatility or range of proficiency that human reason makes possible. Our linguistic competence and rational behavior are well beyond the capacities of any conceivable machine and hence, Descartes concluded, must proceed from some *immaterial* principle lodged within our bodies.

This line of reasoning would not, of course, be accepted as fully compelling today. Descartes was operating with a much too restricted notion of what a "materialist" explanation must be like. Also, in this age of computer technology, we have more reason than Descartes to take a generous view of the possible versatility of "mere machines." Nevertheless, some contemporary philosophers believe that Descartes's argument in the *Discourse* embodies important insight and raises difficulties for certain present-day reductionist theories of human nature. For example, the linguist and philosopher Noam Chomsky argues that the passage reflects an accurate appreciation of the fact that human linguistic competence cannot be explained on traditional empiricistic or mechanistic models (Chomsky, 1966, esp. pp. 3–6). Chomsky does not, of course, think (like Descartes) that we must therefore postulate immaterial substances operating in each human body; however, he does believe that Descartes demonstrated a better understanding of essential features of human mentality than many of his more materialist contemporaries and successors. It does in any case seem clear that within the context of the seventeenth-century conception of materialist explanation, Descartes was justified in supposing that no materialist explanation of human rational behavior is conceivable. (In fact, the adequacy of twentieth-century scientific concepts to account for higher cognitive processes has been doubted by at least one leading brain researcher [Penfield, 1975, chap. 20].)

The Epistemological Argument

Descartes held that considerations about the nature of human reason and language show it is "morally impossible" that a full mechanistic explanation of human behavior can be provided (A.T. VI, 57; H.R. I, 116).

By using the term "morally impossible" in this context, Descartes seems to avoid claiming a logically conclusive demonstration. ("Moral impossibility" tends, in seventeenth-century usage, to mean something that falls short of *absolute* impossibility.) But the most central and well-known Cartesian argument for mind–body dualism does purport to be fully demonstrative. This argument is, in a sense, a priori: It does not depend on any observation of human behavior or other physical facts. Versions of this second argument are presented in most of Descartes's mature philosophical works, although the best-known presentation occurs toward the beginning of Meditation VI (A.T. VII, 78; H.R. I, 190). Because of Descartes's own emphasis and because of the argument's continuing philosophical interest, it is generally regarded as the most important philosophical basis for Cartesian dualism.

The gist of this argument, as I interpret it, is the following.[9] One can, Descartes held, form a very clear conception of oneself as a thinking thing, without including in this conception any attributes recognized as physical. That is—to put it rather loosely—we can clearly conceive *of* ourselves existing as disembodied minds. There is, then, no contradiction in supposing a mind or a thinking thing may exist without a body: The separation of mind from body is a conceptual possibility. Therefore the mind, or thinking thing, is a logically sufficient subject in its own right. Descartes regarded this as sufficient to establish that the mind is a self-sufficient substance (dependent on God alone) and not a mere attribute of body. (He drew here, it must be acknowledged, on some rather abstruse scholastic notions.)

When the argument is fully laid out (I have not attempted to do so here), it proves to involve some readily questioned premises. It is unlikely of itself to persuade anyone to embrace dualism. On the other hand, its virtues should not be overlooked. First, the argument does not appear to assume any particular limit to scientific achievement. Second, it appeals to a fact that really does underlie many people's puzzlement about the mind–body relation: the fact, namely, that we seem to know what it would be like for our very selves to continue to exist in a disembodied state. Finally (as I have argued in the works cited in footnote 8), the argument when rightly interpreted is formally valid—despite the allegations of many philosophers, from Leibniz to the present, that Descartes's position rests on a gross formal fallacy.

When Descartes presented this argument in the *Meditations*, he more specifically contended that we can clearly conceive of ourselves engaging in "pure thought" without having a body. By this he meant, for example, that we can conceive of doing metaphysics, or certain kinds of mathematical reasoning, without a body. Since he did think that our sensations and many of our emotions are caused by bodily states, however, he may not have believed that disembodied spirits could conceivably have experiences just like ours. (I do not think the texts are very decisive on this question.)

Despite the prevailing antipathy to two-substance dualism, at least one feature of the Epistemological Argument has impressed many contemporary philosophers as plausible and significant. This is the key claim that the concept of a conscious experience is not logically dependent on the concept of a material process or vice versa (see, e.g., Nagel, 1970). Unlike Descartes, though, recent philosophers have tended to suppose that if this conceptual distinctness obtains at all, it clearly obtains for sensations as well as for Cartesian "pure thoughts." These philosophers distinguish much more sharply than Descartes between the question of causal dependence of mind on body and the question of whether mental states are just physical states. It is the latter ques-

---

[9] For a detailed discussion and analysis of this argument, see Wilson, 1976, and Wilson, 1978, Chap.6, §3. I have shown in both places that the argument is integrally related to the famous "cogito reasoning" (most fully developed in *Meditation* II). I have also tried to show that the argument, as amplified in Descartes's *Replies to Objections*, is logically much stronger than has generally been recognized in the critical literature.

tion they take to be fundamentally at issue. To illustrate the continued plausibility of this part of the Cartesian position (extended to include sensations), we may take the case of a fairly acute pain. (The best situation of all, for seeing the force of this reasoning, is to be actually having a pain, but merely remembering past pain should suffice.) Now try the following thought experiment. While thinking as concretely as possible about the experience of pain (how it *feels* to be in pain), also think, as concretely as possible, about the firing of A-fibers, or some (perhaps loosely specified) event in the brain, or whatever you take to be the physical basis for the experience of pain. Now try to believe that the experience of pain is just the same thing as the relevant physical state. To many informed people, this thought experiment suggests that there is still much credibility to Descartes's claim that mental states *are* clearly conceivable without reference to physical states. (Again, this is not necessarily to deny the causal dependence of one on the other.) At the very least, Cartesian considerations are still capable of generating considerable perplexity about the ultimate place of mental states or events within the framework of physics or physiology.

The Indivisibility Argument

Descartes's third argument for the immateriality of mind can be passed over more briefly. In the *Meditations,* after presenting the Epistemological Argument, Descartes also argued as follows. Everything material is necessarily extended and hence (in principle) divisible; but the mind or self is completely indivisible:

> [F]or surely when I consider [the mind], or myself insofar as I am only a thinking thing, I can distinguish no parts in me, but I understand myself to be a thing completely one and whole; and although the whole mind seems to be united to the whole body, nevertheless if a foot is cut off, or an arm, or any other part of the body, I know that nothing is thereby taken away from my mind; and not even the faculties of willing, sensing, understanding, etc., can be said to be parts of it, because it is one and the same mind which wills, which senses, and which understands [A.T. VII, 86; H.R. I, 196].

Hence the mind is "altogether different from" the body.

The conception of the mind or consciousness as an indivisible unity has a long and complex philosophical history (Mijuskovic, 1974). Sometimes this conception has been used to "demonstrate" the immateriality of the mind, through claims that interactions of material particles could not conceivably *explain* the unity of consciousness, or the consciousness *of* the self *as* a unity (Mijuskovic, 1974, Chap. 3; Wilson, 1974). Descartes's argument, however, is more simple. He claimed merely that something necessarily true of any bit of matter, that it is divisible, is not at all true of mind.

There are a number of different ways of challenging this argument, but its deficiency can be illustrated by one very simple observation. Even within the terms of Cartesian physics, there certainly seem to be *properties* of body, such as motion, which do not have spatial parts. Unless Descartes was prepared to deny this observation (he did not in fact consider it), he would have had to acknowledge that his argument would only go through if he assumed that the mind is not just a *property* (i.e., that it is a substance in its own right). But then the Indivisibility Argument assumes the conclusion of the Epistemological Argument and is not sufficient in itself—contrary to what Descartes indicated in presenting it. We may conclude, then, that although Descartes's Indivisibility Argument is bound up with an important issue in the history of thought about the mind–body relation, it is not very powerful as it stands.

Historical Objections to Descartes's Position

Objections to the Notion of an Immaterial Thing

One principal aim of the preceding sections has been to exhibit some of the intellectual motivations for aspects of Descartes's dualism and to indicate which of these motivations may be still with us today. The present section will survey a few of the most fundamental objections to his position—each of them already noted by Descartes's contemporaries and often repeated, in various versions, down to the present time.

First, and perhaps most basically, many philosophers from the seventeenth century to the present have found the notion of an immaterial thing incoherent and unacceptable. Thus the materialist Thomas Hobbes (1588–1679), after noting that we can "conceive no act without its subject," continued in objection to Descartes:

> But hence it seems to follow that a thinking thing is something corporeal; for all subjects of all acts seem to be understood only under the concept of body, or under the concept of matter [sub ratione corporea, sive sub ratione materiae] [A.T. VII, 173; H.R. II, 62].

Descartes, in reply, said that Hobbes's inference was drawn "without any reason, and contrary to all practise of speech and all logic [A.T. VII, 175; H.R. II, 63]." He went on to note that both ordinary people and logicians are accustomed to saying there are two sorts of substances, spiritual and corporeal. And indeed Hobbes did not make his grounds for rejecting immaterial subjects (or substances) very clear in his objection. But certain later critics have agreed with Hobbes that there are logical difficulties in the notion of an immaterial particular—and have supported their contentions with careful arguments. It has been shown, for example, that there are serious problems in understanding how immaterial things are to be distinguished from each other at a given time, or reidentified at a later time. If we cannot conceive how this can be done, it is not clear we really can conceive "immaterial things." For the notion then appears to lack the sort of content required for a viable concept of a particular (compare Strawson selections in Morick, 1970, pp. 89-108).

Union and Interaction

Other serious difficulties for Descartes's position emerge when we consider the relation between allegedly immaterial minds and the bodies with which they are supposed to be "intimately conjoined." Where, for example, is the mind positioned? How does it act on the body (or the body on it)? Though it may seem that an immaterial "thinking thing" should not be ascribed any spatial location at all, it also seems that the mind must be located *somewhere* in the body, in order for interaction to take place. Descartes's considered view on the matter of location appears to have been that the mind exercises its volitional control within a special area of the brain but that it experiences sensation by virture of being "in" the various other parts of the body (A.T. XI, 351–352; H.R. I, 345). In other words, the mind is distributed throughout the body, or "joined to the whole body." Unfortunately, this makes it look as if the mind is, after all, *extended*—and hence part of the physical realm of *res extensa*. Descartes naturally wanted to avoid this conclusion but was never able satisfactorily to dissolve the appearance of contradiction.

Descartes's seventeenth-century critics, and most subsequent thinkers as well, were also uncomfortable with the supposition that an immaterial, unextended thing could initiate changes in a body. Thus, one of Descartes's correspondents, Princess Elizabeth, complained that she could not conceive of motion being caused in a body, except by the impact of another body. It was impossible, she said, to understand how the mind could "move the body," as Descartes claimed (A.T. III, 660–661, 683–685; E.D. 376). Additionally, the scientist–philosophers of the later seventeenth century objected that even if such interaction was intelligible in principle, the intervention of mind in nature was incompatible with the basic conservation principle of physics.

The Unity of Science

A third important source of dissatisfaction with Cartesian dualism is found (perhaps ironically) in the Cartesian ideal of a unified and universal science—interpreted more strictly and resolutely than by Descartes himself. On this stricter interpretation, the Cartesian exemption of the mental from the common principles of nature is seen as unacceptable. On this view, "the mental" *must* ultimately be subsumed under "the physical"—just as growth and other phenomena that had been interpreted teleologically by the Aristotelians were subsumed by Descartes under the principles of mechanism. This drive for a unified and comprehensive account of what is, remains to the present day in tension with reasons (some of which we have considered here) for regarding the mental as separate and irreducible.

Some Post-Cartesian Developments of Mind–Body Theory in the Seventeenth Century

Most of the major seventeenth-century philosophers were very strongly influenced by Cartesian notions. At the same time, there were many historically
important deviations from the claims of Cartesian dualism among Descartes's
immediate successors. I will here briefly sketch just three important issues on
which Cartesian doctrine came in for significant challenge in Descartes's own
century: the issue of *unconscious perception* or mental states; the possibility
of a *uniform deterministic model* of the operations of mind (with the connected question of human free will); and the question whether the mind
should be viewed as a distinct particular *res,* or substance. It should be
stressed that the writings of Descartes's immediate successors often show a
mixture of Cartesian and anti-Cartesian positions on these issues. For instance, G. W. Leibniz (1646–1716) affirmed unconscious perceptions in opposition to Descartes. Further, Leibniz held that all physical occurrences, including human behavior, had material and mechanistic causes (see, e.g., G.P.
IV, 537). He also maintained that all events whatsoever, including acts of will,
have their sufficient determining reasons. Yet Leibniz did agree with Descartes
that the mind is an immaterial substance, and he held that mental states in
general had teleological rather than mechanistic explanations. (Partly because
of the latter claim, Leibniz insisted that his form of determinism was compatible with a concept of free will.)[10] On the other hand, the writings of B.
Spinoza (1632–1677) show more systematic departures from Cartesianism.
Like Leibniz, Spinoza affirmed unconscious perceptions and insisted on a
thoroughgoing correlation between thought and matter. But Spinoza also
held, not merely that mental events are determined, but that the same type of
determination occurs on both the mental and physical levels. He openly
denied free will. Spinoza also denied that the human mind is a substance.
Even Spinoza remained a Cartesian, though, in one fundamental respect: he
maintained that thought and extension are irreducibly distinct aspects of
reality—each "conceived through itself" *Ethics,* I, X: Spinoza, 1972, vol. 2,
pp. 51–52.

Unconscious Perceptions

DESCARTES

We have noted earlier in this chapter the official Cartesian dogma that
"there is nothing in my mind of which I'm not in some manner conscious." We
have also observed that Descartes did sometimes acknowledge that I may be

---

[10] Leibniz's position on the mind–body relation involves the bizarre conclusion that mind and
body do not interact at all but each follows "its own laws" (teleological and mechanistic, respectively). He was led to this conclusion partly by the desire to retain teleology while also extending
mechanism beyond its Cartesian bounds, to cover all physical behavior without exception. An
additional factor important in his thinking was the view (alluded to in the preceding discussion of
union and interaction) that Cartesian mind–body interaction was inconsistent with fundamental
conservation laws in physics (cf. G.P. IV, 493–500; 517–554).

only implicitly (not "expressly"), or only potentially (not "actually") conscious of certain things in my mind. In the case of mental occurrences, such as having-the-thought-that-p, or perceiving-0, Descartes's basic position seems to be that I must be *actually* conscious of them. I need not, however, reflect on them or articulate them—and hence need not be expressly conscious of them. In the case of my mental capacities or powers, on the other hand, I may lack actual consciousness of them at any particular time. That is, I may be altogether unaware that I have the ability to perform such-and-such mental operations. Even in these cases, though, it will be *possible* for me to *become* aware of whether I do or do not have a particular capacity, merely by addressing myself to the question—merely by *looking for* the capacity within myself. This position may be connected with Descartes's claim that freedom of will is self-evident, or revealed by introspection: there cannot, at least, be any hidden mental determinants of my decisions (because if there were any I could instantly discover them).

Descartes's underlying reasons for so closely associating the mental with consciousness have not, in my opinion, been sufficiently examined or clarified in the literature. Some of the considerations we have noted in this chapter may provide clues. Consciousness is naturally associated with rational problem solving and decision making, and with perceptual experience (noticing, observing) and sensation. The former processes are, Descartes recognized, altogether outside the scope of the simple mechanistic explanations allowed by his physics. And they are, more specifically, in at least prima facie conflict with the deterministic and antiteleological assumptions reflected in these explanations. Perceptual experience and sensation, on the other hand, stand seemingly outside the scope of physics because they present to the experiencer a range of brute data (sweets and sours, pains and pleasures, louds and softs, russets, crimsons, and golds) that seem to elude adequate description through "geometrical" concepts. Thus, it was precisely those operations associated with consciousness that provided particularly strong reasons for rejecting materialistic monism.

An additional ground for Descartes's close association of the mental with consciousness may be the following. A dualist needs some fairly definite account of what differentiates his two ontological realms. For Descartes, this role was partly filled by consciousness. He lacked any other positive differentiating feature of the mental.[11]

SOME POST-CARTESIAN VIEWS

The acceptance of unconscious mental states, including mental occurrences, among Descartes's immediate successors springs from at least two very notable advances over Cartesian theory. First, there is the incipient development—especially in Leibniz's work—of an alternative account of a mental state: an account strictly independent of the notion of consciousness. Second, there is direct consideration of certain phenomena of both cognition

[11] Descartes also used the claim that he was (or could be on reflection) conscious of everything in his mind as a crucial premise in the argument for the existence of God in *Meditation* III.

and affect that seem to point to the postulation of unconscious perceptions and affects. These points cannot be demonstrated in any detail here, but I will try to explain them briefly.

Leibniz tended to assimilate mental states to representational states; a representation "expresses" what it represents. Further, "one thing expresses another in my terminology when there is a constant and rule-governed relation between what may be said of the one and what may be said of the other [G.P. II, 13]." No doubt Leibniz's account is too schematic to be much help. As he himself pointed out, the relation of expression as he defined it can hold between two *physical* things, for example, a map and a geophysical terrain. He has therefore not shown us how to distinguish mere physical mapping from a state which, while unconscious, counts as mental. Nevertheless, he has perceived the possibility that a mental–nonmental distinction could be theoretically drawn in some way other than direct appeal to consciousness.

The importance to Leibniz of this realization arose from what he saw as the theoretical necessity of postulating unconscious mental states. Behind this theoretical position lay his espousal of two fundamental principles—the law of continuity and the principle of sufficient reason. The former principle led him to suppose that perceptions vivid and definite enough to enter conscious awareness could not come into being *"tout d'un coup"* but must have elements and/or antecedents too faint and momentary to be individually noted. The latter principle led him to conclude that seemingly spontaneous or uncaused acts of will must actually have their source in interior, unobserved "movements" or impulses of the mind (N.E. II, i, §17; II, viii, §13 [pp. 117, 131]).

Spinoza accepted at least the latter part of Leibniz's position. He held on general theoretical grounds that all mental states, including seemingly spontaneous ones, have their determining causes, of which the individual person may be wholly unaware. In addition, Spinoza's observation of human affections and antipathies led him to conclude that laws of unconscious association were of basic importance in determining the course of our mental life, and our reactions to new persons and situations (*Ethics*, Pts. III–IV: Spinoza, 1972).

Psychological Determinism

In the late work, *The Passions of the Soul* (1649), Descartes made some attempt to extend his systematic explanation of phenomena to those aspects of our mental life that he saw as most directly dependent on the body. (These accounts are partly physiological and partly cast in terms of psychological association). But of course he denied that the "activities" of mind—its highest and most spontaneous operations—were subject to such systematic treatment. Other philosophers of the period, however, believed that the concept of thoroughgoing determinism should be extended to all states and occurrences without exception. In Leibniz's terminology, for everything that happens there is a *sufficient reason* for its occurrence; "nothing happens without a cause" (G.P. VII, 309). As already noted, Leibniz did not interpret this to mean that everything that happens has a mechanistic explanation—although everything material does.[12] He held that mental states, which in his view stand in causal relations only to other mental states and not to states of matter, must be explained in terms of immanent purposes or final causes. Leibniz did not attempt to develop a systematic deterministic psychology, however; in fact, he did not even make very clear what his postulated "teleological" determinations really amounted to.

Spinoza and Hobbes also maintained a thoroughgoing determinism but unlike Leibniz did not believe that mental states were distinguished from physical ones by requiring some special sort of explanation. Both considered explanation by final causes unscientific. Both made some attempt to develop a scientific psychology. (These psychological systems are not "experimental" in our sense—but then neither is Descartes's physics!) Hobbes in fact embraced reductive materialism. (He did not defend this position very adequately and did not consider seriously the possible arguments against it.) Spinoza opposed reductionism yet maintained that a mental event is in some sense identical with a particular physical event. Spinoza's position is difficult to make clear in a few words; indeed, his precise meaning still eludes specialists.

Are Minds Substances?

The Cartesian notion of the human mind as an independent thinking thing retained a certain life and vigor at least through the eighteenth century. Even in the seventeenth century, however, it came into question—and not only by doctrinnaire materialists like Hobbes. In Spinoza's system an individual mind, like an individual body, is merely a "mode" of the one self-contained and self-causing substance that he calls "God or Nature." Like the body, the mind is a complex entity, built up of elements in dynamic interrelation (in the case of the mind, these elements are "ideas"). It is equally dependent with the body on external influences. John Locke (1632–1704) followed Cartesian doctrine to the point of saying that human minds are *probably* distinct immaterial substances. Locke argued, however, that we cannot altogether rule out the possibility that we are only bodies to which God has "superadded" thought or consciousness (ECHU, IV, iii, §6: pp. 540 ff.). Locke held, further, that the question of whether our minds are distinct immaterial substances, or only properties of our bodies, is entirely irrelevant to the main aims of morality and religion. He maintained, for example, that personal immortality is an article of faith, independent of any belief about the metaphysical nature of the mind. Thus, in Locke's philosophy the notion of the mind as an immaterial

---

[12] Leibniz's conception of a mechanistic explanation was somewhat more complex than Descartes's; he recognized that the Cartesian theory of matter was oversimple and that Cartesian "laws of motion" were erroneously stated.

substance, while not entirely discarded, is accorded little if any theoretical or practical importance.[13]

Conclusion

As we have seen, the mind–body problem was a major focus of philosophical concern in the seventeenth century. Although religious influences were of some importance, the "problem" in its modern form is still more closely bound up with aspects of the conceptual scheme of modern science. Despite the enormous growth and development of the sciences between Descartes's time and our own, some basic conceptual features have persisted through the centuries. I have suggested that these at least partially account for the persistence of the mind–body problem itself.

In conclusion I want to take brief note of one aspect of Descartes's views about the mind that some contemporary philosophers regard as fundamentally important to his dualism and that I have so far ignored. In the *Meditations* (and other works too), Descartes presented himself as primarily concerned with achieving *certainty*. Deploying some more or less traditional skeptical arguments, he concluded (toward the beginning of the work) that none of his "former beliefs" is really beyond question. In particular, his beliefs in the existence in a material world, including his belief that he has a body, are subject to at least tenuous or "metaphysical" doubt. (Such beliefs, however ordinary and familiar, could be no more than the "illusions of dreams.") But, he found, his belief in his own existence as a thinking thing escaped the most powerful skeptical arguments he could conceive of. This belief, therefore, was his first point of certainty. He then went on to claim that his beliefs about his own "thoughts"—his conscious states generally—are all certain and indubitable. Thus, Descartes drew an important epistemological line between the mental and the physical. Judgments about his own mental states are immediately certain. Judgments about bodies, on the other hand, are not immediately certain. (Descartes thought we can know with assurance that a physical world exists but that justifying this belief requires the long and complex argument of the *Meditations*.) Many contemporary philosophers would hold that this, or a closely related, epistemological distinction lies at the very root of Cartesian dualism (see, e.g., Rorty, 1970). I have argued elsewhere that Descartes's deployment of skeptical arguments in expounding his mature

---

[13] This point has been argued persuasively and in detail by Milton Wachsberg in so-far unpublished writing (Wachsberg, 1977). Systematic criticism of the postulation of mental substances was provided in the eighteenth century by David Hume (1711–1776) and Immanuel Kant (1724–1804). Hume rejected the Cartesian notion of substance altogether. Kant tried to show that currently prominent "rationalist proofs" that our minds are mental substances were all fallacious (although he did not consider explicitly the three arguments of Descartes that I sketched in this chapter).

philosophy must be viewed at least in part as a strategy for gaining acceptance for his new, anti-Aristotelian conception of nature (Wilson, 1978). (This conception requires us to "doubt"—indeed to deny—that the physical world is just the way that it appears to the senses. The skeptical arguments Descartes enunciated are supposed to put the reader in the right frame of mind to entertain this conclusion.) But no one could deny that Descartes's view of the epistemological difference between the mental and the physical has been of immense historical importance. Like some of the fundamental assumptions of his philosophy of science, it has not so far been fully discredited (though many philosophers have tried). This aspect of Descartes's thought has also contributed importantly to the continuing tenacity of the mind–body problem.

References

Chomsky, N. *Cartesian linguistics.* New York: Harper & Row, 1966.

Descartes, R. [A.T.] *Oeuvres de Descartes,* (12 vols.). Published by Charles Adam and Paul Tannery, Nouvelle Présentation. Paris: J. Vrin, 1957.

Descartes R. [E.D.] *The essential Descartes* (M. D. Wilson, Ed.). New York: New American Library, 1969 (a).

Descartes R. [H.R.]*The philosophical works of Descartes,* (2 vols.) (E. Haldane & G. R. T. Ross, Eds. and trans.). Cambridge; Eng.: Cambridge University Press, 1969. (b) (Originally published, 1911.)

Descartes, R. [P.L.] *Descartes: Philosophical letters* (A. Kenny, Ed. and trans.). Oxford: Clarendon Press, 1970.

Leibniz, G. W, [N.L.] *Nouveaux essais.* In G. W. Leibniz, *Sämtliche Schriften und Briefe.* Berlin: Akademie-Verlag, 1962. (Published by the Deutsche Akademie der Wissenschaften zu Berlin, Sechste Reihe, Sechster Band.)

Leibniz, G.W. [G.P.] *Die philosophischen Schriften* (7 vols.). Published by C. J. Gerhardt. Hildesheim: Georg Olms, 1965. (Originally published, 1875-1890.).

Locke, J. [ECHU] *An essay concerning human understanding* (P. H. Nidditch, Ed.). Oxford: Clarendon Press, 1975.

Mijuskovic, B. L. *The Achilles of rationalist arguments* (International Archives of the History of Ideas: Series Minor, 13). The Hague: Martinus Nijhof, 1974.

Morick, H., Ed. *Introduction to the philosophy of mind.* Glenview, Ill.: Scott, Foresman, 1970.

Nagel, T. Armstrong on the mind. *Philosophical Review,* 1970, *79,* 394-403.

Penfield, W. *The mystery of the mind.* Princeton: Princeton University press, 1975.

Rodis-Lewis, G. *La problème de l'inconscient et le Cartésianisme.* Paris: Presses Universitaires de France, 1950.

Rorty, R. Incorrigibility as the mark of the mental. *Journal of Philosophy,* 1970, *67,* 399-424.

Sellars, W. *Science, perception, and reality.* New York: Humanities Press, 1963.

Spinoza, B. *Spinoza Opera.* Heidelberg: Carl Gebhardt, 1972.

Wachsberg, M. *Locke on the substance of the mind.* Unpublished manuscript, 1977.

Wilson, M. D. Leibniz and Materialism. *Canadian Journal of Philosophy,* 1974, *3,* 495-513.

Wilson, M. D. Descartes: The Epistemological Argument for mind–body dualism. *Noûs,* 1976, *10,* 3-17.

Wilson, M. D. *Descartes.* London: Routledge & Kegan Paul, 1978.

Chapter 3

Conceptual Changes in the Problem of the Mind–Body Relation

K. D. IRANI

Understanding the relation between the mind and the body has been a persistent and vexing problem in the history of human thought from antiquity to the present. In the last 100 years, it has been discussed in both the disciplines of psychology and philosophy. In the discipline of psychology, the mind–body problem manifested itself as the problem of the subject matter of psychological science. In contemporary philosophy, newer techniques of analysis have given us valuable insights and generated new formulations of the problem, which have influenced some schools of psychology and been influenced by them. In what follows, I wish to examine in historical perspective some of the significant views on this problem that have appeared in the philosophy of this century, indicate their relations to psychological theories, and suggest a formulation of the relation which is reasonably satisfactory, leaving its elaboration to the advances of future research and wisdom.

The problem emerged in modern thought in the following way: The mind was that which contained the typical mental contents of thoughts, such as beliefs and suppositions or hypothesis, feelings and emotions, decisions and intentions to actions. The material world, on the other hand, was the spatio-temporal matrix in which there was matter undergoing changes of one sort or another through the action of forces. These two worlds were distinct, the distinction having become part of the general conceptual apparatus of philosophy, certainly from the days of Descartes. Philosophers and

57

BODY AND MIND
Past, Present, and Future

psychologists have endeavored to formulate the relation or relations between the two; for at least in the case of the human individual, it was necessary that there be two kinds of relations between the mind and the body. The first is the problem of *perception*, where physical influences from material objects impinge upon sense organs to produce physical effects in the body which then generate sensations and perceptions in the mind leading to judgments about the external world. The second is the influence in the opposite direction, namely, the problem of *action*, where a mental content, that is, an intention to do something, becomes an act through the physico-chemical activation of the appropriate nerves which move the muscles of the body resulting in an external act. These two problems are part of the general problem of how mind and matter influence each other, as they must, and it is known as the mind–body problem.

Over the last 300 years, many types of answers have been suggested. We may divide the traditional set of responses to the mind–body problem into two classes: the monistic theories and the dualistic theories. There are essentially two monistic theories. One is materialism, which asserts the reality of matter alone, making the existence of mental phenomena equivalent to material events. The other is idealism, which asserts the reality of mind alone, making the existence of matter dependent upon mental or conscious contents. These theories in their pure form were prominent in the nineteenth century but have somewhat faded from view today. Turning to dualism, we find that though it asserts the reality of both mind and matter, there is considerable divergence among holders of dualism regarding the philosophic detail concerning their interrelation. In his Tarner Lectures in 1923, C. D. Broad (1937) listed five alternative forms of dualism. In contemporary thought, however, there are three types of relations between mind and matter which have been most discussed and which we shall consider. They are interactionism, epiphenomenalism, and parallelism. Interactionism asserts that some material events in the body generate certain mental events in the mind and also, in the other direction, some events in the mind generate certain changes in bodily states. Epiphenomenalism asserts that all mental events are generated by material events in the body, but no mental events generate bodily events; hence, it is an interaction in one direction only. Parallelism asserts that there is a correlation between mental events and material events in the body, usually with the proviso that though all mental events would have physical correlates not all physical events in the body, or even events in the brain, would necessarily have mental correlates.

These theories were not confined to the domain of philosophical speculation. Each one of the them was embedded in different psychological investigations. For example, the attempts to construct the laws of psycho-physics clearly presuppose an interactionist or epiphenomenalist base, while some explorations in psychopathology proceeded on the assumption of parallelism. The history of ideas concerning the mind–body problem, however, did not move smoothly; there were sharp changes in the approaches and attitudes toward the problem. The changes came from two sources: the development of *behaviorism* in psychology in the United States and the emergence of *logical positivism*, as an approach to philosophic problems of the Vienna Circle in Austria. Both these positions began to be influential in the 1920s and continued to be so directly or indirectly for over 40 years. We shall examine them with a view of extracting the contributions these approaches make to new ways of considering the mind–body problem.

Behaviorism is not typically a theory, it is an approach to the study of psychology and a program for its scientific development. Furthermore, the term "behaviorism" as it appears in the literature is ambiguous. It is advisable to distinguish three senses of behaviorism, which we may call *methodological behaviorism*, *conceptual behaviorism*, and *metaphysical behaviorism*.

The thesis of methodological behaviorism states that the study of psychology is the study of behavior. It is quite clear that this view was strongly influenced by the successful studies of conditioning and the theory of learning based upon that idea. Thus, according to behaviorism, what the psychologist studies is the set of responses manifested by an organism, and since the responses are related to the stimuli that impinge upon the individual subject, the laws of psychology express the relations between stimuli and responses. As the science advanced, it was expected that there would arise more detailed and refined laws relating complex stimuli (i.e., stimuli referring to complicated spatial and temporal organizations of the environment) to responses. The method of psychology was the study of behavior and its modifications as generated by varying conditions in the environment. And these statements relating the stimulus conditions to the behavioral responses constituted the *laws* of psychology. In contemporary psychology stimulus-response behaviorism has been succeeded by another form of behaviorism, which is called *operant conditioning*.

In operant conditioning, the variables that are related are the behavior of the organism, on the one hand, and the environmental situation which is the immediate consequence (or, as some would prefer to say, successor) thereof, on the other. The laws that are formulated account for the modification of behavior or the probability of its occurrence, by relating behavior to environmental outcomes of different sorts. These approaches are called *methodological behaviorism* because in method and content what they claim to study is observable behavior and no more, and the laws that are formulated thereby relate behavior to external conditions, be they stimuli or environmental outcomes. The description of mental events do not enter into the study of behavior nor the laws of psychology. Thus, the science of psychology is viewed as the science of behavior and nothing else.

There are several modified versions of methodological behaviorism in which the state of the organism is taken into account in constructing the laws that explain behavior. Thus one would say that the response, R, of an individual was the result of a stimulus, S, acting upon the individual in state, Σ. If the state, Σ, of the individual was described by using mentalistic predicates, such as the individual's wants, beliefs, hopes, fears, and intentions, the explanatory scheme would violate the requirements of methodological behaviorism. If, however, Σ is specified entirely by behavioral tests, then Σ becomes a set of behavioral dispositions and the constraints of behaviorist methodology remain intact.

We shall now consider *conceptual behaviorism*. This is essentially a philosophic thesis about the meanings of mental terms, such as belief, want, and intention. The traditional philosophic view, and for that matter the view commonly held by the vast majority of human beings, is that there are mental events and that mental terms are required to refer to such events. When we say that Mr. X believes that it will rain tomorrow and Mrs. X intends to buy an umbrella, it is commonly asserted that we are referring to certain mental events or states in the minds of Mr. and Mrs. X. It is this interpretation of the nature of mental terms that is rejected by conceptual behaviorism. According to the analysis provided by conceptual behaviorism, these so-called mental terms do not refer to events or states in the mind, they refer to dispositions to behave; hence, they are behavioral terms after all. There remains however, a problem about the terms "thought" and "thinking," which seemed to refer to certain contents and operations carried on by an individual in his mind. These terms were rendered behavioral by declaring them to refer to speech which was subvocal and accordingly not heard. Though these views were suggested in behaviorist psychology, the full flowering of this position came in some of the philosophic analyses of the logical positivists and somewhat later in the work of Gilbert Ryle (1949) in his very influential work, *The Concept of Mind*. These will be considered later.

There were some behaviorist psychologists who held that behaviorism implied a philosophic position, namely, the denial of the existence of something called *mind*. Some treated mind as coextensive with consciousness and denied the existence of consciousness; but what exactly was denied has remained unclear. This is the view that we have called *metaphysical behaviorism*. The reasons for asserting this position have never been formulated with clarity. We may summarize the most frequently presented argument for this position thus: since all we know and can ever know about the behavior of individuals is obtained by the scientific study of their behavior, and since the laws of this science refer only to behavior, the effective environment, and the dispositional states of the individual, there is no need to use the concept of mind (or consciousness) in the explanation of behavior. And since we cannot see what functions these concepts (i.e., mind and consciousness) could perform other than to explain behavior, these concepts are functionless or empty; a situation which can be expressed in metaphysical language by saying the mind does not exist. This argument seems to take us from an acceptance of methodological behaviorism to an acceptance of metaphysical behaviorism, but the inference is legitimate only if one accepts the view that the sole function of the concept of mind is to explain behavior, that is, it can justify its utility solely as a concept in scientific psychology. Those who accept the existence of the mind are most unlikely to accept this premise. They accept the existence of the mind as the domain of a certain type of events and states, which all of us have and with which we are most intimately acquainted. Thus for the nonbehaviorist, mind is not just an explanatory concept (though it might well be that, too), it is a category of certain types of facts which are given in the sense that they constitute our experience. One may then be a methodological behaviorist without being a metaphysical behaviorist, though the reverse would not be the case.

Most of the philosophical issues considered in the preceding discussion were greatly influenced by the emergence of a form of empiricist philosophy which was formulated by the Vienna Circle and was called logical positivism. We shall consider some of its fundamental tenets and its position on the mind–body problem. The most significant contribution of this school of thought was its attempt to formulate a theory of meaning, that is, to construct clear specifications by which one could distinguish a meaningful sentence from a meaningless (but still grammatically well formed) sentence. Subsequently, techniques were developed for rewriting unclear sentences in clearer language so that one could determine precisely what the sentence meant. One could, from this perspective, look at philosophic problems such as the mind–body problem, and discover which of them are genuine and which are not, the latter being called pseudo-problems.

The theory of meaning as developed in logical positivism underwent some changes; it was the earlier form that had the most influence on thinking in psychology and the social sciences in general, and that is what we shall consider at present. The first part of a theory of meaning is the construction of a criterion for distinguishing a sentence which is meaningful from a sentence which is meaningless. Consider the following two sentences: "Iron is heavier than aluminum" and "Justice is more green than 2^3." The first is meaningful and the second is not. The criterion by which this distinction was made by the logical positivists can be formulated in two parts, in the following way: for a statement to be meaningful it must be either (a) analytic (i.e., one whose truth can be established by a consideration of meaning alone, such as 'all brothers are males') or (b) if not analytic, it must be verifiable in principle. For a proposition to be verifiable it must be possible to formulate a method for its verification. Applying this criterion to 'Justice is more green than 2^3,' one can see that (a) is inapplicable and (b) is violated. For clearly, the sentence "Justice is more green than 2^3" is one for which there is no method of verification, and thus our intuition of its meaninglessness is vindicated by this criterion. Similarly, if a problem in the form of a question is such that no answer can be given to it in the form of a proposition capable of verification, then it is not a meaningful question and the problem is not a genuine one; it is a pseudoproblem. This criterion was not the only provision of the theory of meaning; the theory further declared that the meaning of a proposition which claimed to be factual was given by the conditions of its verification.

The views of the logical positivists on the mind–body problem were developed in the late 1920s and early 1930s. Interesting formulations of these views appear in the papers of Moritz Schlick, the founding spirit of the Vienna Circle, and Carl G. Hempel, an eminent logical positivist, in articles in the *Revue de Synthese* of 1935. Hemple (1949), in the article entitled "The Logical Analysis of Psychology," used the verifiability theory of meaning to argue that when we use a psychological proposition such as "Paul has a toothache," its meaning is given by the conditions of its verification, which are tests such as *(a)* Paul weeps and makes gestures of such and such kinds; *(b)* at the question "What is the matter?" Paul utters the words "I have a toothache"; *(c)* closer examination reveals a decayed tooth with exposed pulp; *(d)* appropriate physiological changes are observed in Paul, etc. Thus, all psychological propositions, when meaningful (i.e., verifiable), turn out to be statements which refer to physical events. In other words, psychological statements, that is, statements using mentalistic words, are translatable into statements that use only physicalistic words. Mentalistic words are merely convenient summary expressions for long and involved materially described test conditions. The relationship between mental terms and physical or material terms is one of translation into verifiable test conditions and nothing more. If one insists on asking what the relation is between the mind and the body and looks for the answer to be anything over and above the translation of terms, one has created a pseudoproblem, which is not a problem at all.

The logical positivist viewpoint became widely known to philosophers in the English-speaking world with the publication in 1936 of A.J. Ayer's highly influential book *Language Truth and Logic*. It discusses the mind–body problem briefly, but there is a significant remark which may be quoted: "The problem with which philosophers have vexed themselves in the past, concerning the possibility of bridging the 'gulf' between mind and matter in knowledge or in action, are all fictitious problems arising out of the senseless metaphysical conception of mind and matter or minds and material things as 'substances' [Ayer, 1946, p. 124]." Here again, the traditional way of looking at the mind–body problem was rejected as a metaphysical pseudoproblem.

A rather detailed discussion of what was viewed as the correct way of dealing with the mind–body problem from the perspective of logical positivism appeared in a paper entitled "On a Relation Between Psychological and Physical Concepts" in *Revue de Synthese* in 1935 by Moritz Schlick (1949). There Schlick writes of "refusing to pose (the mind–body problem) in terms of mental and physical substances; beginning, instead, with the harmless question as to how, in general, we have come by our physical and psychological concepts [p. 393]". At a later point in the paper, he states that "The adjectives 'physical' and 'mental' formulate only two different representational modes by which the data of experience are ordered; they are different ways of describing reality. That in which one counts ordered coincidences in inter-subjective space, is the physical; whereas that which operates by the grouping of intensive properties is a psychological description [p. 403]".

These views coming from Europe found rapid acceptance among those American philosophers who inclined toward the empiricist cast of pragmatism. After exchanges between some American, British, and Viennese philosophers, a slightly modified logical positivism came to be renamed *logical empiricism*, and it became a very influential philosophic viewpoint from the late 1930s into the 1950s. During this period, the mind–body problem was not much discussed, neither was it successfully banished. But in the area with which we are concerned here, one major philosophic contribution did survive from this school. It was the reformulation of the mind–body problem. The problem, as these philosophers saw it, was to analyze the logical characteristics of propositions about mental events and propositions about physical events, and to establish the relation between these two kinds of propositions.

It is not easy to describe the great variety of ideas in psychology and philosophy of mind at the time of the impact of the two intellectual movements, behaviorism and logical empiricism. Prior to the mid-1930s, philosophers and psychologists were still concerned with what they called mental phenomena and theories of mind. There appeared in 1932 a book widely read by philosophers, *Six Theories of Mind* by Charles W. Morris (1932). It presented most of the traditional theories of the mind, including the notion of *mind as function*, which presented the views of the pragmatists, views which were closest to those accepted by experimental psychologists. But profound and rapid changes were taking place, and the laws of behavior, rather than the study of the mind, became the focus of psychological research. These were the laws subject to clear empirical verification and making no reference to contents of the mind. In other words, the product of psychological investigation came to be what the behaviorists and logical positivists required it to be. It must be admitted, however, that the original strict demands of both behaviorism and logical positivism were somewhat moderated. Instead of the logical positivists' original requirement that all psychological terms be translated into observable physical predicates, there was the new logical empiricist requirement that all psychological terms be operationally defined. Similarly, the behaviorist position was modified so that it did not require the rejection of the laws of behavior, which included the description of the state of the organism in terms of intervening variables, as long as the intervening variables were operationally defined and, of course, performed the function of predicting behavior.

This view of the science of psychology was explicitly formulated by C.C. Pratt (1939) in *The Logic of Modern Psychology;* He named the position *critical positivism* and enunciated its program of scientific investigation in psychology.

We now turn to two different and significant influences in the philosophy of

mind. About the middle of this century there appeared in England two important works in philosophy which were to influence the entire field of the
philosophy of mind but whose impact on psychology is very difficult to
assess. The first was Gilbert Ryle's *The Concept of Mind* (1949) and the second was Ludwig Wittgenstein's *Philosophical Investigations* (1953). Many of
Wittgenstein's unusual ideas however, had come to be known by 1949 in one
form or another before the publication of his book in 1953 through the cir-
culation of the notes of his students and the works of his disciples.

Wittgenstein's approach to the philosophy of mind is a critique of the way
in which we interpret the language we use to talk about mental events. We
hold that when we say, for example, that "I have a toothache" or "I am
expecting to see my friend at 4:30" or "I know that this book is on the table,"
we are referring to some mental event or states. This, according to Wittgenstein, is a philosophic mistake. For if we hold, as we are very likely to, that
mental events occur in the consciousness of an individual subject and that the
contents of consciousness are by their very nature private (i.e., X cannot be
aware of the contents of consciousness of Y directly, as Y is of them, although
X may be informed about them or infer their existence from external
evidence), then we could not possibly talk about them.

To talk about a private mental event, we need a word which refers to it,
and such a word would be one which the speaker alone would know how to
use. A language necessarily requires that all members of the linguistic community learn and apply the same rules of use for the words of the language.
This could not be the case if our so-called mental words refer to mental
events, and mental events are private. Wittgenstein goes one step further.
How, he asks, would the user of a mental word himself know if he has used
the word correctly? All he can rely on is his memory, which is fallible. How
can he find out if he has made a mistake or not? The upshot is that if we hold
that mental words refer to mental events that are private, the language
resulting therefrom would produce sentences which could not be established
to be true or false and for which there could be no warrant that anything has
been communicated. This is an untenable situation for any language. Understanding the nature of language requires us to accept that there must be
intersubjective or public rules for the use of all words in the language; hence,
there can be no *private language.* Since our traditional view of the mind implies that mental words are part of a private language, our traditional view of
the mind, mental events, and the language by which we refer to them is
mistaken.

Given the Wittgensteinian critique of the referential character of mental
terms, the questions that arise are: How do we understand mental terms? How
do we learn and teach them? The Wittgensteinian approach to this problem is
to be found in what one may call (although he would probably not) his theory
of meaning. Wittgenstein insisted that instead of asking for the meaning of a
word one must ask for its use. When one knows how to use a word in the con-

texts in which it appears, one knows its meaning. And when two persons, who both know the various uses of a word, employ the word in oral or written exchanges, they are communicating linguistically with each other. There are criteria for the use of a word in particular contexts, and when we learn or teach the use of a word, we are explicitly or implicitly learning or teaching these criteria. And, of course, for the purpose of teaching, the criteria must be public. Private criteria cannot be taught, and unteachable words cannot be part of the language. With most words in the language, however, the criteria of use are not precise and they shift from one context of use to another, which can also be learned. We can see how this approach may be applied to mental terms. Examine the way in which a child or a person unfamiliar with the language learns the word "pain." A pin pricks the skin, a drop of blood appears, and the child starts crying; we tell the child that we know he is crying because he feels pain; we assure him that the pain will lessen and disappear and he will not be crying in a few minutes; and so on. After several such linguistic encounters, the child acquires the criteria of use for the word "pain" and will use the word himself. He then knows the meaning of the word "pain."

Even from this highly oversimplified account of Wittgenstein's treatment of mental terms, one can see its close relationship to conceptual behaviorism. Wittgenstein does not equate the meaning of a mental word with behavior; he moves the discussion of meaning to a consideration of *use* and requires use to be specified necessarily by public or behavioral criteria. It would be fair to say that this part of Wittgenstein's analysis of the meaning of mental terms is widely accepted in contemporary philosophy. The other part of his thesis, however—that mental terms do not refer to internal mental states or events—is not. One could accept the first part and not the second. That is, one could hold that we learn to use mental words by learning the criteria of their use but also hold that the word happens to refer to some state or event in the individual's consciousness which is present when the conditions specified in the criteria are present. As a result of Wittgenstein's work and the extraordinarily rich discussion it generated in the field, a very refined form of conceptual behaviorism came to be accepted—a form which though requiring, on the one hand, the use of mental words to be determined by behavioral criteria, refused, on the other hand, to identify the meaning of the mental word with behavioral conditions.

At the same time that Wittgenstein's work was being discussed, there was also considerable discussion of Gilbert Ryle's *The Concept of Mind*, which may rightly be considered the most influential book on the subject in the 1950s. Ryle undertook the task of freeing philosophy from the Cartesian misconception, which he called the "official doctrine." This doctrine asserted that human beings are composed, on the one hand, of matter located in space and time, which obeys mechanical laws, and, on the other, of mind, wherein are located states and processes given to the consciousness of that individual, with the body and mind somehow harnessed together during life but possibly separated after death. A person's life, according to the official doctrine, consists of two collateral histories, one concerning bodily events, which is public, and the other concerning mental events, which is private. Ryle considered this view to be a myth—he also called it "the dogma of the ghost in the machine"—which was to be destroyed by an analysis of our mental conduct concepts, resulting in a diagnosis of the view as logical error. Ryle proposed to identify the underlying error as a category-mistake. We shall not examine here the philosophic argumentation executed with extraordinary virtuosity. We shall just extract a summary of his position, however distorting it may be to his mode of philosophizing.

When we describe what we take to be mental events or states by such statements as "X believes that coffee is bad for his digestion" or "X wants to visit the Grand Canyon," we are committing, according to Ryle, a logical mistake, because words like "belief" and "want" do not perform the function of naming internal, private states; they are words which refer to behavioral dispositions. The person who *believes* that coffee is bad for his digestion will avoid it when it is offered to him, will be disposed to inquire in a restaurant if some other hot beverage is available, will be interested in finding out if some of the coffee substitutes will satisfy him without affecting his digestion, and so on. Similarly, the person who *wants* to visit the Grand Canyon will inquire into the modes of traveling to the Canyon and the costs of such a trip, will save money to defray the expenses, and the like. These dispositions are formulated as hypothetical propositions, which have the following form: if some conditions are satisfied, then some consequence will (or is likely to) follow.

Ryle's analysis moves successively from a dicussion of cognitive terms to volitional terms, emotional terms, and other mental terms. Generally, Ryle distinguishes between those mental terms which are dispositional and those which are not, namely, those which are episodic (Ryle, 1949, Chap. 5). The latter, he argues, refer either to some events in the environment or in the body, as, for example, a throb of excitement or a pang of remorse. There is another distinction that Ryle makes. There are some words which seem to apply to mental occurrences when in truth what they refer to are performances of various tasks: these are called "task words." Other words that refer to the successful conclusion of these tasks are called "achievement words." For example, looking for one's lost fountain pen is a task, finding it an achievement. Verbs like "know," "discover," "solve," "prove," and "perceive" do not, according to Ryle, refer to mental activities. They refer to no activities at all, because they are logically not the type of words which could refer to activities; they are achievement words and refer to the successful conclusions of identifiable public activities.

Whether or not one agrees with Ryle's analysis, and there are many who have serious reservations, his approach has forced detailed investigations of the nature of individual mental terms. The position of Ryle, more widely held in the 1950s than in the 1970s, gave support from another direction to the position of conceptual behaviorism. Looking at the history of philosophic explorations into the nature of statements about mental activity or events from the 1920s to the 1950s or 1960s, it seems that the thesis of conceptual behaviorism was progressively vindicated, though, undoubtedly changed from its crude and simplistic beginnings into a very sophisticated and multifaceted doctrine. One very powerful reason for the success of this thesis is that, since it does away with mental events as the necessary referents of mental terms, it removes the mind-body problem as a fundamental philosophical issue.

Nevertheless, the mind–body problem is again being actively discussed. There are not only several philosophical theories and approaches involved in these discussions but also psychological theoretical perspectives, for example, from cognitive psychology, psychopathology, and physiological psychology. We shall examine some ways in which the insights of earlier views of mind and body can be incorporated into a scheme for restructuring this problem. So that, as the logical empiricists had anticipated, the problem loses its philosophical perplexity and becomes one which can be progressively solved by the gradual accumulation of empirical information and its appropriate logical organization. But before we come to that point, we must retrace our steps and consider two views which were in opposition to the historical strands that we have considered. One of these was called the *"double-aspect theory"* of mind and matter, and, the other, a later theory, came to be called the *"identity theory."*

Both these theories start by accepting that mental terms refer to mental states and events, and physical terms refer to bodily states and events. And since the problem requires us to focus on the brain, the physical terms will be taken to be terms describing events in the brain with extensions into the nervous system and perhaps also the hormonal system. The double-aspect theory took the view that descriptions of brain states and processes and descriptions of mental states and processes were two aspects of the same situation. The two kinds of descriptions did not describe two different kinds of realities but were aspects of one reality. The descriptions of psychic states were descriptions of "the inner being of brain processes," mind and brain being the same thing seen from two different points of view. This view of the mind–body problem—generally held by the critical realists, such as D. Drake, Roy W. Sellars, and C. A. Strong in the United States, and also by C. Lloyd Morgan and S. Alexander in Great Britain—was widely discussed in the 1920s and 1930s.

When one says, however, that the "mental" and the "physical" are two aspects of the same thing, what is the "thing" one is referring to? D. Drake in a paper entitled "What is a Mind?" stated that "the mind *is* the brain." He stated further "in using the term 'mind' we are conceiving these cerebral events as they are on the inside, so to speak; i.e. we are thinking of their substance.

When we use the term 'brain' we are looking at them from the outside, through our sense-organs" and again "the mind *is* the reality which, when cognized through the senses, we call the brain [Drake, 1926, p. 235]."

Many have felt that this position incorporates a genuine insight, and one that is not altogether new. There is a clear similarity to the views of Spinoza on the subject. And similar views were not uncommon in the medical literature on the nineteenth and early twentieth century. The difficulty with this view is that its crucial assertions are invariably metaphorical, and one can never be confident of knowing exactly what the thesis is. It was, therefore, a matter of great interest when a new and very refined version of this theory was formulated by Herbert Feigl in 1957 and later published as a book entitled *The "Mental" and "Physical"* (Feigl, 1967), which included a postscript to the original essay. This work became the focus of philosophic discussion and influenced much of the philosophical literature on the subject for some time. Before considering this thesis, however, we must go back in time and examine the concept of "reduction" (a significant topic in the philosophy of science), which is presupposed in most of the discussions of the identity theory espoused by Feigl and many others.

When one states that a subject matter or domain of knowledge is reduced to another domain, what is the claim that is being made? We can proceed to answer this by examining the conditions which must be satisfied for an acceptable reduction to be established. Let us say there are two domains of knowledge, A and B, each being a set of propositions. Suppose we are claiming to reduce domain B to domain A. The following two conditions would be required to be satisfied: (*a*) All the terms (other than logical connectives) constituting the propositions of B must be translated into terms which appear in the propositions of A. Thus, when the translation is carried out all propositions of B will now be formulated in the language appropriate to A. (*b*) All the propositions of B, translated into the terms of A, must be derivable by deduction from propositions in domain A. These are reasonably clear criteria for reduction, the only problematic notion being that of translation, stated in condition (*a*), around which most of the philosophic disputes revolve.

Suppose we are concerned with the reduction of the domain of psychology (in this case B) to that of neurophysiology (in this case A). At this point, there is some lack of clarity about what the domain of psychology is to include, but that shall be considered later. Take a single proposition in this domain, that is, domain B; for example, take the proposition "frustration produces agression." In order to satisfy condition (*a*) we shall translate from B to A the three terms "frustration," "agression," and "produces." The only sense we can give to the notion of translation in this connection is that of correlation. That is, we establish that when there is frustration of the individual a certain neurophysiological state is invariably correlated with it; let us call this state X. Similarly, we establish that a neurophysiological state Y is invariably correlated with aggression. The term "produces" may be maintained unchanged

in the translation. Thus, upon translation, the proposition "frustration produces aggression" becomes "X produces Y." At this point, the reduction has
clearly not been achieved; all we have is a translation from one set of terms
into another. But if we can satisfy condition (b), that is, if we can show that
there are propositions in A (i.e., laws in the domain of neurophysiology) from
which one can deduce that a state X will produce state Y, then, as far as this
proposition is concerned, we have achieved a reduction. And in general, when
every proposition of the domain of psychology is so translated into and
deduced from the propositions of neurophysiology, we would be entitled to
assert a reduction of domain B to domain A.

One persistent misconception about reduction which should be mentioned
is that when, say, domain B is reduced to A, domain B is somehow
repudiated, eliminated, or at least rendered superfluous. That is not the case.
In our previous example, if we had an acceptable proposition "frustration produces aggression" in domain B, the fact that it could be derived from the laws
of A does not in any way eliminate it or make it less acceptable or
superfluous. Its stature as a true proposition remains unchanged.

We must return to the notion of translation which we encountered in condition (a) for reduction. All that one can assert in the kind of translation we
have examined is that when a term in domain B, call it T_B, is applicable, we
find that a term or a set of terms in A, call them collectively T_A, are also applicable. What we have is a correlation not an identity of meaning. This
brings us to the philosophic issue which divides the proponents and the op-
ponents of the identity theory. But before we determine that two different
linguistic descriptions are descriptions of the same thing, as supporters of the
identity theory claim, we must consider the relation between different kinds of
equivalent propositions.

The subject of equivalent propositions has generated diverse views in contemporary semantical theory, but the simpler aspects are tolerably free of controversy. Suppose we have two sentences, S_1 and S_2, which are linguistically
different in that S_1 contains the term T_1 and S_2 contains the term T_2. Furthermore, S_1 and S_2 are equivalent, that is, in every situation they are both true or
both false. The following several possibilities may be the case:

1. Terms T_1 and T_2 may be synonymous, so that by a mere inspection of
   the terms any one who knows their meanings would judge that S_1 and 2_2
   are equivalent. For example,
   S_1: X is the brother of Y.
   S_2: X is the male sibling of Y.
2. Terms T_1 and T_2 are not synonymous but can be shown to refer to the
   same object or situation. For example,
   S_1: The conical mountain to the north of X is a mile high.
   S_2: The arched mountain to the south of Y is a mile high.

It takes an investigation to discover that the expression "the conical mountain to the north of X" refers to the same object as does the expression "the arched mountain to the south of Y."

3. Terms T_1 and T_2 refer to different objects or situations but appear invariably correlated. This is the case we are interested in. For example,
S_1: X perceives a flash of light.
S_2: X has a certain (specifiable) neural activity.

Those who say that mental states and brain states are different descriptions of the same set of events consider the relations between the two kinds of propositions to belong not just to type 3 but also to type 2. This is the view of those who hold the identity theory of the brain and mind in its strong form. But there is no way of establishing that there is some common event or entity of which these are two different descriptions. If all one can assert is that the descriptions are always correlated, then one falls short of claiming that they are different aspects or descriptions of one underlying situation. And even if we could achieve a reduction of the mental description of behavior to the domain of the neurophysiological, the assertion of a double-aspect or an identity theory of the relation of body and mind seems unwarranted for a correlation between two descriptions cannot, by itself, support an inference to an underlying identity.

Having surveyed some of the significant contemporary contributions to the problem of the relation between the mental and the physical, one is inclined to ask how, in view of our present-day knowledge and insights, may this relation be construed. Here I should like to suggest an approach which utilizes some findings of contemporary psychology as well as the formulations of phenomenologists and does not go beyond what can be established in scientific investigations.

As we have seen the mind–body problem is a philosophic problem, that is, it is a problem which is to be approached in the spirit of reorienting our conceptual framework rather than constructing new hypotheses or looking for new evidentiary material. The reorienting I suggest is not altogether new; it is really an attempt to clarify and restructure the old distinction of mind and body. The difficulty with the dualism of the Cartesian type is that it views mind and body as two different kinds of substances or two types of realities; but this mode of constructing the problem has changed, and now we look for acceptable ways of *relating mental events* to *physical* or *bodily events*. To this end, we shall now examine the conceptual scheme in which we use mental terms and the scheme in which we use physical terms and inquire into the possible relations that may be established between the items in the two conceptual schemes.

Consider first a purely physical account of the behavior of an individual. This will be in accord with the strictest form of methodological behaviorism. The behavior of the individual is some activity of that individual at some point in his life history, and it must, according to this scheme, be known to be a result of some continuing set of internal events in the organism or the influence of some external event acting upon the organism. Of course, these explanations would be achieved by constructing laws which would tell us how certain states of the organism, Σ, when affected by certain external events, S, would result in some type of response of the organism, R. The form of explanation in this scheme is essentially provided by the notion of causality. The activity of the stimulus, S, upon the state of the organism, Σ, is the causal event which generates a process which terminates in the manifestation of the response activity, R. Notice that in this description the words "individual" and "organism" can be used interchangeably. Indeed, we could compare the individual to a machine functioning in accordance with some causal (either deterministic or statistical) laws. If this scheme can be applied successfully to all behavior, and there is no a priori reason for denying it, then it provides complete explanation. But the nature of these explanations must be clearly understood. The explanations are causal, exactly the same type of explanations we employ in explaining natural phenomena (with the exception of quantum physics). In this scheme mental terms, such as beliefs, wants, and intentions, do not enter.

We shall now consider an entirely different account of behavior. This is given in terms of the states of consciousness of the individual, hence called a "phenomenological description." An individual, X, performs an act, A. We may inquire of X what he was trying to do, and he discloses his intention, which enables us to comprehend the act. We may ask for an explanation of why he did it. An answer may very well take the following form: X wanted to achieve a goal, B, and believed that doing A would lead to B. We may inquire further into why X wanted B or why he held that particular belief, and we would get answers in terms of X's prior perceptions, wants, desires, and so forth. The mode of explanation in this scheme is that of providing reasons in the mind of the individual agent. This is a perfectly satisfactory mode of explanation of behavior; indeed, this is the way human beings offer explanations and come to understand each other's behavior in normal, and not so normal, social interactions.

Thus, we have formulated two conceptual schemes for understanding or explaining behavior. These schemes roughly parallel the traditional distinction between the physical and the mental. However, the distinction that is being made here requires more precise formulation. Let us proceed by establishing the conditions for a *conceptual scheme*. A *conceptual scheme* is determined in accordance with two principles:

1. *Principle of Existence*, which specifies the entities or events that are taken as existing.
2. *Principle of Explanation*, which specifies the conditions for adequate explanation.

Applying these principles, we are in a position to formulate a clear contrast between the two conceptual schemes. In the *physicalist* or *behavioral scheme*, the existent events are the various properties of the physical organism as they are identifed in space and time, and the principle of explanation is causality given by laws which tell us what changes occur in the activity of the organism. On the other hand, in the *mentalist* or *phenomenological scheme*, the existent events are various states of mind or items in consciousness, and the principle of explanation is the scheme of reasons given in terms of wants and beliefs. What this distinction shows us is that it is not enough to distinguish between mental events and bodily events, the distinction is a much deeper and more pervasive one. Indeed, the events in the two schemes are of different kinds: In the behavioral scheme, the event is a bodily manifestation or movement located at a specific point in space and time, whereas in the phenomenological scheme, it is a mental event or state expressed, for example, as "X believes that p" or "X wants q to be the case," etc. and which is related to an individual consciousness at some time but without any possible location in space. But, further and more significantly, each scheme provides explanation in a special way different from the other.

From this point of view, it can be said that the insights of the various traditional dualisms, for example, the Cartesian one of substances and the later one of terms, are preserved and emerge in a clear and logically acceptable form as the distinction between two conceptual schemes, as described in the preceeding paragraphs.

Having formulated the distinction, we must now consider the relation: What possible relations can we establish between the terms in the different schemes? The one relation we can consider as possible is that of temporal correlation; that is, when an individual, X, declares that he is in a particular state of consciousness, a specific, highly complex, neurological state may be correlated with it. It is widely believed that for specific phenomenological states, there will be corresponding specific neurological states, and these relations can be expressed as laws of correspondence between items in the two conceptual schemes. This is a matter of empirical discovery. One may now ask: what other relations can be established between items in the two schemes? Can we not assert that a bodily event causes a phenomenological state or vice versa? These questions would have to be answered in the negative. Causal relations from one scheme to the other cannot be coherently formulated. But whatever empirical information we wish to convey by asserting that a bodily event causes a phenomenological state or event, or vice versa, can be expressed in the structure of the two conceptual schemes with only the relations of correspondence between them. Suppose an individual when injected with a certain substance (a bodily event) comes to feel apprehension about his environment (a mental event). This is frequently taken to be an indication of the bodily event causing a mental event. In the description of the two conceptual schemes, the sequence of events would be described in the following way: the injection of the substance causes physiological changes, that is, a process of continuous physiological changes. One of the neurophysiological states in this causal process corresponds to a phenomenological state of apprehension, which then applies to the perceived environment. A similar description can be given for a mental state leading to a bodily event. The descriptions of events progressing in time can be given in either one or the other of the two schemes. Either they are the movements of thoughts in one scheme, or they are transformations in the neurological structure of the body. The only relation between the two is specified by the *correspondence* of an event in one scheme with one in the other.

Thus, the structure of the two schemes with the sole relations of temporal correspondence between them can be seen to be totally adequate for expressing some of our intuitively obvious statements of causal connections from one scheme to the other. But granting this adequacy, one might still insist that a statement describing a causal connection between mental and physical events has not been ruled out. Why should the structure of describing all events in one or the other of the two conceptual schemes prevent us from asserting a statement such as "shining the light in the corner *caused* him to see the dime"? The reason is that such a causal statement is incoherent, and that can be shown in the following way. When we make a judgment of a specific causal connection, what we are necessarily implying is that there is a continuous process in space–time such that one temporal cross-section of this process can be called the cause and some succeeding temporal cross-section the effect. Notice what happens when we apply this mode of analysis to the example "shining the light in the corner caused him to see the dime." Let us describe the continuous process of these events in the spatiotemporal world. The light shines in the corner; it is reflected unevenly from the objects on which it shines; light waves of different frequencies (colors) and amplitudes (intensities) fall upon the eyes of the observer; various photochemical and electrochemical reactions occur in the retina of the observer, which generate impulses in the optic nerve; these in turn activate impulses in the occipital lobes and other parts of the brain. We can continue this description indefinitely, but it will be limited to continuous changes in the physical variables of the neurological system. Why does the phenomenological description of the *perception* of the dime not appear as an event in this description? Because being a phenomenological state, it cannot (logically cannot) appear somewhere in a spatiotemporal continuity of physical changes. The point is clearly stated by A. J. Ayer:

> Since the mind has no position in space—it is by definition not the sort of thing that can have a position in space—it does not literally make sense to talk of physical signals reaching it; nor are there such temporal gaps in the procession of nervous impulses as would leave room for the mental characters to intervene. In short, the two stories will not mix. It is like trying to play *Hamlet* not without the Prince of Denmark, but with Pepicles, the Prince of Tyre. But to say that the two stories do not mix is not to say that either of them is superfluous. Each is an interpretation of certain phenomena and they are connected by the fact that, in certain conditions, when one of them is true, the other is true also [Ayer, 1950, p. 74].

There has been considerable discussion in contemporary philosophy of the nature of reasons and causes. From the point of view expressed here, we use the term "reason" to identify states in the phenomenological scheme and the term "cause" to identify events in the physicalist scheme, and since the two schemes do not mix, reasons and causes are taken to give two different and independent explanations. It has been argued sometimes (see, for example, Davidson, 1963) that the same event may be both a reason and a cause of one's behavior. Let us say there is an event, E, in the environment of X which leads to X's behavior, B. We can say that, given appropriate behavioral laws, E was a stimulus and thus a cause for the behavioral response B. However, if B is to be explained phenomenologically, the explanation would incorporate X's perception of E, leading to a belief that something (perhaps E itself) is the case, which becomes part of the reason for doing B. E is the cause of X's behavior, but X's belief that E is in the environment is the reason for X's action. Thus, a simple identification of causes and reasons becomes misleading.

A problem which appears at first sight to be purely empirical turns out to be significantly philosophical. It is the problem of how we establish the temporal correlation between events in the two schemes. When as experimenters we proceed to establish such a correlation in X, there is no difficulty in identifying a bodily state in X; but how do we determine the mental state of X at that time? We have to infer it either from X's overt behavior or from a report given by X orally, in writing, or in some other way. This situation should not mislead us into saying that the correlation we establish is between bodily states, on the one hand, and behavior, on the other. As we have seen, the behavioral indications may be the criteria for asserting the existence of the mental state; they do not name or describe it. But if we look at this situation from the perspective of X himself, can we be clear about what he is referring to when he informs us about his mental states? Can X tell us what particular state he has in his stream of consciousness at a given moment? It may well be that X may have to identify a specific mental content of his own consciousness, either by language or by some suitable symbol system, to be able to correlate it with a description of his bodily state. The nature of the correlation cannot be considered to be altogether clear.

Psychologists and phenomenologists have consistently encountered the perplexing problem of how one can accurately report the contents of consciousness. At the same time, it has been claimed that in the phenomenological scheme, we do talk about states of consciousness. We can move in the direction of removing this disparity when we realize that in phenomenological statements we are not just reporting an item in consciousness. When, for instance, X is asked why he went into the coffee shop, X may instantly reply that he wanted to have breakfast. It is unlikely that in the few moments before he was questioned there was such a clearly defined want as an element in his stream of consciousness which X identified by an act of introspection and then reported. The answer which X gave is a social act governed by the rules of the language and having some reference to his state of consciousness. This last element cannot be totally neglected. Suppose X had given the above answer to his interlocutor but had actually entered the coffee shop to meet someone, X would have uttered a falsehood precisely because what he said did not report what he had in mind.

The background of a phenomenological report is very complex. It seems as if part of the mind extracts from the stream of consciousness some information and conveys it in appropriate linguistic form capable of being understood by others. That we are not just naming conscious states is clear from the critiques of Ryle and Wittgenstein. But the full nature of the activity is still unclear.

Some interesting findings in recent brain research seem relevant to our conscious articulation of ourselves. It has been known for some time that our two cerebral hemispheres function differently. It is the dominant hemisphere (in most persons the left hemisphere) which has the language centers. The two hemispheres are connected, and an enormous amount of exchange goes on between them. If this connection is severed (as in an operation sometimes performed in cases of intractable epilepsy) and we control the inputs into the two hemispheres, we find that they are specialized very differently. There are also situations where only one hemisphere is functioning (e.g., where one hemisphere is removed by injury or surgery, or where one hemisphere is temporarily anesthetized), in which the capabilities and incapabilities of the individual hemispheres can be investigated. Generally, we find that the dominant hemisphere uses language and understands arguments, but its discrimination of, and functioning in, complex spatial organization is very weak. The minor hemisphere is very good in comprehension of spatial organization but very poor in linguistic use. More interestingly, one finds that when the hemispheres are separated, or when the dominant hemisphere is anesthetized, the activity of the minor hemisphere is not available to the dominant hemisphere. And later, when the dominant hemisphere is asked about it, the truthful response is one of denial.

The upshot of these findings is that there is conscious activity of which there may be no linguistic expression whatsoever, and of which the linguistic self is indeed, unaware. There have been suggestions to the effect that there are two connected but differently processing conscious systems (some venture to say, selves), one articulate and one silent. An elaborate thesis along these lines has been proposed by R. Puccetti (1973); a more complicated view has been suggested by C. W. Savage (1976). On the other hand, it has been argued, for example, by J. Eccles (1977), that the minor hemisphere, though functioning and conscious of the environment, is not self-conscious. How precisely we can distinguish between these two views is unclear at this stage of our research. However, on the general problem of phenomenological reports, we may reasonably surmise that the quality of consciousness yields contents which become categorized in awareness, which is part of the function of the dominant hemisphere. When a further effort is made to articulate some of this content, it is linguistically processed and then communicated. The criteria for the application of linguistic terms are, of course, behavioral in origin, but the processed content is the stuff of consciousness. It is almost certain that our linguistic reports can cover only a small part of the totality of our conscious activity. There is the stream of consciousness that William James made famous; how much of it we are *aware* of is hard to say. There is a part of this stream which undergoes the processing of categorization and becomes the object of reflection and conscious judgment. Perhaps this is the domain of contents we refer to when we say we are self-conscious. But much of even this content cannot be articulated, because we lack behavioral criteria for terms to refer to these contents. Communication in this domain of the unarticulable must depend upon the complex and subtle associations that emerge in successful works of art. However, from the domain of the contents of consciousness, which has undergone categorization, we can extract elements and complexes which are described by the mental terms of our language. It is just these terms which appear in our phenomenological descriptions.

Thus, when we attempt to formulate the relation between mind and body and construe the relation between propositions describing mental events and those describing bodily events, we are dealing with a small logically circumscribed area of the subject. The minimum degree of precision required to establish the relations of correspondence forces us to ignore a great deal of the life of the mind which escapes the net of our mental language.

The relation between mind and body has gone through a series of reformulations, each expressing an insight or offering a formulation to overcome the defects of earlier versions. In this historical movement, it is hoped that what we discern is a restructuring of our concepts so that the resulting structure progressively incorporates the findings of scientific psychology without becoming incoherent with the essential quality of human experience and understanding.

References

Ayer, A. J. *Language truth and logic* (2nd ed.). London: Victor Gollancz, 1948.

Ayer, A.J. *Contribution to Symposium on the physical basis of mind compiled by P. Laslett.* Oxford: Basil Blackwell, 1950.

Broad, C.D. *The mind and its place in nature* London: Kegan Paul, Trench, Trubner & Co., 1937.

Drake, D. What is a mind? *Mind*, 1926, *35.*

Davidson, D. Actions, reasons and causes. *The Journal of Philosophy*, 1963, *60.*

Eccles, J.C. The self-conscious mind and the brain. In K.R. Popper, & J.C. Eccles, (Eds.), *The self and its brain.* New York: Springer International, 1977.

Feigl, H. *The "mental" and the "physical."* Minneapolis: Unversity of Minnesota Press, 1967.

Hempel, C.G. The logical analysis of psychology. In H. Feigl & W. Sellars (Eds.), *Readings in philosophical analysis.* New York: Appleton-Century-Crofts, 1949. (Translated from the French by W.S. and reprinted from Revue de Synthese, 1935.)

Morris, C.W. *Six theories of mind*. Chicago: University of Chicago, 1932.

Pratt, C.C. *The logic of modern psychology*. New York: Macmillan, 1948.

Puccetti, R. Brain bisection and personal identity. *British Journal for the Philosophy of Science*, 1973, 24.

Ryle, G. *The concept of mind*. New York: Barnes & Noble, 1949.

Schlick, M. On the relation between psychological and physical concepts. In H. Feigl & W. Sellars (Eds.), *Readings in philosophical analysis*. New York: Appleton-Century-Crofts, 1949. (Translated by W.S. and reprinted from Revue de Synthese, 1935.)

Savage, C.W. An old ghost in a new body. In G. Globus, G. Maxwell, & I. Savodnik (Eds.), *Consciousness and the brain: A Scientific and philosophical inquiry*. New York: Plenum, 1976. 1976

Wittgenstein, L. *Philosophical investigations* (trans. G.E.M. Anscombe). Oxford: Basil Blackwell, 1953.

Chapter 4

Darwin on Man, Mind, and Materialism[1]

HOWARD E. GRUBER

When we first begin to *believe* anything, what we believe is not a single proposition, it is a whole system of propositions. (Light dawns gradually over the whole.)
 —Ludwig Wittgenstein, 1969, p. 21e.

On Psychology and Its Relation to Evolutionary Thought

"Multiply, vary, let the strongest live and the weakest die—Charles Darwin. This quotation from the *Origin of Species* was the astonishing title of a presidential address to the American Psychological Association (APA) in 1943 (Stone, 1943).

We may well ask, how much has the theory of evolution affected the history of psychology? If the theory could be adequately summarized in the stark selectionist doctrine just quoted, or in some other simple formula, we might cite a few such historical facts, write Q.E.D., and pass on to the next question. But theories and their histories, like life, are never so simple.

[1] Part 1 of this chapter has been written especially for the present volume. Parts 2–4, headed "Creative Thinking and the History of Scientific Thought," "Man's Place in Darwin's Argument," and "The Citadel Itself," are selections from Howard E. Gruber, *Darwin on Man. A Psychological Study of Scientific Creativity* together with *Darwin's Early and Unpublished Notebooks*, transcribed and annotated by Paul H. Barrett, Foreword by Jean Piaget. New York: Dutton, 1974; 2nd edition, Chicago: University of Chicago Press, 1980.

79

BODY AND MIND
Past, Present, and Future

Consider, for example, the stark contrast between the title of Calvin Stone's 1943 address and the 1909 APA presidential address of Charles H. Judd (1910), entitled "Evolution and Consciousness," in which he wrote, "Psychology. . . deals in a broad way with the evolutionary processes by which consciousness arose and through which the trend of life has been changed from organic adaptation to intelligent conquest [p. 32]."

As I have tried to show in *Darwin on Man: A Psychological Study of Scientific Creativity* (Gruber, 1974), the theory of evolution through natural selection is an exceedingly complex system of ideas; its complexity and density are only matched by those of the creative thought process entailed in Charles Darwin's struggle to construct the theory.

The theory of evolution has indeed deeply affected almost every psychological theory since the beginnings of scientific psychology sometime in the nineteenth century. But without further examination this is not a very illuminating comment, since there is not one theory but a domain of theories of evolution. In most theories, natural selection operating on chance variations is the major factor. But chance can be construed in very different ways. At one extreme, there is the notion of mutations as relatively rare events due to forces extrinsic to and independent of the organism (such as radiation); at an another extreme, there is the view of chance as the systematic exploration, albeit through blind trial and error, of all the structural possibilities open to a given genic organization.

It would seem that a view of organic nature as undergoing perpetual change is the central idea of evolutionary theory. But this is not the idea that psychoanalysts and psychobiologists have drawn from it. On the contrary, in a style that owes more to Newton than to Darwin, they have stressed the existence of *constants* in nature, unvarying instinctual tendencies that lie at the bottom of all human behavior. This is certainly one way to approach the issue of continuity between *Homo sapiens* and other animals. But it is not the only way. There have been other thinkers who have tried to draw from evolutionary theory an understanding of the way in which our species' unusual cognitive capacities and emotional toughness and flexibility, which lead to an enormous variety of cultures and societies, grew *out* of the more limited psychological capacities of our animal forebears.

Finally, there are different theoretical stances regarding the causal relations between behavior and evolution. On the one hand, it is possible to stress the idea that structural changes (through chance mutations) make possible new behavioral adaptations. On the other hand, Piaget is not alone in considering behavior to be the "motor" of evolution. This latter approach is probably more congenial to the incorporation of the idea that with the appearance of our species a genuinely new force appeared in nature: cultural evolution.

The selection from *Darwin on Man* excerpted later in this chapter deals not with the theory as a whole but only with the place of our species, *Homo sa-*

piens, in Darwin's argument. I try also to show the diverse social and intellectual forces with which he was contending.

Now, in these few pages, I want to examine the very partial and disjointed assimilation of evolutionary theory in psychological thought. I will draw heavily upon APA presidential addresses and upon a few seminal writers (e.g., Freud, Piaget), because these sources give a sense of the main alternative theoretical pathways actually available to most psychologists and to their students. But the reader will notice that these pages are not a history of the subject they deal with. Ideas are not presented in chronological order but in a way intended to provide a sketch of some of the major theoretical landmarks in what remains a very contemporary scene.

Approaches Stressing the Role of Evolution in Shaping Behavior

Let us begin with Sigmund Freud and psychoanalytic theory. Freud (1953) hailed Darwin and likened him to Copernicus for his part in dethroning our species from the grandiose view that we are the center of the universe and the highest object of God's creation:

> In the course of centuries the *naive* self-love of men has had to submit to two major blows at the hands of science. The first was when they learnt that our earth was not the centre of the universe but only a tiny fragment of a cosmic system of scarcely imaginable vastness. This is associated in our minds with the name of Copernicus, though something similar had already been asserted by Alexandrian science. The second blow fell when biological research destroyed man's supposedly privileged place in creation and proved his descent from the animal kingdom and his ineradicable animal nature. This reevaluation has been accomplished in our own days by Darwin, Wallace and their predecessors, though not without the most violent contemporary opposition [p. 236].

But Freud and other sociobiologists have borrowed one-sidedly from Darwin. They emphasize the animality of *Homo sapiens* at the expense of our humanity. Insisting on the essential identity of our mentality and behavior with the instinctual behavior of infrahuman species, they advance the idea that *Homo sapiens* is "nothing but" an animal. There is another way of thinking about the subject, more consonant with a fully evolutionary theory. Our long evolutionary prehistory can be viewed as providing the springboard for a radically new event in nature: the appearance of a species capable of elaborate language systems, of cumulative cultural history, and of reflective thought.

This view does not eliminate the task of understanding the relation between emotion and thought, but it does profoundly alter it. At every stage in the growth of an evolving system, the constantly changing relation between form and function opens the way for genuine novelty. In a double sense the system of nature changes itself. On the one hand, it cannot go backward: Evolution consumes its own past; each moment destroys the conditions that made it possible. Thus, it is *impossible* for our species to revert to the instinctual forms of our precursors. On the other hand, every step of evolution makes a new future possible. Thus it is not *necessary* for us to live within the confines of our past.

Although it is true that Darwin did much to show the "animal" nature of our species, he was equally at pains to explore the intellectual accomplishments of other organisms. Not only do we, as evolutionary latecomers, contain traces of the past, they contain promises of the future. It was this well-roundedness of Darwin's thinking about the continuity question that permitted him to close his book the *Descent of Man* with an evocation of man and his "god-like intellect."

Three important currents in psychological thought—behaviorism, psychoanalysis, and social Darwinism (now revised under the name of *sociobiology*)—all drew upon Darwin's work in a similar way. All three were movements that placed overwhelming emphasis on the animal origins of humanity, as against the "far more perfect creature" Darwin (1958) thought he saw in the making.

Darwin's argument for the evolutionary continuity of human and animal mentality was steadily transformed into the antimentalism of behavioristic psychology. Skinner (1938) has acknowledged that this required three steps: Darwin ascribed mental powers to animals; Lloyd Morgan continued the development of comparative psychology by advocating the elimination of mind as a legitimate concept in the study of animal behavior; and J. B. Watson endeavored to "re-establish Darwin's desired continuity without hypothesizing mind anywhere." I believe that Darwin would have been happier with psychologists who, like the Gestaltists, preserved the idea of continuity by developing experimental methods for studying insightful problem-solving behavior in infrahuman species (Köhler, 1925).

By and large, the behaviorists exploited the Darwinian selectionist formula in a strict and narrow way. In his APA presidential address, Clark Hull (1937) began with an obeisance to Darwin. Then he presented his learning theory in the form of 18 definitions, 6 postulates, and 13 theorems. The fourth theorem states the principle of *variation:* "Organisms in simple trial-and-error situations may manifest spontaneous variability of reaction, the objective situation remaining constant [p. 325]." The seventh and eighth definitions state the principles of *selection:*

7. A *correct* or "right" reaction is a behavior sequence which results in reinforcement.

8. An *incorrect* or "wrong" reaction is a behavior sequence which results in experimental extinction [p. 327].

The choice of the term *extinction* clearly shows the evolutionary roots of behaviorist learning theory.

Nor is this kind of learning theory the only place in psychology where the narrow selectionist formula has been applied. For example, this is the theoretical schema underlying much of the experimental literature on creativity. Unable or unwilling to study the creative process as a whole, some psychologists have redefined their problem as the study of *originality*, or the production of unusual responses. The key experimental idea is to separate the processes of variation and selection from each other and to focus attention on the first phase, variation.

There have, however, been psychological theorists motivated by evolutionary thought who did not restrict themselves to the narrow selectionist formula.

Approaches Stressing the Role of Behavior in Shaping Evolution

In spite of the narrow selectionist focus of its title, Calvin Stone's address actually did grasp some of the open-endedness of behavioral evolution. More recently, M. Brewster Smith (1978), in another presidential address to APA, presented the kind of open, continuously evolving perspective of which I now write. Drawing on Jean Piaget, George Herbert Mead, and Karl Marx, he examines the way in which the growth of mind changes the material setting in which it evolves, and vice versa. He elaborates the theme that the growth of language and cognition permit the appearance and development of reflective selfhood, and vice versa. Finally, he conceives of all these as mutually synergetic processes at work in a continuous pattern of spiraling growth.

For Donald Campbell, the use of evolutionary theory as a tool for understanding all knowledge process—"evolutionary epistemology," as he terms it—has been an abiding passion and a productive enterprise. His APA presidential addresss (1975) bore the complex title, "On the Conflicts between Biological and Social Evolution between Psychology and Moral Tradition." He writes:

> The evolutionary theory I employ is a hard-line neo-Darwinian one for both biological and social evolution, the slogan being "blind-variation and systematic selective retention [p. 1104]." . . . this model—which I summarize as "blind variation-and-selective-retention"—is the only and all-purpose explanation for the achievement of fit between systems and for the achievement and maintenance of counterentropic form and order [p. 1121].

In spite of Campbell's epithet "hard-line," the careful reader will notice the use of the word *systems* in the plural. Campbell is not merely speaking of the adaptation of organisms to the system of nature. He has *two* systems in mind: the system of biological evolution and the system of cultural evolution. Their interplay creates complexities that cannot be dealt with through the simplistic use of a purely biological model of evolution. Campbell argues that any evolving system entails the operation of four kinds of mechanisms: variation, selection, retention, and duplication (or reproduction) of that which has been retained. But the exact nature of these mechanisms may be entirely different in a purely biological infrahuman system and in a human cultural system.

Although Campbell insists that variations are "blind," it is important to notice that this blindness is an epistemological constraint meaning only ignorance of the ultimate utility and impact of any innovation or variation. At the human cultural level, Campbell's epistemological blindness is not so different from the philosophers' "learned ignorance." It certainly does not mean that humans are unintelligent or mindless. We grope, but not mindlessly. This is a plea for "epistemic humility" (Campbell's phrase), not a denial of mind.

Campbell uses the same apparatus of evolutionary thought (variation, selection, retention, duplication) at both levels of his two-system model. The resultant situation is not a smoothly functioning coherent world but one that is fraught with inherent contradictions:

> 1. Human urban social complexity has been made possible by social evolution rather than biological evolution.
> 2. This social evolution has had to counter individual selfish tendencies which biological evolution has continued to select as a result of the genetic competition among the cooperators [Campbell, 1975, p. 1115].

Thus, although Campbell's epistemological and social program is broad and subtle, the structure of his argument and the contents of his psychological theory are not so different from Freud's: Biologically evolved, genetically determined instincts or tendencies are controlled by socially evolved cultural mechanisms; instincts that are supposed to have evolved over millions of years remain essentially unchanged.

Approaches Stressing the Role of Behavior in Directing Evolution

The anthropologist Washburn (1978) is among many who are critical of this sort of extrapolation from animals to humans. He writes,

> Students of animal behavior feel free to use the behaviors of nonhuman species when making points about human behavior. For example, in a recent book, the chapter on human behavior cites the behaviors of many nonprimates to make important points. The possibility of atavistic behaviors in human beings is illustrated by a picture of a musk-ox in a defensive position. To show how peculiar this habit of proof really is, consider what the reaction would be if I sent to a zoological journal a paper on the musk-ox with defensive positions illustrated by the British Squares at the Battle of Waterloo [p. 414]!

There is a considerable group of anthropologists, evolutionists, and paleontologists who stress the explosive rapidity of recent evolution toward *Homo sapiens sapiens*, our species. A number of factors seem to have combined in multiplicative fashion to produce the qualitative leap to humanity. In general, this group of investigators tend to stress the role of behavioral changes in driving organic evolution, especially at the hominid level. For example, upright walking permits collecting food (by freeing the forelimbs, or hands): collecting food permits bringing it to a place where it can be shared with others; such sharing permits the development of a stable, homelike abode; this new (for primates) situation facilitates the transformation of a primarily emotional system of communication into true language. These evolutionary events do not happen in a linear sequence. Rather, a little progress along one front opens the way to change on some other front. Not only genes but protocultures are transmitted from one generation to another. Individuals and groups that invent and transmit valuable behavioral adaptations tend to survive; this allows time for neurological and other structural changes to evolve (through mutation and selection) that will make the recurrence and elaboration of these behaviors more probable. The traits that evolve and endure need not be highly specified behavior patterns. As Washburn (1978) writes about one much discussed trait, "There is, obviously, no need to postulate genes for altruism. It would be much more adaptive to have genes for intelligence, enabling one to be altruistic or selfish according to the needs of the moment [p. 414]."

The view that I have just sketched out for the evolution of behavior is quite similar to the geneticist Waddington's (1957) idea of *genetic assimilation*. At the ontogenetic level, organisms increase their chances of survival if they make appropriate phenotypic responses to environmental demands. The preferential survival of those individuals that have such responses within their range of reactions leads to the incorporation of their genic patterns in the gene pool of the population. It should be noted that Waddington still relied basically on natural selection and chance mutation to consolidate gains first achieved at the phenotypic, ontogenetic level.

Piaget goes even further. In his book *Le Comportement Moteur de L'evolution* (1976) (the title of which is inexplicably translated as *Behavior and Evolution* [1978] in the published English version, leaving out the crucial words, "motor of"), he argues that *all* evolution, not only human, is primarily inducted by behavioral changes that lead to genetic changes. He insists that his position is not Lamarckian, and he advances a general hypothesis to explain how appropriate genetic variations could occur, tuned to environmental demands, without relying on occasional chance mutations. Thus, he is arguing not only for the primacy of behavior in evolution but against the role of blind variation.

However, to see in just what measure Piaget rejects the idea of blind variation, we must examine the concept a little more closely. Piaget views the process of variation as a systematic exploration of a set of possibilities. This combinatorial attack or "organic logic" gives the initiative to the organism, rather than submitting it to a process of waiting for the lucky environmental impact that produces an adaptive mutation (Gruber & Vonèche, 1977).

Although the mechanism that Piaget proposes is novel, its consequences are fairly similar to the findings of recent research in genetics: There is far more variation than previously recognized. Many or even most genes exist in a number of allelic forms, expressing the biochemical structural variations of which each gene is capable (Piaget, 1978). Piaget uses this general biological position as a springboard for reiterating his argument that intellectual activity is a biological function and must follow the same law of organization and adaptation, assimilation and accommodation, as any living system. In his earlier treatise on the idea of *phenocopy*, he begins with the "Baldwin effect," well known to geneticists: Phenotypical adaptations arising in the individual life history are *replaced* by changes in the genotype having the same form and the same consequences. Piaget (1974) draws an important parallel between evolutionary–genetic change and cognitive development. In cognition, too, we have phenotypic adaptations, such as imitation, which establish responses that can later be controlled by more fundamental changes in mental structures replacing the ones that gave rise to the response in the first place (Ayala, 1978). In this usage of the phenocopy argument, he is quite similar to Kurt Lewin who also used the terms *phenotype* and *genotype* to distinguish between outward behaviors and underlying structures that control them (Lewin, 1935).

The main outlines of controversy have remained unchanged for nearly a century. In 1898, J. M. Baldwin's presidential address to the American Psychological Association was called "On Selective Thinking." He examined "the supply of thought-variations; . . how certain variations are singled out for survival . . ; and the criteria of selection [pp. 1–2]." In other words, he used the model of evolutionary theory for a theory of cognitive development. Far from casting *chance* variation in the role of prime mover, he criticized this view sharply:

> We do not scatter our thoughts as widely as possible in order to increase the chances of getting a true one; on the contrary, we call the man who produces the most thought-variations a "scatter-brain," and expect nothing inventive from him . . . we succeed in thinking well by thinking hard; we get the valuable thought–variations by concentrating attention upon the body of related knowledge which we already have; we discover new relations among the data of experience by running over and over the links and couplings of the apperceptive systems with which our minds are already filled [p.4].

Baldwin, of course, aimed his criticism of blind variation not at Donald Campbell, who was not born yet, but at Herbert Spencer, who not long before had applied evolutionary theory to learned behavior in a way that anticipated the behaviorism of 1910–1960. Baldwin went on to explain his theory of "organic selection." Some of its highlights are as follows:

1. Mental life, or knowledge, is highly organized; only those novelties can be assimilated into an enduring structure that can be responded to in a coherent way.

2. Of two main phases of the selective function, the first is intra-organic selection: "this transfers the first selective function from the environment to the organism, requires the new experience to run the gauntlet of habitual reactions or habits which organize and unify the system of knowledges, before it can be eligible for further testing by action [p. 10]."

3. The second phase is "extra-organic selection or environmental selection, which is a testing of the special concrete character of the experience as fitted, through the motor variations to which it gives rise, to bring about a new determination in the system in which it goes [p. 10]." It is this phase in Baldwin's theory that is analogous to what is usually meant by *natural selection.*

4. Through this highly organized process of variation and selection the individual constantly rebuilds the "platform" on which further experience, action, and growth occur; this means that the variations that occur are not indiscriminate or blind but a function of the individual's whole life history of organized growth.

5. The growth of the internal organization of knowledge "gradually serves to free the organism from direct dependence upon the control of the environment [p. 21]; this means that the whole process of variation and selection becomes increasingly organized and directed as the person matures.

6. Baldwin, like Piaget—who admires him greatly—attempts to show how there could be an "organic logic" governing both biological and psychological growth.

To conclude this brief survey, it can be seen that there is today not one theory of evolution or of evolution and behavior but a wide array of possibilities. This means that the psychologist, as student of this subject, need not be intimidated by the seemingly greater rigor of the natural sciences. It remains true today, as it was in Charles Darwin's day, that the study of organic evolution and of behavior can enrich each other.

Theories of the relation between mind and body have always been highly colored by their connection with broad social issues. This is especially true of the history of evolutionary thought, which has been seen as relevant to our understanding and ethical evaluation of war, capitalism, slavery, racism, and sexism. There is, in my opinion, no way of avoiding these connections. It may be helpful to be aware of them, to be sensitive to the social roots of all theories.

On the time scale of the history of psychology, a century or so, we see the same issues and theories cropping up more than once, in only slightly altered forms. On the time scale of intellectual fashion, a decade or so, we see a particular form of argument wax and wane in popularity: In one swing it is the heritability quotient, in another it is the sociobiology of aggression and altruism that is called upon to justify the claim that "you can't change human nature." On still longer time scales, there are always a few voices insisting that we must change ourselves. And the joint evidence of many disciplines suggests that over the long reaches of evolutionary time, *Homo sapiens sapiens* has changed his and her nature, that through our own behavior we have indeed made ourselves. The question remains, for the changes we must now make: Have we enough intelligence, courage, and time?

Creative Thinking and the History of Scientific Thought

> Sept 21st Was witty in a dream in a confused manner. Thought that a person was hung & came to life, & then made many jokes about not having run away & and having faced death like a hero, & then I had some confused idea of showing scar behind (instead of front) (having changed hanging into his head cut off) as kind of wit showing he had honourable wounds. All this was kind of wit.—I changed I believe from hanging to head cut off (there was the feeling of banter and joking) because the whole train of Dr. Monro experiment about hanging came before me showing impossibility of person recovering from hanging on account of blood, but all these ideas came one after other, without ever comparing them. I neither doubted them or *believed* them.—Believing consists in the comparison of ideas connected with judgment.
>
> What is the Philosophy of Shame & Blushing? [Charles Darwin, M notebook, pp. 143–144; cited in Gruber & Barrett, 1974/1980, p. 3].

So runs one of Darwin's entries in a notebook he kept in 1838. A person is being executed perhaps for his ideas. He entertains the thought of running away, but stands fast. The dreamer wants to live or return to life, so he changes the method of his execution from hanging to decapitation, which in the dream seems less final. The dream contains a recollected scrap of Darwin's medical education to the effect that hanging is irreversible. In recording the dream Darwin adds a remark about the nature of belief, and in a comment added later raises a question about shame.

In this passage we catch a glimpse of a man thinking. We see the interplay of social and intellectual forces in Darwin's fear of dire punishment for thinking. We see the rapid, easy movement between different kinds of thought: A fragment of a physiology lecture heard long ago, a psychological remark on the distinction between dreams and rational beliefs, and the dream itself. We see, in the change from hanging to decapitation, and the meaning Darwin ascribes to it, the dreamer's wish for immortality; perhaps Darwin would have been satisfied to know that the ideas for which the dreamer was executed would endure a century and more.

The aim of this study of creativity is to describe the growth of thought in a real, thinking, feeling, dreaming person. As in the dream, thinking is not a straightforward advance. From the thinker's own point of view, there are doubts, retreats, detours, and impasses; there are also impulsive moments of decision, leaps into the dark from points of no return. From the standpoint of 100 years of historical hindsight there are reasonable mistakes, nonessentials, and foolish blunders.

The reader may be disappointed if he or she approaches the subject expecting a tale leading up to one climactic moment of great insight, like the dubious stories of Archimedes' bath and Newton's apple. Although the progress of Darwin's thought is punctuated by many vital moments of insight, each one filling him with the joy of discovery, it is hard to find any single insight which in the living moment really seemed more vital than the others to the person thinking.

Perhaps the concept of a single, crucial, sudden insight is suitable for describing someone solving a single well-defined problem. But we are dealing here with a different sort of thinking: A person striving to construct a new synthesis, a new way of looking at many problems, *a new point of view.*

On the time scale of the life history, the classic topics of the psychology of thinking—problem solving, concept formation, and imagery—are not only processes to be explained: Beyond that, they take their places in a longer process of growth, the formation of a point of view. As Thomas Kuhn (1962) has urged, the established point of view, the scientists' "paradigm," provides the shared framework within which problems will be recognized as significant and solutions accepted as valid. But in the psychology of thinking, little has been done to study the growth of a new point of view, although the work of Jean Piaget and his collaborators on the development of thinking in children has done much to show how we might proceed in a study of adult thinking.

As for problem solving, it takes place in a diverse train of activities: reading and observation, imagination and memory, argument and discussion. For all we really know of it, focused problem solving may be a comparatively rare event. The very act of taking up a problem crystallizes a long history of development.

Given a problem-solving process, we may find reflection, sudden insights, and gradual improvement through trial and error. Even the groping trials are not blind or random: They emerge from the problem solver's perception of the structure of the problem, as he has come to recognize and understand it from his own particular vantage point. Thus, the sudden insight in which a problem is solved, when it is solved suddenly, may represent only a minor nodal point, like the crest of a wave, in a long and very slow process—the development of a point of view.

All this is not to say that problem solving is an unimportant part of the creative process. Indeed, Darwin's notebooks show how he attacked and solved a number of problems. But the total creative process of constructing a novel point of view is so complex that it is impossible to identify the solution of some one problem as a step more crucial than any other. The quest for one such step violates the character of thinking as an organic whole, as would a debate on the relative importance of the heart, the brain, and the liver.

Without any one of a number of vital organs, the individual dies; without any one of a number of vital components, an argument fails.

In a case study of creativity one might well expect to find an analysis of the subject's personality and its roots. Although that is not the aim of this study, a description of a man's thinking involves so much of the man that it must reflect something of his personality. For example, in examining Darwin's method of work we find that he is not afraid to examine his own mental processes, including their nonrational components, and something of his own psychosexual life. In the interest of exploring the mind–body problem, Darwin took his evidence where he could find it, and what better place to look than at his own inner world and his own body?

Similarly, we learn something about Darwin as a person by studying the pattern of hesitation and delay which grew out of the purely intellectual difficulties of constructing a theory of evolution when these were multiplied by theological problems and by his fear of persecution and ridicule. A discussion of creativity and personality really ought to deal with the kinds of courage necessary for creative work. While there is no such separate discussion in the present study, the very human, cautious, vacillating yet persistent courage of Charles Darwin will become quite apparent.[2]

The fact that the formation of a new synthesis must be seen as a creative *process* rather than as a sudden creative *act*[3] has a deep significance for the relation between the thinker and the intellectual and social milieu in which he works. An isolated and sudden act might conceivably be thought of as occurring out of all time and place. But a long growth process must be seen as rooted in its total human context. There is plenty of time for the individual thinker to see the implications of his developing work for those around him, to test out colleagues and potential allies, to suffer in private the fear of ridicule and then to recover and persevere, to shape an argument that presents the smallest possible target to critics and produces the largest possible impact on the general movement of public thought.

Man's Place in Darwin's Argument

> Arguing from man to animals is philosophical. . . [Man is] a "Frontier instance. . . [Charles Darwin, N notebook, p. 49, about December 1838; cited in Gruber & Barrett, 1974/1980, p. 339].

Psychologists interested in thinking rarely consider the general architecture of a person's ideas; implicitly, they often write as though its structural form is a set of problems, perhaps organized in a hierarchy of importance, or even

---

[2] Courage is rarely discussed in the literature of academic psychology. "Risk-taking," i.e., gambling, a much studied subject, is hardly the same thing. (See Gruber, 1973).

[3] Compare Arthur Koestler's (1964) treatment of this subject.

just one central problem. Another way of conceiving of this structure is to imagine a network of enterprises. Each enterprise is far more inclusive than a
problem; it is, rather, one domain within which the person works. If the
recognizable problems within that domain were ever all solved, the thinker
might well invent new ones in order to keep the enterprise alive. The enterprises composing the network are mutually supportive, yet in some ways they
have an existence independent of each other, very much as the strands of a
net. And since it is a living network, new relationships are constantly appearing.

In this chapter I examine Darwin's thought about a crucial issue, the evolution of man and mind, with special regard for the period in his life when he explicitly decided that this subject was an enterprise worth differentiating from
the rest of his work.

To anticipate, my examination of Darwin's notes leads me to believe that he
first took up the evolution of mental processes because these seemed to be the
most rapidly modifiable of all biological functions, and therefore the most
useful for testing the "Lamarckian" idea of the inheritance of acquired
characteristics.

I deal first with man's place in Darwin's general argument about the evolution of all organisms. But, for Darwin, the premise underlying this discussion
is the idea that man has evolved according to the same natural laws as other
organisms.

On 15 July 1838, one year after beginning his first notebook on transmutation, Darwin began the third notebook, which he labeled "D." On the very
same day he began another notebook. Skipping some letters of the alphabet,
he labeled it "M," which may have meant Man, or Morals, or Mind or may
have been merely mnemonic. This new enterprise was begun while he was
staying at his father's house, after a 2-week geological expedition in Scotland:
". . . reached Shrewsbury July 13th. Very idle at Shrewsbury, some notes
from my Father. Opened notebook connected with metaphysical enquiries."
(*Journal*) Sometime later he wrote on the cover, "This book full of
Metaphysics of Morals and Speculations on Expression." Perhaps because of
the label, students of Darwin's biological thought have neglected this document. On laboring through it, deciphering Darwin's difficult handwriting, one
realizes that these notes served as the point of departure for *The Descent of
Man*, which he wrote and published 33 years later (1871), and for *The Expression of Emotions in Man and Animals* (1872).

Why did Darwin begin a new set of notes about a subject on which he had
not done any previous systematic work?

A careful reading of the two parallel sets of notes, (those on evolution and
those on man) suggests that Darwin began his systematic study of man and
mind because he hoped to find in that direction answers to questions that
went right to the heart of his search for a theory of evolution. For other evolutionary theorists man and his intellect might pose special problems. But Dar-

win treated man as a unique *opportunity* for the biologist, an opportunity to study intelligence as a central feature of adaptive change, and to study it in that organism in which it is most prominent, man.

For some months, Darwin had been struggling with a group of questions which constitute the genetical problem: How do variations arise? Which variants are heritable? Which survive crossing between different strains? How does hybridization work and when does it fail? Eventually, Darwin had to admit defeat; a complete theory of evolution might explain variation and the hereditary transmission of variation, but Darwin would have to accept these steps as premises, in themselves unexplained. In July 1838, however, it seemed to him of the utmost importance to solve this group of related problems. Without doing so, no matter how well he might marshal the evidence for the occurrence of evolution, he would not have a truly explanatory theory of it.

It is in this context that we must consider the meaning of Darwin's beginning the M notebook. The first 6 weeks of those notes represent an effort to collect all sorts of ideas and information that might bear on the inheritance of acquired characteristics. His basic hypothesis is that an often repeated act may lead to a structural change, which in turn may be inherited.

The belief that habits change slowly fitted in with Darwin's idea that only slowly acquired changes can be transmitted. He rejected the Lamarckian notion that "willing" produces changes. Darwin insisted that it is the real action which must be the prime mover, but then this is moderated by his belief in the efficacy of mental acts of various kinds.

These M and N notebooks on man, mind, and materialism had a second function, to serve as a repository for observations and reflections on the continuity between man and other animals. In this connection, Darwin made many notes on animal intelligence, animal language, and animal emotions— all aimed at showing that the gulf between man and other animals is not unbridgeable.

But Darwin could hardly go this far into the subject of the origin of man without, as he put it, attacking "the citadel itself": man's mind and the way it works. In his day no one could make the effort to develop a scientific psychology without at the same time taking a stand on a fundamental issue in philosophy, the relation of mind and body. In the M and N notebooks we see Darwin's growing awareness that his evolutionary theorizing opened the way for a thoroughgoing philosophical materialism, with all its painful consequences.

The third major function, then, of these notebooks was to explore the possibility of developing a scientific psychology and the relation of that effort to materialist philosophy. Taking that stand, albeit in private, may well have strengthened Darwin for the long struggle that lay ahead. In a sense, these notebooks have not only an intellectual function, the exploration of questions and issues, but an emotional and expressive function, the making of a private commitment. Even as he began to realize that he might not want to say certain things aloud, he felt a need to say them as clearly as possible to himself.

The path he took included a great deal of highly personal introspection. Far from impoverishing the inner life, as some theologians feared, Darwin himself is a case in point for the view that the act of divesting oneself of the protective coat of conventional religion can serve as the point of departure for a deeper examination of oneself.

In short, the M and N notebooks represent the interweaving of three themes in Darwin's thought: searching for the source of heritable variation and testing the hypothesis of habits becoming hereditary; marshaling the evidences for psychological continuity between man and other animals; bringing a variety of methods—introspective, pathological, experimental, and developmental, as well as comparative—to bear on the effort to construct a scientific psychology. Underlying this systematic effort lay Darwin's rapid movement toward a firm decision that only a materialist philosophy of biology could support the whole enterprise.

Are We Not Brothers?

Although the M notebook represents Darwin's first systematic attack on the question of man, it was hardly his first expression of interest in the subject. Indeed, the organization of the manuscript notes during the *Beagle* voyage parallels and foreshadows the later notebooks. On the voyage he kept several sets of scientific notes (in geology and in various fields of biology) and a large diary. The latter was used for general descriptions of scenery, for recording the main events and adventures of the voyage, and for many interesting observations on the different sorts of human being he encountered in his scientific circumnavigation.

From his very first remarks on encountering black people on the island of St. Jago, off the coast of Africa, it is clear that he is interested in the issue of race differences. His description of the behavior of the people he met is sympathetic and emphasizes their intelligence (*Beagle Diary*, 20 January 1832, p. 27).

Six months later he describes the blacks, both slave and free, whom he met in Brazil, in laudatory terms:

> I cannot help believing they will ultimately be the rulers. I judge of it from their numbers, from their fine athletic figures, (especially contrasted with the Brazilians) proving they are in a congenial climate, & from clearly seeing their intellects have been much underrated; they are the efficient workmen in all the necessary trades [*Beagle Diary*, p. 77, 3 July 1832, cited in Gruber & Barrett, 1974/1980, p.181].

In many anecdotes he stresses the essential humanity of the black people he meets, not only in regard to intelligence but in moral qualities as well. For example, he writes of the recapture of a group of runaway slaves from a cliffside retreat: "Excepting one old woman, who sooner than be again taken, dashed herself to pieces from the very summit. I suppose in a Roman matron this would be called noble patriotism, in a negress it is called brutal obstinacy [Beagle Diary, p. 51, 8 April 1832]!"

Members of the antislavery Darwin family circle were well prepared to accept the idea that all men are brothers, sharing both a common fate and a common origin. From the early appearance in Darwin's travel diary of such egalitarian expressions of feeling it seems clear that he shared the family point of view. (See Figure 4.1.)

His sympathetic acceptance of the people of another race and approximately his own civilization stands in sharp contrast to the profound shock of his first encounter with a truly primitive group, the Indians of Tierra del Fuego. On 18 December 1832, he wrote, while still in Tierra del Fuego: "I would not have believed how entire the difference between savage & civilized man is. It is greater than between a wild & domesticated animal, in as much as in man there is greater power of improvement [Beagle Diary, p. 119]."

To his teacher Henslow he wrote in the same astonished vein:

I do not think any spectacle can be more interesting than the first sight of man in his primitive wildness. . . I shall never forget this when entering Good Success Bay—the yell with which a party received us. They were seated on a rocky point, surrounded by the dark forest of beech; as they threw their arms wildly round their heads, and their long hair streaming, they seemed the troubled spirits of another world [LL 1, p. 243, April 1833, cited in Gruber & Barrett, 1974/1980, p. 182].

Darwin's amazement may have been heightened by the dissimilarity between the primitive people of Tierra del Fuego and the Fuegians he had known on board the Beagle. On a previous voyage the Beagle had brought to England a party of four Fuegians, three of whom were now being returned to their native country. (The fourth had died of smallpox.) In their year abroad these individuals had learned some English and grown accustomed to wearing European clothes and other manners. It was these three whom Darwin had in mind 35 years later when he wrote of the

numerous points of mental similarity between the most distinct races of man. The American aborigines, Negroes and Europeans are as different from each other in mind as any three races that can be named; yet I was incessantly struck, whilst living with the Fuegians on board the "Beagle," with the many little traits of character, shewing how similar their minds were to ours; and so it was with a full-blooded negro with whom I happened once to be intimate. [Darwin, 1871/1882, p. 178].

Robert FitzRoy, captain of the Beagle, had succeeded in some degree in educating the transported Fuegians in "English, and the plainer truths of Christianity, as the first object; and the use of common tools, a slight acquaintance with husbandry, gardening, and mechanism, as the second [cited in Gruber & Barrett, 1974/1980, p.183]." His success may have gone much far-

FIGURE 4.1. Wedgewood antislavery medallion, 1788. (Courtesy of Josiah Wedgewood.)

ther than he intended. He himself was a professed Christian, a believer in every word of Scripture, and a natural enemy of all evolutionary thought. But the transformation he helped produce in the three Fuegians must have also had a transforming effect on Charles Darwin's thinking, helping him to see the similarities among different sorts of men, and the continuity between the most urbane, devout Englishman and all other animals.

As he moved over the face of the earth Darwin took advantage of his many opportunities to compare human groups with each other. Often he seems to be forming a scale along which different groups can be ranged. Such efforts appear especially in the later years of the voyage when he had acquired sufficient breadth of experience to warrant such comparisons. For example, he looked with disfavor on the aggressiveness of the New Zealanders (i.e., Maori) as compared with the mildness of the Tahitians:

> Looking at the New Zealander, one naturally compares him with the Tahitian; both belonging to the same family of mankind. . . If the state in which the Fuegians live should be fixed on as zero in the scale of government, I am afraid New Zealand would rank but a few degrees higher, while Tahiti, even as when first discovered, would occupy a respectable position [*Beagle Diary*, pp. 363–364, 22 December 1835, while in New Zealand; cited in Gruber & Barrett, 1974/1980, p. 184].

Darwin consistently took these differences to be the products of history, culture, education, and habitat, rather than the reflection of a fixed inheritance of psychological traits. One passage makes this point very succinctly. Landing on the island of Chiloe, off the coast of Chile,

> Everything I have seen convinces me of the close connection of the different tribes, who yet speak distinct languages. . . It is a pleasant thing in any case to see the aboriginal inhabitants, advanced to the same degree of civilization, however low that may be, which their white conquerors have attained [*Beagle Diary*, p. 251, 26 November 1834; cited in Gruber & Bennett, 1974/1980, p. 184].

But a belief in the educability of primitive people (either through the spontaneous development of their own culture, or through the ministrations of more "civilized" conquerors) has no necessary connection with evolutionary thought. Only if the products of experience are passed on through heredity can they be thought to play a direct role in organic evolution.

Do Habits Become Hereditary?

Several passages in the *Beagle Diary* tempt one to believe that Darwin was, during the *Beagle* voyage, already examining the hypothesis that habits may become hereditary. For example, in discussing the seemingly miserable existence of the Tierra del Fuegians, living as they did in hard country at the end of the world, he concludes:

> There can be no reason for supposing the race of Fuegians are decreasing, we may therefore be sure that he enjoys a sufficient share of happiness (whatever its kind may be) to render life worth having. Nature, by making habit omnipotent, has fitted the Fuegian to the climate & productions of his country [*Beagle Diary*, p. 213, 24 February 1834; cited in Gruber and Barrett, 1974/1980, p. 185].

An early expression in Darwin's notes of the hypothesis of habits becoming hereditary occurs in a quotation from F. Cuvier about "one of the most general laws of life—the transmission of a fortuitous modification into a durable form, of a fugitive want into a fundamental propensity, of an accidental habit into an instinct." Darwin adds, "I take higher grounds and say life is short for this object and others, viz, not too much change [B, p. 118, about October 1837]." He means to say that if such changes accumulate indefinitely in an individual organism, it will lose its identity as a member of a species, and so will its progeny if the changes are heritable. Consequently, the process of death serves the adaptive function of limiting change and maintaining the integrity of species. The changes in question are all the psychological developments that occur in the life of an individual.

The Argument from Continuity and the System of Nature

Darwins' originality lay neither in his espousal of the general idea of evolution, not in his collection of supporting facts, but in his persistent search for a theory of evolution consonant with his underlying image of nature as an irregularly branching tree, an image deeply imbued with the idea of selectivity.

Grasping the importance for Darwin of this image of nature is essential for understanding the second theme of the M and N notebooks, his approach to the problem of continuity between man and other animals, to which I now turn.

We must bear in mind three different types of image of the system of nature, three arrangements of organisms in schemes of classification: the linear model, the branching model, and the "circular" model. As we have already seen, it was possible for either an evolutionist or a nonevolutionist to embrace a linear model.[4] The upward-ascending unbroken chain or Scala Naturae was a widespread image in pre-Darwinian thought. Unfortunately, it left little room for biological systematists to maneuver when they wanted to work out systematic arrangements among related organisms. Lamarck's "ladder image" utilized a second dimension, the horizontal rungs of the ladder, and was somewhat more flexible, but could not do justice to the complexities of the known facts. Lamarck as a systematist certainly could not stick to the simple ladder image employed by Lamarck as an evolutionist.

There was another approach to the issue of continuity in nature, nonevolutionary to the core, with which Darwin had to contend. This was the Quinarian system of William Sharp MacLeay, forgotten now but influential at the time Darwin was thinking things through. It was a "mystical system of classification built on the supposition that at all levels the animal kingdom is based on five groups arranged in a circle, each with affinities to its neighbors on both sides, each containing five sub-groups arranged in a comparable manner with affinities to their neighbors, and so on [Gavin de Beer, 1960, p. 29]."

Demonstrations of continuity in nature were, evidently, necessary but by no means sufficient for Darwin's argument. There were two strong points in nonevolutionary images of nature that Darwin had to attack. He had to show that it was unnecessary to assume a fundamental discontinuity between man and other animals that could be accounted for only by the hypothesis of supernatural fiat. And he had to show that the natural order did not exhibit a mystical and miraculous regularity and perfection but was instead an irregularly branching system.

The tree model (Figure 4.2) saved Darwin the trouble of looking for the "missing link" between man and other primates. If his theory was true, these extant animals represented distinct branchings from a common progenitor, so

---

[4] Lamarck is the evolutionist to whom we have referred on this point in the preceding pages; Wesley is the nonevolutionist.

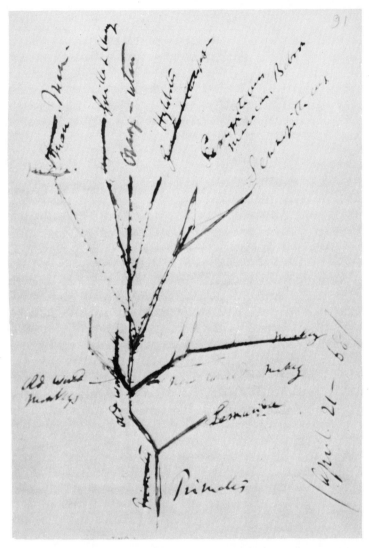

FIGURE 4.2. Taxonomic tree showing hypothetical relation of man to other primates. Drawn by Darwin on April 21, 1868. (Courtesy of Cambridge University Library.)

that the search for living intermediate forms would be misguided: Continuity could be found only by looking backward in evolutionary time to that long-past branching point. He writes, "My theory drives me to say that there can be no animal at present time having an intermediate affinity between two classes—there may be some descendant of some intermediate link [C, p. 201]."

Darwin was sensitive to the analogy between himself and the great cosmologists; he thought of himself as building a new world system, and he enjoyed the thought:

> Before attraction of gravity discovered it might have been said it was as great a difficulty to account for movement of all [planets] by one law, as to account for each separate one; so to say that all mammalia were born from one stock, and since distributed by such means as we can recognize, may be thought to explain nothing [B, p. 196; cited in Gruber & Barrett, 1974/1980, p. 199].

In spite of some similarities between Darwin and other system builders, there was one terribly important difference. The astronomers had constructed orderly orbits which would account for the appearance of irregularity in the wandering of the planets without having to concede that such irregularity in fact marred the face of nature; the physicists had worked out universal laws to explain the orbits. Darwin's task was the reverse. He had to show that the appearance of order, which had been so carefully worked out by MacLeay and other systematists, could be explained as resulting from a random process producing an *irregular* result and furthermore that his hypothesis was not only tenable but more plausible than the hypothesis of a supernaturally created order.

In the long run, it was the chanciness and irregularity of Darwin's system of nature that proved to be the most difficult point in his theory for the religious community. Opposition to the idea of evolution slackened at least a decade before opposition to Darwin's theory of evolution as the resultant of a conglomeration of chance events. God, thought the modern theologians of that day, might choose to operate through natural laws rather than by fiat, but his regime would be more orderly than is provided for by the laws of chance!

The Citadel Itself

> By materialism, I mean, merely the intimate connection of kind of thought with form of brain.—Like kind of attraction with nature of element [Charles Darwin, margin note on p. 28 of Abercrombie, 1838].

One day when the world and my family were agog with the subject, I asked my children, then aged 9 and 11, how they felt about heart transplants. Would they be willing to be recipients? Hesitantly but without too much doubt, they answered yes. Then I asked: "How about a brain transplant? Suppose the only way you could go on living was to have someone else's brain transplanted into you. Would you be willing?" Firmly, without any hesitation, they both answered NO. "Why not?" One said, "I wouldn't be me."

The relation of mind and body is not only an abstract philosophical question. It impinges on a very personal matter, the nature and locus of the self.

The third theme of Darwin's M and N notebooks, the mind–body problem—his early explorations of the possibility of a scientific human psychology
and its relation to philosophic materialism—brought into play Darwin's
awareness of himself as a very human animal.

There is a puzzle in Darwin's life. In a way, the ground had been very well
prepared for someone who wished to advance a theory of evolution. Why,
then, did Darwin wait so long to publish his evolutionary ideas? Why when
he finally published the *Origin* in 1859, did he remain so circumspect about
man and mind? Were his fears and hesitations justified?

Darwin was the beneficiary of a line of distinguished attempts to create an
evolutionary theory. Among nonevolutionists like Lyell the known fact of a
succession of organic beings in successive geological strata had forced many
into a revised interpretation of Genesis and toward the hypothesis of successive creation. Among Natural Theologians there were at least some who,
like John Wesley, had already taken the dramatic step of dethroning man by
recognizing man's place in the great chain of animate beings and by suggesting
the possibility of organisms unknown to us and still higher. In 1844 *Vestiges*,
Robert Chambers' evolutionary book, appeared. That was the year Darwin
wrote his *second* long essay summarizing his views. In 1856 he finally sat
down to write his massive treatise on evolution, "Natural Selection," never
finished because of Wallace's interruption in 1858. But by 1856 *Vestiges* had
gone through 10 editions, clearly demonstrating the possibility of publishing
an evolutionary theory and commanding wide attention of both the general
and the scientific publics. True, *Vestiges* was severely criticized, but Darwin
could hardly have intended to wait until all his potential critics were dis-
armed.

Does this mean that Darwin's fears were groundless or that he was a
cowardly man who retreated in the face of danger? To understand his predica-
ment and his strategy of delay and concealment, a closer look at the subject is
required. His theoretical efforts must be seen not only in the context of the
search for a theory of evolution, but also in relation to the problem of
materialism.

Darwin's Delay: The Specter of Materialism

Darwin realized that it would weaken his whole argument if he permitted
his account of evolution to stop short of the highest forms of intelligence.
Once he admitted that God might have intervened in an act of special creation
to make man's mind, others might argue, "In that case, why not also invoke
the aid of God to explain the worm?"

There was an inherent weakness in the empirical approach of collecting instances pointing to the mental similarities of man and other animals. This
fragmentary, anecdotal approach would be limited in much the same sense

that any purely inductive theory must be. Given the indisputable fact of a considerable difference between man and other animals, Darwin might point to the similarities and assert the plausibility of the evolution of mind; others could point to the differences and cleave to their belief in special creation.

Moreover, Darwin sensed that some would object to seeing rudiments of human mentality in animals, while others would recoil at the idea of remnants of animality in man; he eventually divided the whole subject in two parts, corresponding roughly to these two aspects of the problem. *Descent of Man* deals mainly with the first issue, *Expression of Emotions* with the second. At the time of the M and N notebooks, however, he thought another approach might be possible. If only one could construct a scientific psychology at the human level itself, satisfying the demands of argument and evidence to which the natural sciences are subject, this achievement in itself would constitute evidence for the "naturalness" of mind.

It must be remembered how bitter and pervasive the struggle against philosophical materialism was in those days, and how much of the argument against it rested on the belief that the human mind was not subject to natural law. The intellectual story has been well told by academic historians of psychology, but the venom has been drawn in the telling (Boring, 1950).

Earlier I dealt with the threat of persecution and ridicule of scientists in a general way. As I now examine the controversy over materialism and mind, my primary aim is to see how the significance for Darwin of his ideas about evolution was affected by his view of their place in a still larger argument. But it is not possible to divorce the discussion of the philosophical and scientific issues from the threat of persecution. In countries dominated by an alliance between state and church aimed at maintaining a threatened social order, the allegation that a particular idea was materialistic or tended to materialism or atheism constituted a very serious attack.

In virtually every branch of knowledge, repressive methods were used: Lectures were proscribed, publication was hampered, professorships were denied, fierce invective and ridicule appeared in the press. Scholars and scientists learned the lesson and responded to the pressures on them. The ones with unpopular ideas sometimes recanted, published anonymously, presented their ideas in weakened forms, or delayed publication for many years. The known examples are not very numerous, nor need they be to make the point. Probably one striking case per decade was enough to keep the lesson fresh. If the progress of thought is slowed down enough, any establishment can incorporate new ideas without losing power.

The influential Scottish philosopher–psychologist Thomas Reid, in a letter "on the materialism of Priestley and the egoism of French philosophers" written in 1775, summarized Priestley's view that all "powers that are termed mental [are]. . . the result of such an organical structure as that of the brain," and its corollaries that "the whole man becomes extinct at death," and that the "lower animals. . . differ from us in degree only, and not in kind." Reid (1967) went on to express his disgust:

> I detest all systems that depreciate human nature. If it be a delusion, that there is something in the constitution of man that is venerable and worthy of its author, let me live and die in that delusion, rather than have my eyes opened to see my species in a humiliating and disgusting light. Every good man feels his indignation rise against those who disparage his *kindred* or his *country;* why should it not rise against those who disparage his *kind* [Vol. 1, p. 52]?

Reid thought that Priestley's views of human nature "tend more to promote atheism, than to promote religion and virtue."

The proposition that the brain is the organ of all mental functions received its first great modern impetus from Franz Joseph Gall. Today his name is associated with the discredited notions of phrenology, his misguided but once enormously popular doctrine of a strict relation between the exterior form of the skull and the psychological functioning of the brain within, so that individual character could be "read" from the bumps on the head. It was not, however, Gall's scientific errors but his insistence on a materialistic formulation of the relation between mind and body, as well as the ethical conclusions he drew from his materialism, that led in 1802 to the proscription of his lectures in Vienna as dangerous to religion. Gall migrated to Paris in 1807. There the cautious scientists of the Institute were under considerable political pressure; they did not give his works a fair hearing or elect him a member. His books were eventually placed on the Index Librorum Prohibitorum, and he was forbidden a religious burial, although he was actually orthodox in his own religious beliefs (Young, 1970).

There was a strange law in England dealing with the property rights of authors. The law stemmed from the Star Chamber of Charles I, acting in 1637; in its interpretation in the 1820s, if a work was held to be blasphemous, seditious, or immoral, its author had no property rights in it. A publisher could ask for a ruling, and if the work fell under the disfavor of the court, the publisher could then issue a pirate edition without the consent of the author and without paying him.

Lord Byron was twice a victim of such suits. Another was William Lawrence, an eminent surgeon and for a time lecturer in the Royal College of Surgeons. In 1819 Lawrence published his *Lectures on Physiology, Zoology, and the Natural History of Man.* When the book first appeared, there was such fierce public objection to it that Lawrence had it withdrawn. When the pirate edition appeared, in 1822, he brought suit against the publisher and lost.

Lawrence was an advanced biological thinker for his day. He believed that living organisms obeyed natural laws of higher complexity than the simpler physicochemical laws necessary to account for inanimate phenomena. But he argued against any "vital principle" that could exist apart from the functioning organism, against any life function that could be understood without reference to a bodily organ that carried it out, and consequently against any mental function independent of the highly organized matter constituting the organ of mind—namely, the brain.

When Lawrence first delivered the lectures on which the book was based, in 1816–1817, there was considerable controversy, which remained within a small circle of scientists and students. But immediately after the publication of the book he was attacked for materialism and atheism, both from the podium and in the press. In July 1819, the *Quarterly Review* condemned this expression of "the doctrine of materialism, an open avowal of which has been made in the metropolis of the British Empire in the lectures delivered under public authority by Mr. Lawrence [Quoted in Goodfield-Toulmin, 1969, p. 285]." The *Quarterly Review* demanded that the offending passages be purged from his book. Lawrence withdrew the book and resigned his post as lecturer. He was thus able to continue a brilliant medical career, but at the cost of his scientific freedom.

Lawrence, then, was in Darwin's day a living document of the price of dangerous ideas. Darwin owned his book, marked it up with marginal strokes, and referred to it in his transmutation notebooks and later on in the *Descent of Man*. Huxley knew Lawrence and mentioned the story of his near-ostracism. Darwin probably knew him too; in any event, he could not have avoided knowing all the circumstances of the case. Lawrence lived until 1867. In the Darwin circle he was not a forgotten man.

In 1826, less than a decade after the suppression of Mr. Lawrence, young Charles Darwin attended a meeting of the Plinian Society in Edinburgh and witnessed the expunging of his fellow student's paper, Mr. Browne's argument that "mind is material."

In 1830–1833 the volumes of Charles Lyell's *Principles of Geology* appeared, just in time to play a major part in shaping Darwin's intellectual growth during the *Beagle* voyage. Lyell pursued a policy of caution in expressing himself on geological matters that contradicted accepted interpretations of Scripture. This policy was related to his views on creation and on the relation between mind and matter. To account for the fossil evidence of innumerable extinct creatures, Lyell supported the hypothesis of successive creations extending into an indefinite past, repeatedly repopulating the globe with new sets of organisms. For Lyell, this view harmonized perfectly with an extended version of the argument from design. As the physical state of the globe was altered ". . . the species likewise have been changed; and yet they have all been so modelled, on types analogous to those of existing plants and animals, as to indicate throughout a perfect harmony of design and unity of purpose [1872, p. 401]."

As early as 1841, while going through the sixth edition of Lyell's *Principles of Geology*, Darwin took cognizance of the latter's position on man. As was his habit, he used the back flyleaf of the book for notes and comments, among them: "Lyell always considers that there is *saltus* between man & animals [S. Smith, 1960, p. 391]."

Much later, after Darwin had published the *Origin*, in *The Antiquity of Man* Lyell (1963) addressed himself both to the argument from design and to the mind–body question. On design he concluded, "The whole course of nature may be the material embodiment of a preconcerted arrangement; and if the succession of events be explained by transmutation, the perpetual adaptation of the organic world to new conditions leaves the argument in favour of design, and therefore of a designer, as valid as ever." He went on: "As to the charge of materialism brought against all forms of the development theory. . . far from having a materialistic tendency" the evolution of mind culminating in ". . . Man himself, presents us with a picture of the ever-increasing dominion of mind over matter [1963, p. 506]."

Lyell's private notebooks, only recently published, show that the thoughts expressed above reflected his real thinking.[5] On 6 December 1859, after he had read the *Origin*, he wrote in his notes, "May not creation consist of four powers or principles," variation, natural selection, inheritance of acquired characteristics, and "the progressive tendency to more complex organizations, both physical & spiritual, material & immaterial [Wilson, 1970, p. 327]."

The essential point is that Lyell could easily compromise with religious believers in matters of phrasing and timing because he was himself a believer. To the extent that Darwin was an agnostic and a materialist, he was far more isolated in the scientific community, and his compromises would be harder to make.

Vestiges—An Evolutionary Theologue

While it is often said that evolution was "in the air" in Darwin's time, not enough attention is paid to the crucial differences between Darwin and other evolutionists. Robert Chambers' *Vestiges* appeared anonymously in 1844. Although it was published after Darwin had worked out his main ideas, *Vestiges* is worth dwelling on because it was the most popular and immediate precursor of Darwin's published work. The differences between himself and Chambers help us to understand how Darwin might feel a wide gulf between himself and his potential audience, not simply because he espoused an evolutionary theory but because of its utterly materialistic tone.

The title of Chambers' book, *The Vestiges of the Natural History of Creation*, was well chosen. The whole tenor of the book is a continuation of the tradition of natural theology. The author pauses repeatedly and lengthily to expound his fundamental theme that "the Divine Governor of the world conducts its passing affairs by a fixed rule, to which we apply the term natural law [Chambers, 1853, p. *v*]."

---

[5] These notebooks record Lyell's ideas during the years 1855–1861.

Chambers was not content with a creator who set the world in lawful motion and then abandoned it to the operation of natural law, nor did Chambers' God leave anything to chance:

> God may be presumed to be revealed to us in every one of the phenomena of the system, in the suspension of globes in space, in the degradation of rocks and the upthrowing of mountains, in the development of plants and animals, in each movement of our minds, and in all that we enjoy and suffer, seeing that, the system requiring a sustainer as well as an originator, He must be continually present in every part of it, albeit He does not permit a single law to swerve in any case from its appointed course of operation. Thus we may still feel that He is the immediate breather of our life and ruler of our spirits [p. 323].

Chambers was aware that postulating a world in flux implied imperfection at any given moment. Moreover, he was concerned with the meaning of human suffering, war, and death and the questions they raised about the benevolence of God. He wrote, "To reconcile this to the character of the Deity, it is necessary to suppose that the present system is but a part of the whole, a stage in a Great Progress, and that the Redress is in reserve [p. 324]."

Like Darwin, Chambers insisted on the continuity of human intelligence with "the lower animals." But their theological conclusions from this continuity take entirely different directions. Chambers, after expatiating on the gulf between humans and lower animals, especially with regard to human powers of "veneration. . . hope. . . reason. . . conscientiousness and benevolence," concludes that our belief in God is evidence for His existence. "The existence of faculties having a regard to such things is a good evidence that such things exist. The face of God is reflected in the organization of man, as a little pool reflects the glorious sun [p. 299]."

Darwin's treatment of the origins of religious belief was, by contrast, entirely naturalistic. He likens primitive interest in the inexplicable to a dog's disturbance at some unfamiliar event; he assumes that sophisticated human theologies evolve from a general belief in "spiritual agencies" to account for inexplicable events; he repeatedly emphasizes the continuity of human religious beliefs with tendencies to be found in other animals, citing one author who claimed that "a dog looks on his master as on a god [*Descent*, p. 96]."

Like Darwin, Chambers drew on a human invention for an analogy to clarify his theory of evolution. Darwin drew the analogy between natural and artificial selection; at the heart of his thinking lay a probabilistic conception of the process of evolution. Chambers drew on an entirely different sort of invention, Charles Babbage's celebrated calculating machine. What is significant about the analogy is that Chambers treats the machine as operating in an entirely deterministic way: in a very long series of numbers generated by the machine, increasing regularly by steps of one, eventually a seeming irregularity appears; if we understand the machine fully, we know that the change is not an irregular violation of its laws, but expresses the fact that the machine is preset to generate numbers according to a more complex or "higher" law than first appeared to be the case. Chambers quotes Babbage to the effect that both the simple numerical series, analogous to inheritance without evolutionary change, and the apparent irregularities, analogous to such change, were "as necessary a consequence of the original adjustment, and might have been as fully foreknown at the commencement [Babbage, 1838, p. 838]."

Was Darwin a Materialist?

Was Darwin a materialist? We cannot quite say. Wherever he included a reference to the creator or creation, one reader may claim that Darwin was really a believer, another that he was only propitiating prevailing opinion or, as he put it himself, "truckling."

In the *Origin*, Darwin was repeatedly explicit on one point: The hypothesis of independent creation of each species explains nothing. He went further, attacking the idea that there is a natural system which "reveals the plan of the Creator"; because of the vagueness of such an idea, "nothing is thus added to our knowledge [*Origin*, p. 413]."

Publicly, on two points he conceded something, leaving some room for a creator. First, on the origin of life, he wrote, "There is grandeur in this view of life, with its several powers, having been originally breathed by the Creator into a few forms or into one; and that. . . from so simple a beginning endless forms most beautiful and most wonderful have been, and are being evolved. [Darwin, 1859, p. 490]."

Second, his printed words admit the possibility that the whole lawful system of material nature might have had a supernatural creator, a first cause, who then left all else to "secondary causes [*Origin* p. 488]."

How seriously should we take these occasional allusions to creation? A careful reading shows that they do not permeate the *Origin* in the way that the argument from design permeated Chambers's *Vestiges*.

Privately, in a letter to his close friend Joseph Hooker, Darwin confesses, "I have long regretted that I truckled to pubic opinion, and used the pentateuchal term of creation, by which I really meant 'appeared' by some wholly unknown process."[6]

Apart from the concluding passage of the *Origin* discussed above, the chapter in which concessions to creationism are most marked is Chapter 6, "Difficulties on Theory." Darwin saw the immense difficulty for his contemporaries of believing that an organ so wonderful and perfect as the human eye could have evolved by the haphazard process of evolution proposed in his theory. He devoted eight pages to the problem posed for his theory by "organs of extreme perfection and complication." Reminding his readers of

---

[6] LL 3, p. 18, letter to Hooker, 29 March 1863. However much he may have regretted his compromise, he did nothing to strengthen his stand in the three editions of the *Origin* which appeared after 1863: 1866, 1869, 1872.

the argument from design, he agrees that it is natural to infer that the eye was made by a process analogous to that of a skilled human making other optical instruments. He asks, "But may not this inference be presumptuous? Have we any right to assume that the Creator works by intellectual powers like those of man [*Origin*, p. 188]?"

This is one of the more heavily revised sections of the *Origin*. From the third to the sixth edition, 1861–1872, Darwin kept on adding new information about the eye, to bolster his contention that even an organ so marvelous might have evolved by natural selection. One year after his last revision of the *Origin*, a lecture on vision by Hermann von Helmholtz, the German man-of-all-science, appeared in English translation.

Helmholtz was a master physicist, mathematician, and biologist, the author of a great treatise on physiological optics. He was also devoted to a completely materialistic biology. Indeed, as a young man in 1845 he was a member of a group of physiologists who formed a pact to struggle against vitalistic theories and for the view that no other forces than common physical chemical ones are active within the organism. Helmholtz's famous paper on the conservation of energy, written in 1847, actually grew out of an effort to show the physical transformations of energy involved in muscular activity (Gruber & Gruber, 1956).

In the lecture that Darwin read, "The Recent Progress of the Theory of Vision," almost every passage that Darwin marked dealt with defects of the normal eye as an optical instrument. After a discussion of the psychological complexities of vision, Helmholtz concluded:

> The inaccuracies and imperfections of the eye as an optical instrument, and those which belong to the image on the retina, now appear insignificant in comparison with the incongruities which we have met with in the field of sensation. One might almost believe that Nature here contradicted herself on purpose, in order to destroy any dream of a preexisting harmony between the outer and the inner world [1873].[7]

Darwin also marked some of the passages in which Helmholtz explicitly drew the connection between the peculiarities of the visual system and the Darwinian theory of evolution. How could he have failed to appreciate the support of a great physicist who concluded that "Darwin's theory contains an essentially new creative thought. It shows how adaptability of structure in organisms can result from a blind rule of a law of nature without any intervention of intelligence [Helmholtz, 1873]"?

Although Darwin did not make it easy for us to say exactly where he stood on certain philosophical matters, we can profitably ask what role these issues might have played in his argument. In rephrasing the question—was Darwin a

---

[7] Darwin read Helmholtz's essay on the imperfection of the eye in time to use it in his second edition of *Descent*, 1874, p. 441.

materialist?—it is important to distinguish the concept of a creator as a first cause and the concept of God as omniscient and omnipresent in the universe. Darwin's theory of evolution dealt only with the laws governing the ongoing operation of the organic world; he had expunged the question of origins from his theory, which in its developed form said nothing about the origin or life or of matter and energy and the universe. Consequently, his theory could not be affected either favorably or adversely by the introduction of a supernatural creator as first cause.

On the other hand, the idea of either a planful or an intervening providence taking part in the day-to-day operations of the universe was in effect a competing theory. If one believed that there was a God who had originally designed the world exactly as it has come to be, the theory of evolution through natural selection could be seen as superfluous. Likewise, if one believed in a God who intervened from time to time to create some of the organisms, organs, or functions found in the living world, Darwin's theory could be seen as superfluous. Any introduction of intelligent planning or decision making reduces natural selection from the position of a necessary and universal principle to a mere possibility.

Something of Darwin's agnosticism appears in various letters and in his *Autobiography*, all posthumous. The only publication in his lifetime expressing these ideas was the concluding passage of *The Variation of Animals and Plants Under Domestication*. There Darwin stated the issue baldly, but left something for each reader to decide for himself:

> If we assume that each particular variation was from the beginning of all time preordained, the plasticity of organisation, which leads to many injurious deviations of structure, as well as that redundant power of reproduction which inevitably leads to a struggle for existence, and, as a consequence, to the natural selection or survival of the fittest, must appear to us superfluous laws of nature. On the other hand, an omnipotent and omniscient Creator ordains everything and foresees everything. Thus we are brought face to face with a difficulty as insoluble as is that of free will and predestination [1868, Vol. 2, p. 432].

In this passage, published in 1868, Darwin went almost as far in public as he had gone in private many years before. Either the theory of evolution through natural selection or the idea of an omnipotent and omniscient creator is superfluous.

Using the idea of God merely to get the whole system of nature started puts God permanently outside the system and in a very real sense reduces his importance. This accords well with what Darwin has told us about the development of his religious views. "Quite orthodox" as a young man, his faith faded gradually and, as he remembered it, painlessly. He became an agnostic in a dual sense: He had no reason to believe in God, and no desire to disprove His existence.[8]

---

[8] See the unexpurgated version of his *Autobiography*. For many years his family permitted the publication only of a version in which his views of religion were severely censored. This reduced

The fact that Darwin seemed to vacillate on certain philosophical issues, and that he was willing to be conciliatory in his eventual public posture, might conceivably mean that he had adopted a definite, subtle, middle-ground position. More likely he decided that these were secondary questions on which he could afford to be conciliatory because they did not affect his ruling passion, the theory of evolution through natural selection. Whether God had created the universe a long time ago, whether it had always been there with God standing by, or whether God was an out-moded hypothesis—none of this really mattered to Darwin, so long as the world of nature operated according to discoverable natural laws. If Darwin had been willing to compromise on questions he deemed fundamental, he would not have been the great Darwin we know. Strangely, the decision that God's existence was not a fundamental question for his purposes may have been a much more profound change in Darwin's ideas than for him to have adopted the view that He did not exist, but that the question remained fundamental.

The rejection of the idea of a planful or intervening providence carried with it an important implication for Darwin's ideas about man. Without such a providence there was nothing except the laws of nature, including the principle of evolution through natural selection, always governing the entire natural order. There was absolutely no reason to exempt man, in either his past or his future evolution, from the Darwinian mill. Regarding man's past, Darwin's views are plain enough, all the way from the M and N notebooks to the *Descent of Man*.

The Future of Humanity

As for man's future, there is a mysterious idea that Darwin reiterated at least six times in his early notebooks: "If all men were dead, then monkeys make men.—Men make angels [B, p. 169 cited in Gruber & Barrett, 1974/ 1980, p. 446]."

This is an idea that must be read at two levels. He is saying that organisms evolve in such a manner as to fill up ecological niches, and there is a place in the world for an intelligent, manlike creature. If chance had not brought forth *Homo sapiens*, a progenitor similar to ours would have evolved into an intelligent hominid, because the evolutionary conditions would have favored it. By emphasizing the point that this hypothetical creature would not have been the species *man* as we know it, Darwin brings home the idea that chance plays a large part in evolution. Whatever total set of conditions happens to prevail will determine the outcome.

On another level, Darwin means to say something about evolution as an

---

version was included in the *Life and Letters of Charles Darwin*, edited by his son Francis. The unexpurgated version was published by his granddaughter, Nora Barlow, in 1958, 76 years after his death.

ongoing process applicable to man today. At first he seems optimistic: Man will evolve into something still higher, "angels." Later on he is not so definite. Of man, he writes "he is not a deity, his end under present form will come" [C, p. 77; cited in Gruber & Barrett, 1974/1980, p. 449]."

Darwin realized that he was dethroning man from his boasted place at the pinnacle of creation in at least three senses: past, penultimate and ultimate futures. Man would no longer have the divine right of kings; he was born not of God, but of the lower animals. Worse, future evolution might put man in the shade, inferior even in intelligence to some new species that would evolve, probably out of man. Worst of all, whatever man becomes, Darwin believed that in the end the sun and all the planets will grow too cold to support life: "Believing as I do that man in the distant future will be a far more perfect creature than he now is, it is an intolerable thought that he and all other sentient beings are doomed to complete annihilation after such long-continued slow progress [*Autobiography*, p. 92]." An intolerable thought it may have been, but Darwin thought it: The "angel" that man is becoming will be annihilated.

The question *Was Darwin a materialist?* has one other important side to which we must attend, the issue of *vitalism*. Granted that all organismic phenomena have a material basis in that they consist of highly organized forms of matter in motion and of specialized energy transfer systems. Is there not, in addition, something else, some "vital principle" necessary to account for the special properties of living things? One might believe that there are such special "vital" properties and suppose that they derived from non-natural or supernatural sources. Alternatively, one might interpret the "vital principle" as a qualitative leap, a group of emergent properties inherent in the very nature of matter and energy when they occur in the highly organized forms we label "alive." In the latter case one would be a sort of materialist, believing that life and mind are "nothing but" matter and energy, but the sting of nothing-but-ness, so painful to the faithful in Darwin's time, would be lessened. Perhaps this second position might be labeled *naturalistic vitalism*.

Today we seem very close to synthesizing simple forms of life in the laboratory, to controlling precisely the pattern of development of more complex forms, and to simulating thought processes in computing machines; but we have also come to recognize that there is nothing at all simple about the whole subject. As we come a little closer to this godlike control over nature, our respect for its enormous complexity grows again. But in the nineteenth century there was far greater uncertainty as to the distance to be traveled from inanimate matter to complex living forms. The very effort to understand the innermost secrets of life and thought seemed to set the scientist against the gods. As Thomas Huxley put it, probably with relish, "Most of us are idolators, and ascribe divine powers to the abstractions 'Force,' 'Gravity,' 'Vitality,' which our own brains have created [L. Huxley, 1908, p. 358]."

By dint of some effort, Darwin managed to place the question of the origin of life outside the scope of his theory, In that way he avoided dealing with the nature of life insofar as that phrase means understanding the differences between inanimate and animate matter and the transition from one to the other. Logically, and therefore publicly, he could exclude the origin of life from his theory. But psychologically the preservation of his intellectual comfort required that he arrive at some understanding with himself on the answer to these ultimate questions.

The Question of "Special Creation"

With respect to the emergence of all the major forms and functions of living things, of course Darwin's main theoretical life task was to show that these could be accounted for in an entirely natural way. But that left one crucial question hanging, and to Darwin it felt like a hanging matter: With the evolution of complex nervous systems, does there at last appear in the pantheon of nature a type of process, mind, which can no longer be thought of as natural?

In all the manuscript material Darwin wrote most fully and openly on these questions in the bundle of papers he later labeled "Old and Useless Notes about the moral sense and some metaphysical points . . ." written between 1837 and 1840. The date is important because it shows that he immediately felt the need to resolve these metaphysical questions which were thrown open by his theoretical work in biology. True, in his eventual published work very little of this "useless" thought appears. But in his private intellectual economy it did not seem to him at all useless to speculate on such ultimate questions as the nature of life, purpose, and mind.

On the whole, his position is clear. He is drawn to a relatively straightforward materialism: "Sensation is the ordering contraction. . . in fibres united with nervous filaments. . . ."[9] From the simplest sensations to the most complex thoughts, mental processes can be explained as the activity of the nervous system. He cites experiments done with planaria (a simple flatworm, not to be confused with the earthworms which Darwin also studied). By their adaptive, seemingly purposive behavior, planaria display the rudiments of consciousness; we can split one planarian and produce three functioning organisms, and the adaptive behavior or consciousness of the resulting individuals is "multiplied with the organic structure. . . ." For Darwin it follows that consciousness is the effect of "sufficient perfection of organization" of bodily structure.[10]

In the *Origin*, by limiting his treatment of the evolution of mental functions

---

[9] Old and Useless Notes, #9.

[10] "Old and Useless Notes," #16. Psychobiologists are still interested in the redistribution of planarian intelligence, although modern efforts, rather than splitting the whole organism, involve the injection into untrained individuals of RNA extracted from planarians trained in a simple conditioning task. Planarians are interesting because they are among the simplest organisms in which the transition from a nerve net to a central nervous system occurs.

to the subject of instinct, Darwin essentially sidestepped the problem of purposeful behavior and motivation. But in the "Old and Useless Notes" he deals with it forthrightly. "Every action whatever is the effect of a motive. . . . Motives are units in the universe . . . The general delusion about free will [is] obvious."[11] As human beings, we *feel* as though there is some incorporeal self controlling the actions of our bodies, but in fact even the mechanism of control represents the functioning of a part of the body, the brain.

At least transitorily, Darwin entertained the possibility that there are emergent levels of organization, that life may display properties not predictable from any knowledge of inanimate matter, that it may represent "matter united by certain laws different from those that govern in the inorganic world. . . ." But he goes on immediately to ask, "Has any vegetable or animal *matter* been formed by the union of *simple* non-organic matter without action of vital laws?"[12] We can see here how, at every turn, Darwin was concerned to keep his speculations as clearly as possible within the domain of natural phenomena. From the sequence of these notes, we can also see how his botanical work, done much later in life, was guided by a philosophy of biology. Darwin wanted to show that seemingly purposeful acts in plants as well as in primitive animals could be explained according to the same general laws as the voluntary behavior of more complex animals, and, consequently, that the simplest forms of mind, such as the photosensitivity of plants, are parts of the same evolutionary net as the more obviously purposeful acts of human beings.

The title of Part 4 of this chapter has been drawn from the N notebook, where Darwin wrote: "To study Metaphysics, as they have always been studied appears to me to be like puzzling at astronomy without mechanics.— Experience shows the problem of the mind cannot be solved by attacking the citadel itself.—the mind is function of body.—we must bring some *stable* foundation to argue from [N, p. 5, 3 October 1838; cited in Gruber & Barrett, 1974/1980, p. 331]." Just as we cannot directly see the full nature of the stars but only points of light, we cannot study the mind directly. Just as Newton was able to solve astronomical problems by applying to celestial motions a deep understanding of terrestrial mechanics, so we may be able to come closer to understanding the mind and solving the profoundest philosophical and psychological problems if we . . . what? Darwin does not quite say what this "stable foundation" might be.

To the modern reader, knowing about recent great advances in neuropsychology and computer science, these might seem to provide the foundation

---

[11] "Old and Useless Notes," #25–28.

[12] "Old and Useless Notes," #34. In 1828 Friedrich Wöhler had synthesized urea from potassium cyanate and ammonium sulphate. This step is often regarded as the first laboratory production of an organic compound and as a great blow against vitalism. Perhaps Darwin did not yet know about Wöhler's work; more likely he did not regard it as decisive, since the substances with which Wöhler began were not exactly "simple."

for understanding the mind, by giving us knowledge of the structures which carry out mental processes. Perhaps Darwin thought something similar, but his actual work never took him in that direction. Instead, he addressed himself to the task of understanding how evolution might proceed in such a manner that the changing structures can perform the adaptive functions we wish to understand, including the functions called *mind*.

References

Abercrombie, J. *Inquiries concerning the intellectual powers and the investigation of truth* (8th ed.). London: Murray, 1838.

Ayala, F. J. The mechanisms of evolution. *Scientific American*, 1978, *239*, 56–70.

Babbage, C. *The ninth bridewater treatise* (2nd ed.). London: John Murray, 1838.

Baldwin, J. M. On selective thinking. *Psychological Review*, 1898, *5*, 1–24. (APA Presidential Address, 1898.)

Boring, E. G. *A history of experimental psychology* (2nd ed.). New York: Appleton-Century-Crofts, 1950.

Campbell, D. T. On the conflicts between biological and social evolution and between psychology and moral tradition. *American Psychologist*, 1975, *30*, 1103–1126. (APA Presidential Address, 1975.)

Chambers, R. *The vestiges of the natural history of creation.* London: John Churchill, 1853.

Darwin, C. *On the origin of species.* London: John Murray, 1859.

Darwin, C. *The variation of animals and plants under domestication* (2 vols). London: John Murray, 1868

Darwin, C. *The descent of man, and selection in relation to sex.* London: John Murray, 1871. (2nd edit., 1882.)

Darwin, C. *The autobiography of Charles Darwin.* Nora Barlow (Ed.). London: Collins, 1958.

de Beer, G. Darwin's notebooks on transmutation of species. *Bulletin of the British Museum (Natural History) Historical Series*, 1960, 2 (2), 25–73.

Freud, S. *A general introduction to psychoanalysis.* New York: Doubleday, 1953.

Goodfield-Toulmin, J. Some aspects of English physiology: 1780–1840. *Journal of the History of Biology*, 1969, *2*, 283–320.

Gruber, H. E. *Darwin on man: A psychological study of scientific creativity* together with *Darwin's early and unpublished notebooks*, transcribed and annotated by Paul H. Barrett, Foreword by Jean Piaget. New York: E. P. Dutton, 1974; 2nd edition, Chicago: University of Chicago Press, 1980.

Gruber, H. Courage and cognitive growth in children and scientists. In M. Schwebel & J. Raph (Eds.), *Piaget in the classroom.* New York: Basic Books, 1973.

Gruber, H. E., & Gruber, V. Hermann von Helmholtz: Nineteenth-century polymorph, *Scientific Monthly*, 1956, *83*, 92–99.

Gruber, H. E., & Vonèche, J. J. (Eds.). *The essential Piaget.* New York: Basic Books, 1977.

Helmholtz, H. *Popular Lectures on Scientific Subjects.* E. Atkinson (Trans.). London: 1873.

Hull, C. L. Mind mechanism and adaptive behavior. *Psychological Review*, 1937, *44*, 1–32. (Reprinted in E. R. Hilgard (Ed.), *American psychology in historical perspective.* Washington, D.C.: American Psychological Association, 1978.

Huxley, L. (Ed.). *Life and letters of Thomas Huxley* (Vol. 2). London: Macmillan, 1908.

Judd, C. H. Evolution and consciousness. *Psychological Review*, 1910, *17*, 77–97. (quoted in E. R. Hilgard (Ed.), *American psychology in historical perspective.* Washington, D.C.: American Psychological Association. (APA Presidential Address, 1909.)

Koestler, A. *The act of creation.* London: Hutchinson, 1964.

Köhler, W. *The mentality of apes.* London: Routledge and Kegan, Paul, 1925.

Kuhn, T. *The structure of scientific revolutions.* London: University of Chicago Press, 1962.

Lewin, K. *A dynamic theory of personality.* New York: McGraw-Hill, 1935.

Lyell, C. *Principles of geology* (11th ed.). London: Murray, 1872.

Lyell, C. *The antiquity of man* (2nd ed.). London: John Murray, 1963.

Piaget, J. *Adaptation vitale et psychologie de l'intelligence: Selection organique et phenocopie.* Paris: Hermann, 1974.

Piaget, J. *Le comportement moteur de l'evolution.* Paris: Gallimard, 1976.

Piaget, J. *Behavior and evolution.* New York: Pantheon, 1978.

Reid, T *Philosophical works.* Vol. 1. Hildesheim: Georg olms Verlagsbuchhandlung, 1967.

Skinner, B. F. *The behavior of organisms: An experimental analysis.* London: Appleton-Century, 1938.

Schwebel, M., & Raph, J. (Eds.). *Piaget in the classroom.* New York: Basic Books, 1973.

Smith, M. B. Perspectives on selfhood. *American Psychologist,* 1978, *33,* 1053–1063. (APA Presidential Address, 1978.)

Smith, S. The origin of "the origin." *The Advancement of Science,* 1960 (64), 391–401.

Stone, C. P. Multiply, vary, let the strongest live and the weakest die—Charles Darwin. *Psychological Bulletin,* 1943, *40,* 1–24. (APA Presidential Address, 1942.)

Waddington, C. H. *The strategy of the genes.* London: Allen and Unwin, 1957.

Washburn, S. L. Human behavior and the behavior of other animals. *American Psychologist,* 1978, *33,* 405–418. (The Invited Address, APA, 1977.)

Whyte, L. L. *Internal factors in evolution.* New York: Braziller, 1965.

Wilson, L. G. (Ed.). *Scientific journals on the species question.* New Haven: Yale University Press, 1970.

Wittgenstein, L. *On certainty.* G. E. M. Anscombe & G. H. von Wright (Eds.). New York: Harper and Row, 1969.

Young, R. M. *Mind, brain and adaptation in the nineteenth century: Cerebral localization and its biological context from Gall to Ferrier.* Oxford: Clarendon Press, 1970.

PART II

CURRENT THEORY
AND RESEARCH

Chapter 5

On the Effect of Mind on Matter

DAVID BAKAN

The essential assertion of this chapter is that the mind can and does affect matter, and it is foolish to think otherwise. General A would be more interested in General B's battle plans than in his nervous system. Even if General A could have secret access to General B's nervous system, it would be of strategic value only if the battle plan could be deciphered from it. For even if there were a perfect isomorphism between battle plan and pattern of neural activation, battle plan is decisive whereas neural activation is only necessary, just as tanks may be necessary for a tank battle but not decisive in the same sense that battle plans are.

I do not intend to offer either a theory of mind or theory of action in this chapter. I do, however, want to indicate that there is a real intellectual territory to be explored here. I do not, at this point, pretend to report on explorations of that intellectual territory.

The existence of an effect of mind on matter is, to say the least, empirical. By *empirical* I quite specifically intend the dictionary sense. My desk Webster's *New Collegiate Dictionary* says that empirical means "depending on experience or observation alone, without due regard to science and theory." The dictionary betrays great profundity in suggesting a contrast between that which is empirical and that which is based on "due regard to science and theory." Divergence between science and theory, on the one hand, and the universe of empirical observation, on the other hand, may speak to

117

BODY AND MIND
Past, Present, and Future

either a defect of science and theory, or a defect of empirical observation, or both. I do not derogate science and theory generally. Nonetheless, scientists and theorists must be able to offer powerful and cogent arguments if they ask that the results of experience and observation be dismissed as illusion.

There is the commonplace observation that talk can effect physical events, as, for example, when one person gives a direction and another person follows the direction. We are aware these days that one word, say, from the chief executive officer of the United States, or of Russia, could set certain physical events in motion that would result in planet-wide destruction. The commonplace empirical observation that underlies the clinical psychological enterprise is that "just" talking with people often has designable effects, hopefully beneficial, on their physical behavior. To make this point, one does not have to enter into the quarrels among the various forms of psychotherapy. They all entail talking. This is true if the therapist just gives instruction, or so-called verbal rewards, right through the spectrum to depth psychoanalysis. Even the practice of physical medicine largely entails talking that has an effect on the physical world, as when a physician instructs the patient, "Have this prescription filled, and take one pill every six hours." This instruction is truly the "cause" of a whole series of subsequent events in the physical world, since it is unlikely that they would otherwise occur.

Such observations are so ubiquitous as to appear banal. Yet, we are given pause should we try to connect them with the position of those nineteenth-century giants of physiology, Helmholtz, Brücke, Du Bois-Reymond, and all of their followers. Their position was that only common physical and chemical events could be causative of physiological events. Clearly this gang and their followers would probably be able to handle the chemical and physical effect of the pill on the patient. But they would have a hard time explaining how the pill got to the patient if they limited themselves purely to the terms of common physical and chemical events.

One might be able to discourse at length on the effects of lubrication on the performance of my car in terms of common physical and chemical events. But no one could do as well with the various events that ensue when I say, "Please change the oil," to my mechanic.

There is a sensible way of comprehending how it may be that mental events can affect physical events. It may be difficult to persuade many who may read this chapter. For we live in a schizophrenic world in which, on the one hand, we commonly assume that mental events do affect physical events, while, on the other hand, our scientific assumptions make the effect of the mental on the physical incomprehensible. Our scientific assumptions are at fault. Quite specifically, *the defect of the scientific universe of discourse is that it has no place in the objective world for information, except information in the bound condition.*

It may be of value to introduce a distinction at this point. When I say to my mechanic, "Please change the oil," there is my talk and there is its message. The talk may, perhaps, be described in terms of the sounds or the pattern of air movements created by my speaking. There is also the whole set of events of a patently physical and chemical character that are set up in the body of my mechanic. But all of this is quite different from the message, the instruction, the information, which has been transmitted from me to him. It is the same as the difference between the message that is transmitted over the telephone system and the physical and chemical events in the telephone system. The telephone system may *carry* the message, but in no sense are the message and the characteristics of the telephone event the same. The message may have been encoded into a set of electrical impulses, but the message and the encodement of it are different.

Or, consider the following. On Mars there is a box that was sent up from Earth and that is under the control of, I believe, some people in Houston, Texas. Imagine such a box with mechanical arms, scooping up Martian dust, taking the dust into the box for analysis, and returning the dust to the Martian ground. Imagine two Martians watching this. Imagine them discussing the question of how this phenomenon might be explained. Imagine one of these Martians to be the Martian equivalent of Helmholtz or Brücke or their intellectual descendants. Imagine the other to be the Martian equivalent of St. Peter or St. Paul or one of their intellectual (and spiritual) descendants. Helmholtz says that every movement of the box can be explained by common physical and chemical principles. But St. Peter says it can only be adequately explained in terms of control by a being in the Martian heaven.

St. Peter clearly betrays a better understanding of the situation than Helmholtz. For Houston, Texas, is in the Martian heaven. Furthermore, between Houston and Mars there is no air channel for conveying the sound waves and no telephone wires. It is empty space. There is some view about *energy* going through empty space to explain this. But for sure it is not *material* in the more ordinary sense.

Thus, in the face of this mental experiment in which we placed the Martian equivalents of Helmholtz and St. Peter as witnesses to a landed space instrument the materialist must retire from a strict matter-materialism. He must allow that there can be nonmaterial causation across empty space. We have inched a bit closer to the position that perhaps what is really important when I tell my mechanic to change the oil is indeed the message and not the various material media that carried the message from me to him. For, after all, if I were on Mars, I could have ordered an oil change from there, with a little cooperation from the people in Houston.

One more introductory thought before I get into the details of the argument. This thought arises out of the context of the study of psychological disorder. There is a particular disorder that plagues the contemporary world. That disorder is *depression*. It is very widespread and is characterized by the sufferer's belief that his mental acts can have no impact on the world. I would observe that the materialist and the depressive share the same belief, that mental events are not causative.

Thus, not only is the position of the materialist empirically invalid, but it is also depressing. And this is in a world in which one of the most frequent psychological disorders is depression.

Brief History of Materialism

How did materialism come to exist? (I use the word materialism to indicate the belief that there can be no nonmaterial causation.) The history is too long and complex for me to deal with it adequately here. But there is some value in indicating some of the more important sources. Descartes and Newton are two major sources of contemporary materialism. From Descartes we have the notion of the body as a machine. From Newton we get the notion of the world as machine. These intellectual giants of the seventeenth and early eighteenth centuries (whose mental states were certainly causative of a great deal) started a process that produced a breathtaking set of propositions, propositions intrinsically intelligent yet not reliant on an intelligent being. These propositions "worked," especially in connection with nonliving things.

Following Descartes and Newton there was a period of accelerated world travel and exploration, in which Europeans were considerably exposed to previously unknown plants and animals. The seeming intelligence displayed by biological adaptation was more than could be contained in, and explained by, a mechanical view. But Darwin came along in the middle of the nineteenth century and seemed to show, quite convincingly, that all of the intrinsically intelligent life mechanisms could have derived from a single mechanism, the principle of natural selection. Now, both Darwin and Newton looked on the laws they discovered as divine decrees. Yet, all of the discovered intelligence in the universe was now *immanent* in the created universe, without control from God in heaven on any day-to-day basis. If there was an intelligent God at all, he completed all of his work in endowing the world with the laws that continued to regulate it. And since the human body is equally part of this same universe, as Darwin indicated in tying man into the rest of the animal kingdom, man too is completely regulated by these immanent laws. Man's apparent intelligence in guiding his own body is at best an illusion, or an epiphenomenon. It cannot be an agent in directing what that body does.

The materialism that began in the seventeenth century thus received a new boost in the second half of the nineteenth century from Darwin. At the same time, giant steps in technology were also taking place. The seeming ideological success, on the one hand, and the seeming practical success, on the other, served to reinforce the view that all observable movements of observable things could be exhaustively explained by a unified scheme of physical explanation. Thus, the conclusion that mental events can have no effect upon physical events, and the view of Helmholtz, Brücke, and Du Bois-Reymond was announced.

The Separate Reality of Information

A major turning point, however, took place with the publication by Leo Szilard, of later fame in connection with the release of atomic energy, of his 1929 paper entitled "On the Decrease of Entropy in a Thermodynamic System by the Intervention of Intelligent Beings" (Szilard, 1964). I have previously discussed the implication of the Szilard paper that information must be conceived of as having an ontic status quite on a par with physical reality (Bakan, 1974). Szilard's argument is essentially that *either* the second law of thermodynamics is invalid, *or* there can exist separate intelligence systems interconnected with physical systems in a manner such that, while the entropy in a physical system decreases, corresponding rise in entropy in the intelligence system takes place. Given the choice, Szilard opts for accepting the latter.

Entropy is a physical measurement. A thermodynamic system is a physical system. Szilard talks freely about the effect of the intervention of intelligent beings on a physical measurement of a physical system, or what appears to be the effect of mind on matter.

Szilard's contribution can be better appreciated if we digress to discuss a feature associated with probability theory. It is to be recalled that the mathematics of probability had been brought to bear on the problems of heat with some powerful consequences prior to Szilard and that it is in that context that Szilard wrote.

There are certain differences between the application of probability theory and the otherwise ordinary application of mathematics to measurement. In virtually every other branch of mathematics, the empirical universe of application is *actual*. Contradiction is characteristically eschewed. But contradiction is an intrinsic part of probability theory. *When probability theory is used in measurement, both the possible and the actual are involved.* Consider a 6-sided die, with numbers on the sides 1, 2, etc. Then, in the context of probability theory, we say that the probability of a 1 coming up topside is 1/6, the probability of a 2 is 1/6, etc. Then we go further to indicate that the sum of all of these probabilities is 1, and on to a variety of other mathematical operations.

But when a die falls with the 1 topside, it is not a 2, or 3, etc. That it is 1 on top is in *contradiction* to it being 2 on top.

This is not a trivial observation. There can be no contradiction in the realm of the actual. Contradiction only exists in some realm that is not actual. Contradiction only exists in the informational realm. Thus probability theory in application deals with the realm of the informational as contrasted with and in relation to the realm of the actual.

It is important to point out that this is not to say that probability theory does not deal with the *objective*. But actual is not the same as objective. Objectively, a die can fall in six ways. Actually, it can only fall one way.

Consider the problem of thermodynamics that Szilard dealt with. Two basic observations can be made:

1. If there is a hot gas in one chamber and cooler gas in an adjoining chamber, the hotter chamber will grow cooler and the cooler chamber will grow hotter. That is, it will be as though the heat goes in one direction only.
2. If the gases in both chambers are of equal temperatures, no matter how hot, no work can be derived from the system.

Entropy is the measure of unavailable energy in a thermodynamic system.

The mechanical theory of heat envisioned a gas as consisting of moving molecules. The faster the molecules moved, the hotter the gas.

Ludwig Boltzmann brought to bear the theory of probability on the mechanical theory of heat. How many ways can a given number of molecules be spatially distributed in a chamber? Some of the molecules are moving faster than others. How many ways are there for the molecules, fast and slow, to be distributed more or less homogeneously all over the chamber? Many. How many ways are there for all of the fast molecules to be over on one side and all of the slow molecules over to the other side? Fewer. Therefore, it is more likely that the molecules will move to a condition of homogeneous distribution all over the chamber. When they are homogeneously distributed all over the chamber, the entropy is high. When they are distributed with fast molecules to one side and slow molecules to the other, the entropy is low. When it is hot on one side and cold on the other, the system can produce work, and the entropy is low. And generally the trend will be toward increasing entropy.

The important thing to recognize is that the measurement of entropy involves not only the actual but the nonactual possibilities as well. The numerical value assigned to a system is based not only on what it actually is but also on what it actually is not but could be. This contribution by Boltzmann constituted a major change from more classical measurement in which measurement was of actuality only. Allowing the distinction between the realm of the actual, where contradiction never exists, and the realm of informational, in which contradiction may exist, the concept of entropy critically depends on the latter.

The next natural step after Boltzmann was taken by Szilard, in which he indicated specifically the role of the informational realm on a thermodynamic system. Szilard's contribution was essentially to combine a problem posed by James Clerk Maxwell in his work on the development of the mechanical theory of heat, with the contribution of Boltzmann in defining a state in terms of nonactual possibilities. Indeed, Maxwell saw the possible role of the informational realm, even before the bringing to bear of probability theory and its employment of contradiction in the informational realm. Maxwell implicitly drew on the contradiction feature of the informational realm.

Maxwell suggested that one consider a being who sat by a hole with a door at a partition in a chamber. The "demon," as Maxwell's being was named later by William Thompson, opened the door for fast molecules but kept it closed for slow molecules. Eventually, there would be many fast molecules in one chamber and slow ones in the other, making for a rise in the difference of the temperatures, which was against the observation that heat goes from the hotter to the cooler side.

What Maxwell had here, obviously, was the similar entertainment of contradiction, open–closed, while in actuality it could only be open or closed. Open–closed exists only in the informational realm.

Essentially Szilard amplified the Maxwell demon argument with a number of similar thought–experiments using the Boltzmann contribution. The most important contribution of the Szilard paper was to identify the informational realm as part and parcel of the thermodynamic system.

His argument is as follows: It is possible to set up thought–experiments that appear to violate the second law of thermodynamics. The Maxwell demon is one such thought–experiment. Szilard outlined several others. He demonstrated that if one considers the total system to consist of *both* the intelligence system and the physical system, the second law of thermodynamics is not violated.

The idea that there could be influence of intelligent beings on physical systems is the natural extension of the bringing to bear of probability theory on thermodynamics. For the application of probability theory is based on the assumption that the realm of the possible, including the contradictions that can exist in the realm of the possible, are determinative of the actual. Boltzmann showed that it was meaningful to measure the actual by reference to the possible in the entropy concept. And Szilard showed that this could be interpreted as meaning the influence of intelligent beings on physical systems.

Two major developments followed quite directly on Szilard. One was the identification of thermodynamic theory for the analysis of communication systems by Claude E. Shannon: information theory. The other was the use of this mode of thought for the analysis of control systems by Norbert Wiener: cybernetics. In both cases, communication, on the one hand, and control systems, on the other, what is critical is precisely the relationship between the actual and the realm of the possible with its contradictions.

Shannon took the measure of information to be a function of the region of possibility. The greater the total region of possibility, the greater the amount of information. The measure of information was the entropy. He advanced the concept of the basic unit of information, the "*bit*," as the amount of information associated with the simplest contradiction in the realm of the possible, the two-alternative equally probable case. Wiener equally came to conceptualize control systems by bringing to bear the fundamental notion of analyzing control systems in terms of the relationship between the actual and the possible.

Information

The word *inform,* as a verb, has two meanings. On the one hand, it means to communicate from one mind to another, and that which is thus communicated is called *information.* On the other hand, it also means to give form to, or to put form into. *Information is nonmaterial substance that imparts form. The human mind is a nonmaterial container, as it were, that can accept and store and process information, and inform the action of the body in such a way that the body can inform other parts of the world.* One of the major characteristics of information, when it is not involved in actuality, is that it can be internally contradictory, whereas information that is bound in actuality is never contradictory. Thus, whereas a door may be open or closed in the nonmaterial realm and not actualized, actual doors are only open or, otherwise, only closed. If they are not open, then they are closed. But in the nonmaterial realm open and closed coexist in a way different than in actuality.

If I may return for a moment to the materialist position, I would like to point to one immediate consequence of these considerations in helping us to understand the materialist position. While the materialist is deeply preoccupied with the lawfulness *of* the material world, he has essentially left no place for the existence of lawfulness *in* the objective world. Consider any law associated with motion. The materialist argues that the universe is exhaustively described in terms of matter and energy, or perhaps as matter, energy, and law. Now, what is law? Law is the information that *informs* the physical motion. Otherwise, what then is it? It is certainly not matter and not energy. The materialist might then answer with some version of the constructionist argument, indicating that law is something that is constructed by the scientist. But then, what is the locus of the law? In the mind of the scientist? If it is in the mind of the scientist only, then the materialist has been forced to allow another category of existence: mind. Furthermore, if he takes any form of constructionist position, he has no way by which to assert the lawfulness of the universe prior to the evolutionary production of human beings. For any kind of constructionist position is contingent on man's existence. Indeed, what answer would any materialist have to the question of, say, what happens to any law if, in any time interval, there is no system in which the law is immediately operative in actuality? Does the law cease to exist for that interval? On the other hand, the acceptance of the notion of the nonmaterial objective existence of law avoids these difficulties.

The whole question of the existence of information *in time,* which the foregoing opens up, is important. But I would like to postpone its consideration until later in this paper. At this stage in the argument, I would like to move to a consideration of the world of practical men.

Information and Practicality

Having earlier alluded to the seeming success of the materialist viewpoint, and having indicated a possible alternative, I would like now to return to the discussion of materialism and ask whether too much has not been granted to the materialist position in the first place. Is it really true that the materialist position has been as successful in the practical world as it is reputed? That, of course, is an empirical question. I am not about to embark upon a study of the history to assess the success of materialism in the practical world. But if one were to engage in such a historical study, one should be careful not to fall prey to the *post hoc ergo propter hoc* fallacy. In other words, just because certain great technological developments took place *after* the development of the materialist viewpoint does not mean that these developments took place *because* of that viewpoint. Indeed, I tend to believe that the contribution of the viewpoint was principally in allowing the perception of regions of possibility that were otherwise not manifest to the observers, rather than the reverse, as the materialist position appears to self-consciously proclaim. The materialism of the chemist led to the recognition of the *possibility* of new chemical compounds, which had prior existence only in the realm of the nonactual. The avowed materialist position has no locus for such possibilities, for the realm of possibility, even though that realm is decisively involved in the successes.

I do want to say more about the world of practical affairs. But let me enter that discussion with an observation concerning the historical problem of contradictions between the propositions of science and the propositions of common sense. One of the classical examples has been that of the relative motion of the earth and the sun. There is an old story detailing a conversation between a country bumpkin and his sophisticated city cousin that ends with the country bumpkin saying, "What do you mean the sun does not move. In the morning I see it over there in the east. And at night I see it over there in the west. How does it get from east to west if it doesn't move?" The point is, of course, that the common sense observation is an illusion that is created by the rotation of the earth.

However, we would be no less stupid than the country bumpkin if from this type of consideration we should conclude that a presumptively scientific version is always sounder than a common sense belief.

I do not want to get into a discussion concerning what it means when I say I want to raise my arm. I do want to point out that, short of muscular or neural defect, fatigue, unconsciousness, compulsion, hysteria, orders by the commanding officer, etc., most people raise their arms if they want to. Furthermore, the wish is generally decisive in connection with the event.

I have not done a survey, but I suspect that the majority of human beings believe that they can raise their arms if they want to if they are free to do so. Nor is there any misunderstanding about this except perhaps among infants, the mentally disordered, and persons of certain philosophical persuasions.

If one can raise one's arms if one wants to if it is possible to do so, then a mental event can affect a physical event. As I have indicated, the realm of possibility is beyond the world of actuality, and the materialist would have some difficulty with that. So, for him, the proposition which is the first sentence of this paragraph is simply that the mental event can affect the physical event (the idea of possibility deleted). Yet he would deny even this.

I stress that the burden of proof is surely upon him to demonstrate that it is an illusion, just as the burden of proof would be on the shoulders of the sophisticated city cousin to demonstrate that the apparent movement of the sun across the sky is an illusion. To the best of my knowledge, there exists no cogent proof to show that the contingency of arm movement or the wish to move the arm is an illusion. There are numerous instances in which it is *assumed* that the apparent effect of the mental on the physical is illusory. But, to the best of my knowledge, there is no cogent demonstration. There are numerous demonstrations of the *necessity* of certain physical conditions to allow physical movement. For example, there is no doubt that intact neural connections are *necessary* for the movement of the arm. But the argument of the materialist is that the physical is not only necessary but also *sufficient.* Of course, the *hope* of investigators of a materialistic conviction is that their enumeration of purely physical factors will reach a point in which the physical factors are so total in the determination of the event that there will be no room left for mental input. But hope is hope. And wishful thinking is not scientifically excellent.

The materialist position has not, in my opinion, allowed itself to be sufficiently impressed by the existence of devices constructed to be indeterminate and generative of possibility. There are numerous machines whose principle property is precisely to allow possibility and thus to be informed by mental events. We have built them. They are steering mechanisms, typewriters, telephones, television sets, radios, computers, or tinker toys, bricks, and blank paper for that matter. *These are devices that are designed to be indeterminate* and thus able to receive informational input. These are machines designed precisely for the purpose of being influenced by mental events. Why then should the idea of mental events affecting physical events be such an alien thought? No examination of telephones and the like will ever yield a hint of the messages transmitted. These devices are made indeterminate, and they are indeterminate. This is not a fancy Heisenberg-type indeterminacy. It is that we build equipment with deliberate intention of introducing indeterminacy. And it may well be that the nervous system is precisely such a system of indeterminacy, like a television set or telephone or computer.

I am aware of the LaPlacean-view-informed reply to this last point, to the effect that the position of determinism calls for knowledge of *all* matter and energy in the universe. But to build a strategy on that possibility does not appear to be very wise, whatever metaphysical or epistemological merits it may appear to have.

Which brings me back to the consideration of the world of practical men. Do practical men believe that mental states affect physical conditions? Do practical men concern themselves with mental states, or do they just regard them as epiphenomenal? Judges concern themselves with the mental state of the accused. They are interested in whether there was intention to murder or not, or whether there was an intention to discriminate or not. A United States Supreme Court decision on discrimination ruled that disproportionality itself could not be taken as discrimination. The court ruled that there had to be evidence of intention to discriminate. Lawyers are concerned with the mental states of judges and juries. Politicians concern themselves with the mental states of their constituents and others. Military commanders are particularly concerned with the mental states of those against whom they are warring, as well as the mental states of the people on their side. Spies are deeply interested in the mental states of those upon whom they spy. The mental events in the minds of Einstein, Fermi, Szilard, and other physicists, in connection with atomic energy, were of no small moment with respect to the physical world. Deceivers are very concerned with the mental states of those whom they deceive and vice versa. Lenders are concerned with the mental states of those who borrow. Salesmen and advertising agents are concerned with the mental states of potential and actual customers. Everybody has an interest in the mental states of motor vehicle operators. Swindlers have an interest in the mental state of those whom they are attempting to swindle.

Or consider the group of people who have a greater effect on the physical world than any others. These are the heads of the large corporations and large governments. One of the keys to being successful in their work is in *planning*. And certainly without the assumption that mental acts affect physical events, the very idea of planning has no sense in it whatsoever.

Indeed, the very word *rational* not only means logical but also means *engaging in planning*. The very concept of rational, as it is used in the expression, say, the "rationalization of industry," critically involves the assumption that mental events affect physical events.

The very concepts of *conflict* and *power* in social relations entail the assumption that mental events can influence physical events. Conflict among persons is precisely competition with respect to *whose mental condition*, whose *wish*, will prevail in influencing the physical world. Conflict results precisely from the fact that within the nonphysical world there is contradiction. In the actual world there is no place for both sides of a contradiction. Persons are in conflict because one wants it to be A and the other wants it to be not-A, whereas in the world of actuality one or the other must prevail.

And power is what the proponent of A has that makes A prevail over not-A in actuality. Or more simply, the person who has power is more likely to have his wish affect the physical world.

In the light of what goes on in the world of practical men, it appears that the materialist owes very cogent reasons if he is to persuade the world of practical men that mental conditions are not effectual in changing the physical world.

If one were to make an appeal to Occam's Barber Shop, then it is reasonable to ask who needs the shave, the one who argues that mental events affect physical events or the one who says they do not?

Let me leave off the argument with the materialist. I will attempt to indicate some of the features of information.

1. *Information is substance.* What is substance? From the dictionary: (a) Substance is that which underlies manifestations. (b) It is that in which qualities inhere. (c) It is essential import or gist, as, for example, the *substance* of what he said.

2. *Substance refers to that identity which is subject to transposition.* One important example of the use of the concept of substance is to be found in the concept of energy in physics. Energy, as such, has no manifest existence. It is only manifest as mechanical force, electrical force, etc. But that identity that is transposable and itself unmanifest is referred to as energy. Similarly, information, as such, has no manifest existence. It is manifest only when it is bound. Thus, information may be bound into a pattern of air vibrations in English. In the same way that energy can be converted from a mechanical to an electrical manifestation, so can the information of an English sentence be converted into another pattern of air vibrations in French.

3. *Information can be measured.* Energy is measured by work, that is, by what it has, as it were, triumphed over. So may information be measured by the possibilities over which it triumphs. Citing a textbook on information theory:

> As an example, let us suppose that a baby has just been born at a neighbour's house and the question is asked, "What is the baby?" The answer, "It's a boy," then gives a specific amount of information. . . . namely,
>
> $$\text{quantity of information} = -\log(1/2) = \log 2$$
>
> In the above equation, it has been assumed that the baby was equally likely to have been a boy or a girl [Goldman, 1953, p. 4].

It is evident that the amount of information associated with the message "It is a boy" is contingent on the *nonactual possibility that it could have been a girl.* If there were the possibility of more than two sexes, the announcement would have a larger informational value, having triumphed, say, over two equally probable possibilities instead of one. Although there is no doubt that the measurement is quite objective, we must note also that it is contingent in a very special way on the realm of the nonactual.

4. *Material actuality is made up out of three components:* matter, energy, and bound information. For example, an operating electrical motor consists of the energy that is coming into it, its materials, and its form including a variety of so-called physical laws. The form of the energy input is electrical. The form of the energy output is mechanical. The materials are in the form of an electrical motor, steel, wires, etc., all shaped in certain ways. Information was bound into it in its construction. And its information as an electrical motor can be dissipated by, say, exposing the system to intense heat.

5. *While matter and energy are subject to conservation laws, there is no conservation law with respect to information.* The history of the planet suggests ever-increasing amounts of bound information. The information, say, of organic chemistry, biology, sociology, and economics have become manifest only in the last 4 billion years (the presumptive birthday of the organic molecule). The information is the result of creation, and creation takes place variously in history.

6. *Information may exist in an unbound state.* The prime candidates for consideration as information that exist in unbound states are logical and mathematical relationships. Another way of saying this is to say that essential information can exist in an unbound state, if one can lean on the Aristotelian distinction. Thus, for example, it is essential that the diagonal of a square shall be longer than its side. And this information has an existence quite outside any actual square objects and beyond the accident of its discovery by man. That information existed to inform events before the existence of man on the planet and is available to inform any construction of squares at any time. Indeed, the information was available to inform the constructing of squares even during some historical interval during which there were no square objects in the universe at all.

7. *Information in the unbound state has no locus in space.* There is no sense to the question "Where is the information that the diagonal of a square is longer than its side?" Space is not a matrix for the existence of unbound information.

References

Bakan, D. Mind, matter and the separate reality of information. *Philosophy of the Social Sciences*, 1974, *4*, 1–15.

Goldman, S. *Information theory*. Englewood Cliffs, New Jersey: Prentice-Hall, 1953.

Szilard, L. On the decrease of entropy in a thermodynamic system by the intervention of intelligent beings. A. Rapoport & M. Knoller (trans.). *Behavioral Science*, 1964, *9*, 301–310. (Originally published as Über die Entropieverminderung in einem Thermodynamischen System bein Eingriften intelligenter Wesen. *Zeitschrift für Physik*, 1929, *53*, 840–856.)

Chapter 6

Mind as Life and Form

MILDRED BAKAN

The view of mind that follows is in many ways neo-Kantian, though it draws from a perspective that is informed by Hegel's development of Kant and, in turn, Marx's development of Hegel. What is particularly Kantian is the concept of structure or form as immanent end that develops as it is achieved and, more generally, the concept of mind as organizing or systemizing experience in terms of a world. It was Hegel who stretched this concept of mind into a concept of dialectically developing structural organization in nature as well and, moreover, emphasized the significance of work as a uniquely human activity lying at the foundation of man's special relationship to nature. Though Marx was critical of the Hegelian concept of structure as mind at work, Marx nevertheless retained the Hegelian logic of the dialectical development of structure as he developed Hegel's insight into labor and work as man's special mode of relation to nature.

The tie between language and thought has been at the fore of contemporary philosophical concern. Indeed, it is primarily through the analysis of this tie that Kantian reflections have been absorbed. In effect, what follows relates the Hegelian–Marxist emphasis on work as uniquely human to our contemporary philosophical conception of the importance of language as a clue to mind.

131

BODY AND MIND
Past, Present, and Future

Mind as Subjectivity: Descartes versus Plato

The so called mind–body problem has sociocultural as well as metaphysical aspects. Defining the mind–body problem in terms of the metaphysical relation of mind to matter has the merit of sharply confronting us with the mystery of the mind–body relation. If, however, we simply define *body* as spatially extended material and *mind* as purely thinking, as Descartes does, the very terms of the relationship preclude any further insight. The mind is so effectively disembodied that its integration with the body as material is either an illusion or a miracle, evading any further elucidation.

It is important to note that for Descartes neither bodily feeling nor sensation qualify as mental. Feeling, as the mere affectation of the body, is taken, like sensation, to belong to the material mechanism of animal bodies: in principle, no different from fire, a powerful material force, generating heat and light and capable of transforming things, but as comprehensible as a clock (Descartes, 1956, pp. 29 ff.).[1] Thinking, on the other hand, is the *free* activity of a radically different nonextended substance, which, in contradistinction to matter, can be wholly self-determining. Though the mind can will freely, its efficacy is, strictly speaking, mediated by thought. The free will aims (!) to determine itself by knowledge. And indeed, only the mind as self-determining can know. Nevertheless, Descartes recognizes that distinctively human feelings require a mysterious mix between mind and the mechanically explicable analogue of animal feeling. Descartes's reasons for selecting the pineal gland as the intermediary between mind and the material body are interesting. He argues (Descartes, 1975, pp. 345 ff.) on physiological grounds that the pineal gland is the locus of a literally common sense (a concept derived from Aristotle) and is therefore especially suited to mediate between mentally apprehended form and the body's firelike animal spirits. The mind can apprehend the representation of things in the pineal gland and, generally speaking, out of representation of some desired object can move the ethereal animal spirits of the pineal gland.

The Cartesian split between mind and body arises in the context of a philosophical concern to justify (and find) necessary truth and, with that, to extend a new mathematical mechanics of motion to the study of living bodies. To know nature in terms of mathematical laws that can characterize motion as a mechanism demands a concept of mind as both nonsensory and independent of natural law. If the mind were subject to mechanical law, it could not freely know, and, if the mind could not free itself of sensory determination, it could not grasp abstract mathematical truth. Thus, the Cartesian distinction be-

---

[1] Descartes analyzes fire and felt heat as aspects of the *material* realm. In the *Discourse,* he writes: "The [circulatory] motion . . . . follows necessarily from the mere disposition of the parts of heart visible to the naked eye, from the heat which one can feel with the fingers [1956, p. 32]." Please note that the dates cited in this chapter for Descartes and other early philosophers are to recent publications. The dates of original publication are given in the References.

tween mind and matter incidentally drives a wedge between thought, on the one side, and sensation and feeling, on the other.

Indeed, if we take sensation and feeling as themselves sharing something of the mental (being experiential), then the mind–body relation takes on a somewhat different cast. The mind–body distinction becomes fuzzier, as the relation between the mind as knowing and the body as experiencing. The relationship between mind and matter acquires a puzzling intermediate stage: the relation between inert matter and life.

On the Cartesian conception, animal life is itself to be understood in terms of the same mechanical principles that explain the motion of inert matter. Aside from obscuring the distinction between what is alive and what is simply material, the Cartesian view renders any experiential subjectivity—both human and animal—functionally suspect. If, as Descartes says, bodily sensation and feeling share the mysteries of fire, fire as material is also mechanically comprehensible, and the causal efficacy of thought, as mere awareness or consciousness, on the motion of material substance is, to say the least, highly problematic.

The conception of subjectivity as functionally superfluous is peculiarly modern. Until the development of Western physics, material things were by and large thought of as something like bodies, rather than the reverse; that is, as appearing individual beings oriented, on the Aristotelian model, by their nature to their own proper place in the cosmic order of things. All material things were taken as themselves embodying something like the entelechy of living bodies. According to Plato (and Aristotle), mind is itself the entelechy of the human body, which in the case of man is informed by the perception—and in that sense knowledge—of the entelechy of things.[2] The mind, as the entelechy of the body, brings order into avaricious impulse by ordering the object of desire. So, for Plato, the relation of the body to the mind is essentially a relation of the appetitive—chaotic desire or want—to harmonious ordering. This harmonious ordering amounts to the recovery of one's true self. In effect, the recovery of one's true self brings stability into practical or sociopolitical activity by establishing the true objects of desire and allotting them their proper place as ends. Though Descartes and Plato share the concept of mind as essentially knowing—gaining access to what is true as corresponding to what is real independently of the mind—Plato understands the body not as simply spatially extended matter but as intrinsically informed by desire and alive.

The treatment of the mind–body problem has suffered from its restriction, on the one hand, to a concept of mind as only knowing and, on the other, to a concept of body as akin to inert matter. In fact, for neither Plato nor Descartes is the mind wholly separate from the self. For Plato, *nous*, by bring-

[2] For Plato (1974, pp. 164 ff.), mathematical knowledge is itself a kind of seeing, a perception of abstract form.

ing order into the appetitive, allows the achievement of personal integrity as the recovery of one's true self. For Descartes, the clue to thinking substance—the personal awareness implicit in thinking—is a self-reflexive awareness. By doubting, one becomes reflexively aware of that which one cannot doubt—that one is doubting. The awareness that one is doubting achieves awareness as personal reality. Self-reflexivity, in just this sense, has been widely recognized since Descartes as uniquely characteristic of human beings. But reflexive awareness characterizes the awareness that one's body is one's own as well as the awareness that one is thinking. The awareness that one's body is one's own points to the undeniable ontic unity of body and mind, whatever difficulties we may have in comprehending this unity (as Descartes, indeed, knew). The awareness that one's body is one's own arises in the context of the functional unity of body and mind in practical activity. It is important to note that Descartes loses the Greek sense of the relation of mind to social practice as the pursuit of human virtue. In Cartesian thought, the quest for truth loses its relation to political and social integrity. The body can be conceived as a machine going its own way only by ignoring the larger context of human practice.[3]

The Order of Meaning versus Physical Reality

From an evolutionary point of view, which belongs as much to our contemporary perspective as does physical science, the persistent superfluity of experience—and with it mind—makes no sense. We can distinguish between two modes of mutual influence among entities, to which, indeed, our own daily lives bear continuous testimony. Whenever we do such things as cut meat, chop wood, push a table, or strike another person, we use the force of physical contact, a mode of mutual influence we attribute to other material entities as well. But there is another mode of mutual influence that we restrict largely to the human order, social and solitary: communication through language. The first mode of influence belongs to the physical domain, the second to what we recognize as a domain of meaning. The influence of language is effected by the transmission (to use a term heavily laden with overtones of physical influence in order to sharpen the point) of *meaning*. Though the transmission of meaning may require a physical medium—material marks of one sort or another—and though human violence is never devoid of meaning, we can draw a distinction between influence by force and influence by communication.

The Cartesian split between mind and body amounts to a split between the

---

[3] The concept of the body as a machine in effect rationalizes depersonalized domination. The other is seen as merely a thing rather than as one who can be addressed. See, in this connection, also footnote 4.

human order of meaning and the natural order of physical force. By assimilating the dimension of mind to the dimension of meaning we have, however, stretched the concept of mind beyond that of only knowing or thinking or awareness. We have placed the philosophical concern with mind as knowing in the larger context of mind as meaning. As we shall see, by broadening the concept of mind in this way, we can recover the mind–body relationship as, in effect, a relationship of self to body which (a) allows a place for subjectivity in the order of things; and (b) recovers the Greek sense of the living body as itself oriented.

Whenever we act with any sense of what might be—to bring something about or to avoid some eventuality—we bring body and mind together. Whenever we reach for something, look for something, indeed whenever we speak to another or otherwise use language, we also bring body and mind together and, moreover, attribute their unity to others as well. The very act of speech to another presupposes that the other can understand what we say by hearing our words. Moreover, to request—even command—another to do something is to suppose that the other is open to the alternative of refusing to comply. Speech presupposes acting not merely in the sense of linguistic activity but also in the sense of the bodily manipulation of things as an intersubjective context for the relevance of speech itself. Our daily life presupposes that we are comprehending intersubjectively related actors, not mere robots. Actors are guided by linguistically formulable possibility and, therefore, can participate in dialogue and cooperatively assign and assume responsibility for socially organized action. The human social order would collapse if we did not relate to each other as somehow embodied minds. And interestingly enough, Descartes took the use of language–speech as *the* criterion for distinguishing the human from the mechanical (the mere machine) (Descartes, 1956, pp. 34 ff.).

We have had great successes in physiological studies since the time of Descartes, who, indeed, advocated a theory of the body as mechanical to advance medical knowledge. Just as we have been able by the analyses of color spectra to attain more precise criteria for the definition of material substances, we dream of gaining by physiological analysis more precise definition of thoughts and feelings as well. But this conception of the relation of physiology to the study of mind is something like seeking to understand art by a study of the physical principles of colors or sounds. Though we may gain much that is interesting this way, we miss something—precisely the artist's intent, which uses the colors and sounds as material but is not reducible to colors or sounds, even if taken qualitatively. On the other hand, it is a mistake to suppose that the artist's intent can develop apart from his materials, though he may rehearse his work beforehand in models, in sketches, or simply in imagination. At some point, creation takes place as a development of intent in terms of appropriate materials, much as our thoughts develop in terms of their verbal formulation. But just as the words that formulate our thought take on meaning in the context of the guiding and self-clarifying thinking, the materials in terms of which intent develops are no longer simply physical entities. Like words, they take on meaning relative to each other and as a coherent whole. They assume a qualitative dimension in terms of their relevant contexts. We can say of the artist's intent that it functions something like a final cause, which, without violating the laws of physics and chemistry, is nevertheless not reducible to them either. The artist's intent is informed by a sense of the future and of the possible and actual coherence of his materials in terms of their felt qualities. If mind plays something of this role with respect to the body, then physiological study will not provide the clues we need.

There is a sense in which whatever is material is exhausted by the here and now; that is, materiality can be conceived spatially without reference to the temporal, except as an externally related successive order of what is earlier to what is later. In what is describable as spatially material, we will not find the past or the future, neither of which is physically present. Yet mind has, as an essential dimension, just this sense of future and past. Somehow mind allows the future and past to be present as future and as past. We remember what once occurred as having occurred and live in terms of the anticipation of what may be. We are not simply creatures of habit in terms of learned reflexes that effect an alteration of the material body. In anticipating the future, we anticipate the possibly physical, and in remembering the past, we suffer a sense of its physical absence.

In so far as we are aware of what we are doing, mind and body are clearly fused. But insofar as we are aware of what we are doing, we are aware of ourselves as acting. Humanly, we become selves insofar as our acts exclude alternate possibility, however undefined. Action, as opposed to mere movement, is informed by possibility, and the sense of possibility, as the presence of what might be in the context of action, is also the sense of alternatives that demand decision.[4] (For the sake of completeness, we should also distinguish between behavior as goal oriented and acting as deciding among alternate possibilities. Only the actor can put his ends in question and so confront an open future.)

The Body as Minded: A Neo-Hegelian Perspective

Indeed, we can make a case for claiming that insofar as the body is alive, the body is itself, so to speak, minded. Some biologists speak of the living body as centered to preserve its organization. The body as centered regulates

[4] D. M. Mackay (1962, pp. 89 ff.) points out that the attribution of possibility to automata is marked by conceptual confusion. He distinguishes between possibility as underspecification of physical states, which are, however, as physical states fully determined, and possibility as requiring decision to exclude relevant alternatives. Mackay adds that a Buberian dialogical relationship is a commitment to respond to another in terms of mutual possibility in the second sense.

itself so as to maintain its organization or form. In effect, the centered body already achieves a level beyond the merely material, for its own formal identity as an organized body is self-generated and maintained.

The German biologist Adolph Portmann,[5] who emphasizes the relevance of ethological considerations, analyzes living bodies in terms of two key characteristics: display (in German, *Selbstdarstellung*, which translates literally as "self-presentation,") and centeredness (in German, *Weltbeziehung durch Innerlickeit*, which translates literally as "world relation through inwardness"). He points out that every living body is bounded by an appearing surface that mediates the body's relation to its environment so as to maintain its internal organization. On the other hand, this very regulation in terms of the maintenance of internal organization amounts to a centeredness that, in relation to the organized body, is something like the human relation of self to body.

According to this conception, every living entity is centered and every living entity has a body boundary. As centered, every living entity takes some account of its body boundary. An interesting description of varieties of forms of life, which is, moreover, suggestive with respect to evolutionary development, emerges in terms of an analysis of levels of interrelatedness of centeredness and display. Portmann and other ethologically oriented biologists[6] point out that among some animals their mutual bodily appearance enters as an important component of their biological life. Bodily appearance effects a communicative link in terms of the body itself. Among the higher animals, this communicative link mediates both sexual and social behavior. Body display takes on a communicative role that is recognizably continuous with the development of language.

More particularly, Portmann attributes to the body boundary two functions: (*a*) separation of the organism from its environment by controlling the access of what is external to the internal organization of the organism; and (*b*) the presentation, or display, of the organism in its environment and to other organisms. This second function is often recognized by more Darwinian-minded biologists as protective environmental adaptation. But Portmann points out that among higher animals, at any rate, the very appearance of animals to each other enters as an indispensable component of their own

---

[5] In my characterization of Portmann's thought, I am indebted to the work of Marjorie Grene (1965). Grene puts Portmann's thought in the context of a wider school of philosophical biology. In this connection, special attention should also be drawn to the work of Hans Jonas (1966). Jonas takes the most important characteristic of every living entity to be the metabolic maintenance of an identity of form in time.

[6] Konrad Lorenz is perhaps the most widely known biological ethologist in the English-speaking world. However, Lorenz (1975, pp. 205 ff.), unlike Portmann (and Jonas), seems to conceive of the communicative role of mutual appearance among animals as somehow effected by *mutually triggered* responses. The concept of triggered response makes sense once the motor responses begins, but it is not at all clear how the *appearance* of another animal can *trigger another* animal's movements.

biological life. Ethological investigation has yielded extensive evidence that highly specific patterned sequences of behavior, invariant within a species, are indispensable for such vital relations among members of a species as mating. There is also evidence that the appearance of the body plays an indispensable role in the social organization of some species of animals. In all these cases, the body of one living entity influences other living bodies not simply by physical force—though the body belongs to the physical order of things—but by its *appearance* to other living bodies. Though this sort of body presentation is hardly voluntary, we can recognize it as a communicative transmission of something like meaning in terms of the very appearance of the body. Bodily appearance itself effects a communicative link regulated by heredity.

Correlatively, animal centeredness is to be understood as something like our human self-experience, without, however, any experienced distinction of self from body. Indeed, to attribute centeredness to animals is to suppose that experience plays some role in their relation to their environment, though this sort of experience may be taken as inseparable from its bodily context (much as pain and hunger are). At any rate, it is as centered that one living body experiences the display of another.

Centering allows a progressively novel order of identity to emerge in terms of meaning. Thus, at a sufficiently developed level, one can presume centeredness to involve inwardly showing the body and its environment (which includes other living bodies) in terms of the promise or threat of that environment to the organism's continuation as a living entity. Such experience can be taken as a primary affectivity that does not, as experience, separate body, environment, and others. We need not suppose among nonspeaking animals a purely objective reference to others or to things as simply there. Nevertheless, it is quite plausible to suppose some sort of objective reference, however vague, which is inseparable from a situated context of promise or threat with respect to the animal's own future. We can recognize this primary affectivity in our own lives as a bodily, merely felt, objective reference, which is, however, complicated by our also being speaking—or linguistic—creatures.

We can find historical roots for this biological perspective in the Hegelian conception of the relation of self to body, which understands the body as a living entity, distinguished from the nonliving, in that its form is self-generated through metabolic exchange with the environment. In effect, the form of the body functions as a guiding final cause, to be maintained or developed as the organism lives.[7] Metabolism becomes the clue to life, but metabolism transforms the inorganic to generate and maintain a form as the organization of a living body. According to Hegel, all living things must die because they somehow use themselves up in that metabolic transformation of the inorganic on which they feed. Hegel places the emergence of desire in this

[7] According to Herbert Marcuse (1976), Hegel's conception of life is central to Hegel's thought. It should be noted, also, that Marx (1970) adopts the Hegelian concept of metabolism.

biologically organic context. He conceives of elemental desire as oriented to what is required for the body's ongoing life (Hegel, 1910, p. 225). However, though future oriented, desire cannot itself achieve awareness of its desired object as such nor of its future orientation as such. In the context of desire, the sense of future remains inseparable from the merely felt relation to its object. For in the context of desire, the object, though experienced as independent, cannot be known as independent but only as satisfying or unsatisfying. Indeed, Hegel held, it is only through work, a uniquely human practical activity, that the sense of future arises as the merely possible, though not yet actualized, object. Work transforms things so that they embody what is intended as the thought-informed will of the worker (Hegel 1910, p. 238). But work develops out of desire in the context of a split between desire and the desired object.

Hegel spins a wild but fascinating and highly suggestive tale of the developmental course from elemental desire to work. He envisions a forced split between desire and the desired object in terms of a prehistorical master–slave struggle that goes to the point of, but not beyond, biological death (Hegel, 1910, pp. 232 ff.). The combatant who is ready to die becomes the master of the other, who, terrified, yields to become the working slave. The master, in risking himself, has discovered his identity as not simply biological. But it is the slave who learns to think by embodying his will in the transformation of things. The master's desire has developed into that of an aristocrat, who, despite his physically forceful power, is dependent on others to gratify bodily needs. The slave, however, develops real competence through work. He establishes his personal identity through mastery of nature, not others. In the course of history, he will gain the courage to risk his biological life as well, and so gain that recognition from the master that he forfeited in combat.

In any case, work itself lies at the origin of human thought as the distinction between possibility and actuality. By embodying intent in things, work is the first desiring relation to an independent object that does not destroy its object in achieving gratification. Work allows its object to endure through its transformation so as to be used by another. Thus work brings thought into the metabolic relation of the body and its environment. Hegel's concept of the relation between work, thought, and, indeed, self-consciousness was incorporated by Marx (1967, p. 57). On the other hand, ethologically minded biologists like Portmann have picked up the biological side of Hegel's story.

A New Look at the Body–Mind Relationship

Along the lines of Portmann's analysis of living bodies, we can speculate that evolution allows the development of levels of centeredness of increasing complexity and that mind at the human level is an extremely complex centering of the body, which allows knowledge of what is independently real and action in terms of alternate possibility. It is certainly not excessive to suppose that this sort of centering involved the evolutionary development of speech in the context of the social use of tools. Human centering is achieved in terms of a thought world that allows us to relate to things not simply in terms of desire-regulated metabolic exchange but in terms of the possible transformation of things as well. On the other hand, the development of language allows possibility to be so distinguished from actuality that possibilities are formulable as the possibilities of things. These possibilities are formulable not only as the possible presence or absence of things but as their possible predications. It is in terms of language that we formulate and structure the possibilities of things, converting our environment into a world. In relation to things, these formulated possibilities (especially as predicative) structure the range of alternate but mutually exclusive transformations. Such structuring incidentally defines our concept (or concepts) of reality, opening our future in terms of a shared world and, correlatively, our own personal identity as actors, in relationship to others who share that world.

Since concepts of reality are incidentally defined by alternative possibilities for the transformation of things as the limits of our world, the concept (or concepts) of reality carried by language is itself relative to our mode of transforming our environment. But language also brings us together socially and is thus itself an aspect of our larger communicative relation to each other and to our environment. From this perspective, mind is situated in the context of a communicative relation to others and to our world, which, as communication, is not separated from our work-mediated, metabolically relative, relation to the things about us. Work as an activity and language as a mode of social communication are mutually related.

It is important to note that, if the body boundary of living bodies is communicative, this communication is inseparable from its particular context, though the pattern of display, through genetic control, repeats itself across varying contexts. Thus a communicative structure is established through heredity. In the case of human beings, centeredness (and with that selfhood) is complicated by a radical change in communicative style. The specific structure of language is not genetically controlled, though there is undoubtedly a genetic disposition to the development and use of language in suitable social contexts.[8] Clothes, manners, political organizations, religions, myths, and other aspects of culture are not genetically controlled either. Nevertheless, human beings are centered in terms of a world disclosed as a structure of possible objects distinct from the human beings themselves. The criteria for validity of disclosure are themselves aspects of the way in which a socially shared world is disclosed. Such criteria are carried by the accepted grammatical structure of language and its accepted vocabulary as used in the con-

---

[8] Even Chomsky must grant that *apparent* structures of languages differ. In contrast to Chomsky and his followers, I would stress the *social* context as the nexus in which language develops.

text of socially organized activity. But the criteria are supported by the experiential disclosure of a world in the context of this socially organized activity. Indeed, language itself correlates with a socially shared world by so formulating possibility that activity can be intersubjectively guided so as to achieve identification of what is the same across varying experiential contexts.[9] Thus language, by formulating possibility, allows human beings to communicate in terms of a structure that establishes invariance across specific experiential contexts. Whereas genetically controlled appearance is tied to its specific context, nongenetically controlled linguistic structure is supracontextual. Language intrinsically achieves reference beyond the experiential context of its use.[10] Thus, the criteria for validity of disclosure are not themselves simply derived from experience but rather structure experience as a coherently supportive order (Bakan, 1974, pp. 28 ff.).[11]

Furthermore, though we are centered in terms of a world of independent objects, the reality of these objects is not indifferent to our own identity–not merely as bodies but as persons. With language, an order of selfhood emerges that does, indeed, recognize the distinction between itself and its body and its environment. Ego or self-identity is relative to an order of meaning that structures possible experience as a real world in terms of which self-identity finds its own place. Indeed, the real world is personally meaningful only insofar as our practical activity is integrated with that world in terms of the real prospective possibilities for personal action opened by our concepts of reality. In effect ego identity is a prospectus for practical activity, which takes place, to be sure, in a social context in relationship to others who share a world in terms of socially organized practical activity.

Now, in all living bodies we can recognize something like mind insofar as experience informs their action as the presence of the possible. The biological is then not merely an order emerging from the material as the maintenance of the body in terms of its needs but also an order in which communication functionally informs motion. Indeed, we can cast metabolically relative relations to things in a socially communicative context as well. Certainly, what is desired is experientially enticing. The experience of the desired object is a

---

[9] See discussion of identification on pp. 143, 145 ff.

[10] Gregory Bateson and Karl Pribram both draw on something like this distinction between language as supracontextual and gesture as context specific. Bateson (1972, pp. 177 ff. and pp. 128 ff.) distinguishes between animal communication, which he takes to be context dependent, and normal human communication, which he maintains is dependent on a conceptual metaframe. Pribram (1971, pp. 369 ff.) distinguishes between signs as context free and symbols as context dependent.

[11] It is interesting to note that the work of both Wittgenstein and Husserl support this conception of the relation of language to social life. Wittgenstein stressed the rule-regulated aspect of language and argued that rules to be rules must be social conventions. Husserl, in his later writing (1960, pp. 89, ff.), stressed the intersubjective dimension of concepts of reality and, as early as his *Logical Investigations* (1970), analyzed reference as the identification of an object as the same, tying the process to both perception and language.

beckoning lure. Thus, desire can itself be conceived as a social relation to the objects of our environment in which the experience of objects guides behavior. Again, such experience functions as a regulative final cause (in the sense of immanent emergent end)[12] that motivates the behavior it elicits in terms of a more or less clearly perceived entity that can be approached, avoided, or rejected. Affectivity of this sort orients behavior by making present what is factually only possibly physical—the promise or threat (which indicates the future) to the organism inherent in its physical relation to the object felt. The very presence, in terms of experience, of what is spatially distant, requiring time to establish physical contact, is achieved through smell, hearing, and sight in other animals as well as in the human. In the case of the human being, language allows the presence, also, of what is temporally distant, though experientially absent. (Indeed, the development of language allows us to entertain what is physically not even capable of being actualized.) Thus, subjectivity, including sensation and feeling, transcends the merely physical by paradoxically introducing into the present more than the physically present. Generally speaking, subjectivity achieves an evaluative temporal synthesis that goes beyond the physically present by indicating the future. In nonspeaking animals, this temporal synthesis indicates the future in terms of the possible relation of the identity of the experiencing body to the experienced object. In human beings, subjectivity is more complicated.

Anthropologically speaking, the human being is, of course, an extraordinarily social animal. The human animal requires prolonged nurture before being able even to walk, let alone assume mature responsibility. This nurture takes place in a social situation, in which the infant's cries are an essential aspect of the mode of gaining response. But the infant's cries communicate in a context-specific way, like animal gesture rather than like language. It is on the basis of parental response to cries and other gestures that the infant develops a sense of an other as someone who addresses (speaks) and can be addressed (spoken to). Thus, the development of the mind rests not on a merely informational base concerning the things of the world but rather on a context-specific socially communicative base, which ties one person to another. Care is, in a sense, interpersonally communicative only in a context-specific way. Without such care as a foundation, the addressive order of speech does not itself develop and we are not open to the meaning of the things of the world either. Nevertheless, the development of language is *not* simply continuous with context-specific communication. After all, the barking of dogs does not develop into language. The human mind as centering reaches beyond context-specific bodily disclosure to a world shared by others.[13]

---

[12] This concept of end is developed by Kant (1974) as purposeless purpose, in the context of his treatment of aesthetic judgement.

[13] Though this view of the child's development of language is Buberian, I would not want to exclude a Sartrean perspective. For Buber the glance of the other *acknowledges* me; for Sartre it threatens to rob me of my freedom by reducing me to an object. In fact, the look of the other can

W. R. Bion, a noted British psychoanalyst with Kleinian sympathies, speculates that the child's positive relation to his absent mother marks the beginning of thought and the birth of the ego (1962, pp. 28–37). Bion writes that the critical step in the development of the infant ego is the emergence from a global and undifferentiated sense of deprivation when hungry to the sense of an absent, caring parent who is nevertheless present—that is, in the world. Bion is, in effect, trying to locate the social basis of the development of language as reference to what is experientially absent. Following Bion's thought, it is plausible to suppose that the initial step on the way to language in the (parent) mother–child relationship is a relationship to an absent mother (parent) as one who is in the world though absent, as one who can be called, summoned.

But the centering mind also informs human bodily activity. The shared world informs our perception of the environment as alterable, possibly otherwise (and coincidentally identifiably what it is by excluding alternate possibility, however vague and unspecified). What we ordinarily call *feeling* is not simply biologically based desire but a mind-informed, bodily or context-specific, social relation to others in the context of a world taken as real (thus Descartes's point concerning the distinction between human and animal feeling is well taken). Our context-specific bodily relatedness to others reflects our complicated social being—more precisely, our cultural being. Thus, our biological desires, as affectivity, are themselves interpreted in terms of our intersubjectively shared concepts of reality, as our sensory experiences are. Indeed, it is plausible to suppose that the normal human infant is disposed at birth to develop both socially and culturally. (The disposition to see predicatively—that a cube has a top, a side, etc. or is yellow rather than green, etc.—invites the conceptual interpretation of things in terms of language.)[14]

The achievement of the awareness of feelings is not a simple matter, as Descartes has suggested. Awareness of our feelings amounts to a dialogical relation with our desires that allows our desires to persist as desires without moving to gratification. To suppose that animals are aware of feelings as we are is assuredly absurd. Feelings, of which we can be aware, are not simply

do either, depending on the power relationship between oneself and the other and, perhaps more particularly, the interplay of one's orientation to the world with the orientation of another. Whereas Sartre points to the dialectics of power underlying social relationship, borrowing from Hegel's dialectics of the master–slave relationship, Buber points to the dialogical aspects of social relationship. Sartre leaves out what Buber takes into account; Buber leaves out what Sartre takes into account. Social relations are both dialogical *and* dialectical. At the limits of dialogue, we find the dialectical relationship of power.

[14] Predicative perception implies a distinction between perceived object and predicate through the entertainment of alternatives with respect to the characterization of things. Wolfgang Köhler (1957, p. 132 and 122 ff.) points out that his apes cannot take account of the top side of things in their instrumental activity. His chimpanzees have great difficulty in building boxes *on top of one another* to reach an objective.

impulses. Impulse must be arrested or deflected to allow cognizance.[15] Hegel is correct in his emphasis on the human split between desire and the desired object. But it is by virtue of our being speaking creatures that we can be aware of our feelings. Correlatively, desires that escape the conceptual map of reality sketched by our language escape awareness as well. Whatever inclinations, wishes, or impulses we may have that take us off the conceptual map of reality are not even linguistically formulable. The expression or realization, even imaginatively, of such inclinations threatens—indeed disrupts—our personal self-conception (our individual ego identity) associated with the socially shared world that our language maps. Such wishes and inclinations escape our voluntary control and are bodily rather than thought centered. Wishes that are bodily centered are communicative—or rather they are meaningful—but the meaning is wholly context specific, in the sense that the meaning is tied to the concrete experience of oneself and others (including other entities) in terms of a body-centered identity that obliterates the distinction between self and other in a manner similar to that sketched for nonlinguistic, bodily carried communication. Such desires can only be deflected as dream or fantasy or erupt as blind action (which, however much like impulse, is still not simply biological). On the other hand, it is by virtue of our capacity to desire without moving to gratification—that is, to wait and so to demand and point—that we can learn to speak.

Ego identity is the correlate of a socially shared, linguistically carried concept of reality, however vague. Plato (1974, p. 101) argues in *The Republic* that, in the case of human beings, intellect must assent to desire as if it were an "answer to a question". Assent to desire amounts to a coherence of ego identity and desire. Desire that has no coherence with ego identity can only erupt as a psychotic episode—a loss of self, an overwhelming impulse that intoxicatingly draws one into the immediate present, like a call from the gods beyond, without integration with that sense of past and future that is tied to the socially shared real world of practical activity. Indeed, the integration of ego identity and desire is unavoidably problematic.

Desire is never without a context-specific communicative base, but ego identity is the correlate of a supracontextual order of meaning carried by language. Language allows a split to develop between an affectively body-centered self and a thought-centered self. But the split is itself engendered by the thought-centered self, which integrates possible experience as a world. Feeling that is integrated with thought is intelligible. But thought also has the capacity to stay in its own domain. Thought can refer to thought. It is this

---

[15] Only humans, so to speak, stop time to be aware of what is *now* before them. Only humans can cling to the immediate as evanescent, wishing the moment could remain forever. Correlatively only humans, of all the animals, or rather, only a speaking animal, achieves an *aesthetic* sense of experience. Kierkegaard (1944) is, in this respect, fascinating. He characterizes the instant as an intersection of eternity and the temporal.

aspect of thought that allows the critique of thought in terms of thought, on the one hand, and the avoidance of possibly disruptive experience, on the other.

We must be careful, nevertheless, to avoid reducing human feeling, however context specific, to desire defined only in terms of biological urge. Human desires themselves develop in the context of our capacity to become thought centered. It is difficult to conceive of loneliness as biological deprivation. Loneliness is a deficiency of a kind of perceptual involvement, which at the human level amounts to a deficiency of a cultural involvement. Human loneliness and isolation make sense in terms of a cultural rather than merely physical—or even merely social—isolation.

Human beings, besides experience of the situation itself, can alter what occurs in terms of the possible. Though we will not find any appearing guiding final cause if we dissect the brain, we can expect the human brain to be more complicated, because it coordinates physical activity, which transforms things, and linguistic activity, which develops in a social situation and structures the possibilities informing our physical activity. Mind as opposed to feeling thus moves in terms of what may be otherwise, alternative possibility, allowing us to be free of situation and to be critically evaluative of what is occurring and of bodily desire as well.

Whereas the horizon of possibility is experientally immanent at lower, nonlinguistic levels of centeredness, at the human level the horizon of possibility is tied to a world in terms of opposing, or mutually negating, alternatives. Language allows us to be open to the being of things in terms of an order of meaning that is not simply related, as biological desire is, to the body's internal organization. Language allows the negation of what is physically present to be thought and formulated (as excluded *alternative*, or as altering, changing, or modifying what is physically present). The chair ahead of me may be light or heavy, of wood or painted metal, soft or hard, etc. Indeed, I might prefer the chair to be removed or to be replaced by another more suitable chair. I approach the chair itself in terms of such alternative possibilities, and I can direct someone else to the chair I have in mind by a description. As vocabulary develops, vague and, indeed, unspecified alternatives acquire more precision in the context of the demands of more complicated activity. In this connection, it should however be noted that it is the identity of something as the same thing that governs the possibility of alternative predications.

By carrying meaning in terms of the mutual exclusion of possible alternatives, language allows the deliberate transformation of things. Thus, the order of meaning generated in terms of language allows the development of a choice of activity itself in terms of the anticipation of—and actual (physical) exclusion of--possible consequences. Correlatively, language allows the development of the sense of future as future—that is, as open-ended horizon.

The effortful fulfillment of anticipated (not merely expected) possibility identifies what is later with what is earlier as the same.[16] Language orients, but it is
important to note that this orientation retains a background of open-ended
horizon, which can indeed be recovered as the opening to the being of things,
per se, as the possibility of things, per se, that is, as possible alternatives that
remain unformulated. The recovery of an open-ended horizon, in effect,
achieves the suspension of ends. A speaking creature can wonder at the being
of things precisely because speech introduces an order of meaning that orients,
providing direction, which is not simply hereditary. It is by virtue of being
radically open-ended that we can be aware of ourselves as acting in the sense
of originating what we do, determining ourselves with some self-direction in
terms of intention that could itself be otherwise.

This openness to the future is itself the correlate of the infant's primordially
open dialogical relation to another as an addressive person, who provides
orientation, a source of meaning adopted by the child.[17] And it is by virtue of
being radically open-ended that we can become objects to ourselves as (a)
simply there (or rather here) bodily, like things in the world, excluding the
merely conceived (thought) possibility of our worldly absence and (b) volun-
tarily realizing (embodying) our intentions through our own bodily activity in
a world.

As the structuralists point out, linguistic meaning is essentially relational.
The physical marker (visual or oral) gains meaning by taking on a grammatical relation to other markers differentiated from itself. The marker's
meaning—quite apart from the question of truth—is a relational presence carried by the marker itself. (According to contemporary biological theory,
something like this takes place in the biological order itself in the expression of
the genetic code. Perhaps the mutual appearance of living bodies motivates
behavior in analogous fashion.) Our capacity for achieving relational meaning constitutes the potentiality for reading, artistic creativity, objective
perception, and speech through the indication and the fulfillment of a larger
whole in terms of a mutually relative but serial specification of alternate possible elements whose possible relational structure amounts to a grammar. What
is taken, or generated, as the same is identified as the same by virtue of its
structural differentiation from what is other. Yet it is a mistake to suppose
that what is excluded as other need be further specified or for that matter can
be fully specified. Though all meaning implies coherence (at the biological
level, the desired object furthers the maintenance of the body), it is important
to note that linguistic meaning is carried by the realization and exclusion of
alternate possible specifications, however vague, of interrelated elements.

---

[16] Anticipation is open to alternative possibility—as this or that—which though not necessarily
formulated allows *confirmation* of "this" as the negation of "that." Expectation, on the other hand,
is either fulfilled or frustrated. Expectation is a species of desire; anticipation is a species of
thought.

[17] See footnote 13.

Grammatical relation is constituted by opening up an intended locus of indeterminacy (as something to be further specified) and subsequently specifying that locus. A chair may be soft, hard, red, blue, high, low, etc. To speak of a chair, then, is to open up the anticipation of a limited range of further possible specifications. But truth itself is not simple coherence. Indeed, language itself allows the truth and falsity of anticipated possibilities to emerge and with that the deliberate predictive making of things and the critical revision of belief.

The Larger Picture

We can, then, isolate three levels in the development of life: the biological, the social, and the cultural. Each builds on the preceding level and complicates the preceding level as well. Also, each level presupposes the preceding level as its potentiality. For each introduces a more complex level of integration in terms of which the lower level itself takes on direction. The cultural level legitimizes ends (as practice) that in the human case are themselves open. Because human ends are open, direction is fragile. Direction is informed by culture rather than by heredity and, therefore, capable of breakdown. It is in terms of cultural legitimation that we achieve a social organization, which in turn transforms our environment on the basis of possibility rather than of mere behavior regulated by heredity.

As the mind–matter problem, the mind–body problem concerns the emergence of integrating orders that serve as forms or ends organizing matter by unifying their constitutive elements in terms of their relational possibilities. Experience itself achieves integration that is intrinsically social, by making what is distant and possibly future present as an experienced relation to an object physically independent of the organism itself. Cartesian reflexivity can occur, however, only in an animal that can change its orientation, to change its situational evaluation, its direction, and also the concept of its own identity as a project of its own goals.

That communication can occur is itself an intrinsic developmental potentiality inherent in matter insofar as matter takes on any form whatsoever, any coherence that allows a stable order or pattern. However, communication in terms of meaning achieves integrative relation while, however, maintaining some autonomy of the related parts.

Francois Jacob, the noted French biologist, points out (1976, pp. 299 ff.) the survival advantage of this sort of integrative relation.[18] Though particular autonomous parts may disappear, the integrative relation may continue, pro-

---

[18] Jacob blurs the distinction between integration and communication. I would prefer to restrict communication to integrative relation which (a) is achieved while maintaining autonomy of the related parts and (b) relates a body in terms of its surface to an environment (a characteristic that Jacob acknowledges can be attributed only to living beings).

vided other like autonomous parts take their place. However, living bodies are characterized by an extraordinary capacity to regenerate parts of their own bodies by healing and, of course, to regenerate themselves as a whole by reproduction. So Jacob takes a special kind of communicative integration to be coextensive with life: a communicative integration that is "open" to its environment so as to be able to draw selectively from it whatever is necessary to maintain and reproduce itself. According to Jacob, life behaves in terms of pattern, per se. He adds, evolution itself "depends on setting up new systems of communication just as much within the organism as between the organism and its surroundings" (Jacob, 1976, p. 308).

On this conception, the universe has something of Leibniz's monadic harmony about it. The monadic harmony is not, however, preestablished, but rather emergent, and only a potentiality for harmony, even as embodied. Living beings that enact harmonious relations can survive; but such harmonious relations require the mutuality of the activity of beings. For living beings, at any rate, persistence depends on the enactment of harmonious relations, whose preservation, however, is always precarious.

What of Neuropsychology?

In *Languages of the Brain*, Karl Pribram (1971, pp. 369 ff.) evolves a conception of the brain as an information-processing mechanism that monitors bodily action, not as a disconnected successive series of movements, but as an organized achievement. Pribram hypothesizes that movements, monitored by the brain, are regulated by a so-called image of achievement, which is predictively regulative. In just this sense, says Pribram, the organism acts. Conversely, the brain can be taken as regulating movements to process information.

Pribram points out that such activities as attending and searching reduce uncertainty by information. Indeed, according to Pribram, information is information only in the context of uncertainty as the possibility of alternatives. He argues that the reduction of uncertainty is *itself* reinforcing and habituating. Thus psychological description and theory can use either a stimulus language or a response language. As a stimulus language, discrimination is emphasized; as a response language, action is emphasized. But each language must take account of the other, inasmuch as experience and action are interrelated. Meaning is on the stimulus side; achievement is on the response side.

This story is further complicated by Pribram's distinction between the "world within" and the "world without." The latter is constituted as "images" attributed to external objects, the former as "images" attributed to interest and emotion. The "world without" is perceived; the "world within" is felt. The "world without" is external reality; the "world within" is internal reality. Internal reality is "caring"; external reality is "meaning."

Pribram's language reflects impressive sophisticated sensitivity to the complexities of individual and even social psychology by the use of such concepts as meaning, images of achievement, and care (according to Pribram, reflected in symbols that structure contexts through context-dependent language). In the end, however, Pribram consistently reduces the experiential order to the organization of matter in motion in terms of the interrelation of neural electrical discharges and encompassing electrical potential fields. The constitution of both the world within and the world without is analyzed as an electrical encoding and recoding system that regulates and is regulated by neural discharge in the context of surrounding electrical potential fields: hypothetical neural activity supported by the evidence of ingenious research, usually neurobehavioral, but frequently merely behavioral. This hypothetical neural activity renders the human being an interesting, complex self-regulating machine, whose electrical (I suppose one should add, chemical) substance determines every move. Indeed, a marvelous critique of conventional stimulus–response conceptions concerning the presumed workings of the machine is achieved. But experience, thinking—in short, subjectivity—remain confused appearance, which, on further analysis, reduce to matter-in-motion, just as, say, the appearance of water (as slippery, wet, transparent, etc.) is the confused appearance of H_2O molecules (according to Pribram, the appearance of water is, of course, achieved by neural organization). The world without reduces to a miraculous world within, which itself reduces to a subsystem of the world without.

Thus Pribram is an ingenious epiphenomenalist, who reduces mind to the organization of matter. Mind is really the organization of matter, for mind as appearing subjectivity remains devoid of any causal efficacy. If mind is to be real, somehow feeling and thought must themselves be causally efficacious. And despite his ingenuity, Pribram does not avoid the absurdities of epiphenomenalism. Colors, tastes, smells, thoughts, even things (as perceptual achievements) are to be found within the neural organization. Pribram indiscriminately speaks of the perception of objects as images or as ideas, in the tradition of a confused British empiricism. Though the physical analysis of the so-called primary qualities has altered, the basic materialist conception of objective reality as reducible to matter in motion has not. The miracle of appearance occurs within the neural organization. Temporal organization is itself analyzed as a "feedforward-" but really feedback-monitored successive series of states, and spatial organization is analyzed as a simultaneous mix of neural receptivity and neural-generated lateral inhibition. Both remain essentially brain-monitored neural states.

This is not to deny that this type of neural organization does not occur or *cannot* occur. It is interesting to note that occasionally Pribram speaks of the neural organization as merely "involved" in acting, feeling, thought, etc., but his more responsible theoretical ascription takes the brain as itself acting by monitoring, that is, as exhaustively causally efficacious. Pribram never picks up the problem implicit in taking appearances as monitoring. He uncritically accepts appearance itself as the epiphenomenon of the brain's monitoring activity. Thus, the question remains: Why any appearance at all? But if appearance is the way possibility itself is present, appearance is the very processing of information as meaningful. Though appearance as meaning resolves uncertainty with respect to antecedent alternatives, as Pribram almost concedes, the resolution of uncertainty once complete, destroys appearance as meaningful. We are left with an inert "image." All appearance retains what Edmund Husserl [19] calls a horizonal dimension, as something more to be seen: the further, hidden side of the front of the chair that I now see, as the presence of future possibility, the expected and the anticipated, which become explicated by further relevant specification. Uncertainty is resolved only by "going on" (to use Wittgenstein's happy phrase) in this way. Appearances themselves arise in the context of "going on," as precisely the guide of "going on," as its organization and its direction, which is irreducibly relevant to subjectivity in terms of caring or concerned responsibility for what is beyond subjectivity itself.

In the end, the epiphenomenologist must suppose it possible to study the world by studying neural organization itself. But neural organization is perceptually effective by virtue of selectively focusing objects independent of the neural organization. This focusing is, in effect, an effortful problem solving, an achieving, that brings about the clarity of perceptions in terms of coherent figure–ground relations that have something to do with what is going on in the world without and are in relation to real others, whose own actuality and response are integrally involved. One can indeed speculate that a problem is physiologically encoded as a hologram. But Pribram substitutes the physiological hologram for the problem itself. A problem is puzzlingly out of focus. The resolution—the establishment of focused clarity—carries with it the scar of its birth. What is on the subject side is effort and attainment, confusion working toward clarity of perception, always in relation to others and dependent upon their coherence or cooperation. For the others must be such that clarity *is* possible. In human beings, this problem-solving capacity goes far beyond perception in terms of the development of thought. Certainly with regard to thinking, we cannot hope to inject into the brain by suitable electrical stimulation the solutions to the problems that are yet to be worked out in relation to the appearing problems themselves. Even if we could, the

---

[19] Husserl (1970, Vol. 1 pp. 269–297, Vol. 2, pp. 675–705), the founder of phenomenology as a philosophical school, develops Brentano's concepts of intention in terms of intentional aim at fulfillment. Experience, as fulfilling intention, also develops intention through intrinsic horizonal aspects that indicate further possible experience. Aron Gurwitsch (1966) takes Husserl's development of the horizonal aspect of experience as fundamental to phenomenology.

materialist hypothesis makes sense only in terms of an omniscient knower, who has at hand the solution to every conceivable problem. But could such an omniscient knower have a problem? (A materialist monism emerges as a metaphysical residue of a particular conception of God.)

Wilder Penfield, another distinguished neuropsychologist, notes that the human brain is marked by a vast increase of area that is hereditarily undetermined with respect to its specification, allowing its "programming" or "encoding" by learning (1975, pp. 18 ff.). Why should encoded or programmed specification in this region of the brain not carry with it the sense of the larger horizonal ground, precisely because its neural facilitation is acquired and is not tied at birth to specific sensory or motor bodily routes? It is in a part of this region, which he calls the interpretative cortex, that Penfield takes experiential memories to be registered. He argues, however, that these experiential memories are not themselves the mind. He identifies the mind itself as awareness. Indeed, Penfield argues for an interaction between mind and brain on the ground that he cannot avoid taking awareness or consciousness as itself acting. He calls upon physicists to be open to the exploration of an as yet unknown kind of energy that does not itself course through neural pathways but nevertheless selectively generates neural innervation and thus arouses memories. Precisely with respect to what Pribram isolates as the role of attention (in the symbolic organizing of contexts as contexts and in the separation of aspects of these contexts as identical signs), Penfield puts the question sharply: Is the brain merely involved in this activity, or is the brain the agent of this activity?

Epiphenomenalism takes the brain's relation to the mind to be akin to the relation of the aggregate of H_2O molecules to the appearance of water. The water's appearance proves to be, on deeper analysis, nothing but the aggregate of H_2O molecules in their interrelation. As Pribram himself acknowledges, in living beings, organization takes on a different role. It seems to be itself achieved as an organizing. For Pribram, however, this organizing amounts to organization of neural states. What is organized are aspects of the organization itself. But we can distinguish organizing from what is organized. Organizing acts, or behaves, or moves in terms of the possibilities of what is organized. In just this sense, organizing centers what is organized and thereby amounts to an emergent level of order with respect to what is ordered, constituting an emergent level of being or reality beyond what is ordered, without being separated from what is ordered. In effect, the centering ordering constitutes a metalevel to what is centered as its object-level.[20] Now, mind is clearly a centering activity. Indeed, feeling, sensations, and even images are themselves such that they can be centered as experiental content that is organized, whereas the centering activity is precisely awareness (or mind) as

---

[20] Howard H. Pattee (1973) sets the concept of centering as a relation of metalevel and object-level in the context of a larger systems theory.

act.[21] From this perspective, we can say of human communicating and meaning that it is achieved in the context of a metalevel that can recover itself as a metalevel, by recovering horizonal possibility as such, a freedom from every specific context, an opening to the world per se, as, perhaps, physiologically, the potential (or rather possible?) innervation of neural pathways. Attention, after all, occurs as a selective act that excludes possible alternative acts, on the subject side, and possible alternative objects, on the worldly side. Perhaps the mind, the spirit, the beyond-the-brain-dimension of awareness—the recovery of the metalevel per se as the possibility of a specific object-level (Gregory Bateson [1972, pp. 177 ff.] refers to this metacommunicative or metalinguistic metalevel as a frame)—correlates with (without being reduced to) a brain, which is, to use Penfield's terms, largely uncommitted at birth, that is, precisely underspecified yet under the integrative control of what he calls a highest brain mechanism. This is not to say that the infant has available the adult's sense of formulated, or even, open possibility. But when the infant smiles at another, that metalevel consciousness or awareness as primordial *self*-awareness is there as originating direction into the object-level stemming from the metalevel organizing act itself. But notice, however accurately the mind may correlate with the brain, the mind organizes the brain, or we revert to either dualism or epiphenomenalism.

Does consciousness have a strange sort of energy? It is capable of generating, or rather working out, direction, and is itself highly dependent on a complicated energy system (the brain uses a great deal of glucose). What is significant is that we have here a highly developed centering, which as centering, makes a difference by virtue of its position in the hierarchial ordering of the body: an activity, which though dependent on matter, is no longer simply material and yet is efficacious with respect to that matter by introducing order. I find it a tempting position to suppose that the organizing energy or force comes from matter itself, the mere guiding, organizing, or directing from mind. But mind is the organizing, and the organizing is itself efficacious: It is itself energizing, if only through the medium of the organized matter. Perhaps mind, by returning to the metalevel, allows energy to accumulate, which though drawn upon to work out or develop organization, then effectively releases energy by directing the rest of the body in relation to its environment. But this direction still retains, as its horizonal background, the absence, or rather the lack, of direction. Mind as directing, organizing, in the case of human beings, achieves direction.

In any case, we can make sense of the mind as directing, by, in effect, focusing, achieving clarity, through the brain, much as a blind man may focus, achieving definition of an object, with his hands or even through a probing cane. In terms of this model, the mind as focusing projects through the body.

---

[21] But see discussion of the mind as focusing on pp. 150 ff.

In perception, the mind projects through the body into the world, toward a possible object, achieving definition by the felt, though antecedently anticipated or expected, specification of the object as possible. Thus the mind sees (taking seeing in the broadest sense) by projecting a possible object. The manner of projection may be physiologically not that different from what is involved in visual seeing as the achieved sighting of an object (through an achieved encoding of a neural image or message). But visual images, as messages, only allow objective perception to take place by guiding action (with, to be sure, something like feedback) in terms of further possible movements of the body, which achieve further relevant definition of the focused object. At the perceptual level, mind is thus open to the possible real object, which must itself contribute something to its further definition if this objective something is to be taken as real. At the perceptual level, at any rate, mind is then the informing intention that opens up the future as one's future—as opening to another as precisely addressive, demanding response by and from that other in terms of the possible appearance of the other. Thus, on the one hand, the mind as centering is an essential aspect of human selfhood. On the other hand, if the mind is informing intention, what is perceptually intended is no image but rather a possible appearing object. Moreover, what appears discloses a real object only because that object is selectively intended by a bodily incarnated act. Generally supporting this view of mind is Jacques Monod's (1971, p. 156) suggestive assessment of thinking as a simulating activity whereby "abstract 'reality' offers itself directly to our imaginary experience." (It should incidentally be noted that the simulation of abstract reality is singularly appropriate to, if not required by, the fashioning of artifacts—the making of things.)

Finally, it is interesting to note, that though Pribram in his concluding chapters of *Languages of the Brain* speaks of his own theory as providing an image of man, he provides no systematic analyses of the problems involved in achieving ego identity and its breakdown, or of the sense of future as open-ended horizon, or of the relation of ego identity to the broader human world. Though he acknowledges the key role of structure, in the end, he assimilates culture to biology, emphasizing the achievement of constancy and stability rather than ongoing dialectical process. He speaks of the brain as generating and transforming structure by encoding and recoding and of thought as a neural brain activity that achieves control over the internal state of the organism through the resolution of uncertainty. Though he avowedly takes as his starting point behavioral research in a biological context, his setting is experimental, not ethological. So Pribram loses touch with communicative practice in the social and political spheres. As a question of the generation and transformation of structures worked out in terms of the appearing world in relation to others, much more is at stake than the encoding and recoding capacities of the brain itself.

References

Bakan, M. Between body and thought. In D. Shugarman (Ed.), *Thinking about change.* Toronto: University of Toronto Press, 1974. Pp. 20–37.

Bateson, G. *Steps to an ecology of mind.* New York: Ballantine Books, 1972.

Bion, W. R. *Learning from experience.* London: Heinemann, 1962.

Descartes, R. *Discourse on Method.* (L. J. Lafleur, Trans.). New York: Bobbs-Merrill, 1956. (Originally published 1637.)

Descartes, R. *Passions of the soul.* In R. Descartes. *The philosophical works of Descartes (Vol. 1) (E. S. Haldrane & G. R. T. Ross, Eds. and Trans.). Cambridge: University Press, 1975.* Pp. 329–427. (Originally published 1649.)

Grene, M. *Approaches to a philosophical biology.* New York: Basic Books, 1965.

Gurwitsch, A. The problem of existence in constitutive phenomenology. In *Studies in phenomenology and psychology.* Evanston: Northwestern University Press, 1966. Pp. 116–123.

Hegel, G. W. F. *Phenomenology of mind.* (J. B. Baillie, Trans.). New York: Macmillan, 1910. (Originally published 1841.)

Husserl, E. *Cartesian meditations.* (D. Cairns, Trans.). The Hague: Nijhoff, 1960. (Originally published 1950.)

Husserl, E. *Logical investigations,* (2 vols.). (J. N. Findlay, Trans.). New York: Humanities Press, 1970. (Originally published 1900.)

Jacob, F. *The logic of life.* (B. Stillman, Trans.). New York: Vintage, 1976.

Jonas, H. *The phenomenon of life.* New York: Dell, 1966.

Kant, I. *Critique of judgement.* (J. H. Bernard, Trans.). New York: Hafner, 1974. (Originally published 1790.)

Kierkegaard, S. *The concept of dread.* (W. Lowrie, Trans.). Princeton: Princeton University Press, 1944. (Originally published 1844.)

Köhler, W. *The mentality of apes.* (E. Winter, Trans.). London: Penguin, 1957.

Lorenz, K. Kant's doctrine of the a priori in the light of contemporary biology. In R. Evans (Ed.), *The man and his ideas.* New York: Harcourt Brace, 1975.

MacKay, D. M. The use of behavioral language to refer to mechanical processes. *British Journal for the Philosophy of Science,* 1962, *13,* 89–103.

Marcuse, H. On the problem of the dialectic. *Telos,* Spring 1976 (27), 12–39.

Monod, J. *Chance and necessity.* (A. Wainhouse, Trans.). New York: Vintage, 1971.

Marx, K. *Capital* (Vol. 1.) (S. Moore & E. Aveling, Trans.). New York: International Publishers, 1967. (Originally published 1807.)

Marx, K. Alienated labor. (T. B. Bottomore, Trans.) In E. Fromm (Ed.), *Marx's concept of man.* New York: Ungar, 1970. Pp. 93–109. (Originally published 1932.)

Pattee, H. H. *Hierarchy theory.* New York: George Braziller, 1973.

Penfield, W. *The mystery of mind.* Princeton: Princeton University Press, 1975.

Plato. *Plato's Republic* (G. M. A. Grube, Trans.). Indianapolis: Hackett, 1974.

Pribram, K. *Languages of the brain.* Englewood Cliffs, New Jersey: Prentice-Hall, 1971.

Chapter 7

Brain-Based Limitations on Mind

MARCEL KINSBOURNE

The Brain Basis of Subjective Experience

The dependence of various cognitive skills on the integrity of specific areas of the brain is well established (e.g., Kinsbourne, 1976). Selective performance deficit after focal brain damage is often easily demonstrable. One can debate how justifiable it is to infer from such data how the brain locus in question controls normal behavior. But it would be generally agreed that different cognitive skills depend on the integrity of different parts of the brain. Can one say the same about subjective experience?

If parts of the brain are disconnected from input, this must limit the amount and variety of information that becomes available to experience (just as disconnection of output channels restricts the response repertoire) (Geschwind, 1965). But someone who is blind or numb can *imagine* a visual or a tactile experience (just as a paralyzed person can *imagine* moving). Even if the deficit is congenital, subjective experience within the deficient modality is potentially available. If a congenitally blind person's central visual projections are stimulated electrically beyond the locus of the lesion that blocks his vision, he experiences a visual impression. Stimulation of a paralyzed person's central system of motor control may lead him to imagine he has moved (Penfield & Roberts, 1959). After amputation a "phantom" limb may be experienced. Thus, while the everyday content of subjective experience can be grossly

155

BODY AND MIND
Past, Present, and Future

depleted by input or output limitations, this is in principle no different from the way in which experience may be impoverished by a depleted environment. In other words, obstructions in the body's communication channels are *environmental* as far as subjective experience is concerned.

The potential for subjective experience remains unrestricted by such changes (in the body's periphery, in sensorimotor projections, and even in the first cortical relay of input and final cortical pathway for output).

The integrity of input channels determines the extent to which information is faithfully coded for cortical analysis. The tuning of brain stem amplification mechanisms seems to determine the extent to which this information will have impact on conscious awareness (Pribram & McGuinness, 1975). Mechanisms of selective attention legislate among stimuli competing for control of the organism's limited response capability. At most times, some information will form a substrate for conscious awareness, while other information is left unattended. But it is hard, perhaps impossible, to maintain information passively in awareness. Biologically, awareness is the subjective concomitant of information processing. It selectively invests information with regard to which there is response uncertainty, that is, novel or problematical inputs. Once the uncertainty is resolved, the input slips from awareness ("habituates"), unless deliberate action is taken to maintain it in conscious focus, perhaps by elaborating it in diverse ways. Now the tuning of brain stem modulators will determine the range of information brought to awareness (i.e., Easterbrook's [1959] range of cue utilization) and the depth to which processing proceeds before response uncertainty is "sufficiently" resolved and new content admitted to awareness. Thus, if two individuals differ in their habitual range of cue utilization, they will experience differently a physically identical situation. If two individuals differ in the extent to which they habitually resolve uncertainty before deciding on a response, they also will experience most everyday situations differently. The anxious person, restricted in his cue utilization, will be oblivious of much that the calm individual notices in the same setting. The underfocused individual, who processes to a shallow level only, will experience a subjective information underload in situations in which the deeper processing overfocuser is subjectively overloaded (Kinsbourne, in press). Such differences in information-processing strategies go far to account for individual variation in behavioral responses to the same situation. In a setting in which the underfocuser rapidly exhausts processing options and, bored, sets up his own turmoil or distractions, the overfocuser remains riveted and deeply preoccupied, evading any further stimulation until he has resolved residual uncertainty to his individual satisfaction. As representing pathological extremes of this dimension of temperament, we may identify underfocusers with individuals lacking in impulse control, such as hyperactive children and certain psychopaths, and overfocusers with individuals who function at a pathological pitch of hesitancy and resistance to novelty, such as certain autistic patients (Kinsbourne, in press). So, subjective experience is not a faithful passive reflection of external change, nor even a reflection of such change qualified by personal adaptive necessity. It is further shaped by attentional proclivities that characterize individuals, which are determined by the balance of competing control mechanisms in the brain stem and in many cases are demonstrably heritable, presumably on a genetic basis. In other cases, a deviant phenotype is established subsequent to focal brain damage, such that the individual's attentional preference changes, and so does his subjective experience. A variety of drugs that modify the action of catecholamine neurotransmitters can have the same effects for the duration of their action.

As we have noted, the moment-to-moment content of subjective experience is determined, not only by the stimulus situation (and stimulus history) of the individual, but also by brain-based mechanisms that control range and depth of information processing. As information being processed is the essential substrate of conscious experience, it is clear that these control mechanisms are powerful determinants of the content of awareness. But while they modulate the *balance* of subjective experience, the manner in which it is distributed across potentially attention-attracting events, they are distinct from the brain basis of the subjective experience itself, which comprises the collective activity of cerebral cortical mechanisms.

In this discussion, we will address the mind–body problem from a neuropsychological point of view. We will show how brain organization limits mental activity. Then we show how anomalous and abnormal brain function modify behavior in ways not predictable purely on the basis of mental considerations. Specifically, we will first show how functional specialization in the brain makes it possible to distribute attention between simultaneous unrelated activities and how the topography of that specialization limits the extent to which this is possible. Given the same mental content, different brain organizations differently limit this ability to think and act simultaneously in unrelated ways.

Our second illustration reveals the impact of brain organization on the physical expression of mental processes. We show that certain forms of thinking engender typical patterns of corollary movement. In a minority of people, brain organization deviates from that of the norm. These individual differences in brain organization among normal people result in predictable differences in the motor accompaniments of thought.

Thirdly, we demonstrate that strategically located lesions in the cerebral hemispheres can limit not only an individual's behavioral repertoire but also his conception of what his behavioral repertoire should or could be. The damage induces in its victim a loss of awareness of behavioral options. It constricts the range of his consciousness. Whereas most performance deficits following brain damage can be thought of as restricting information flow to the "mind" or limiting the ability of the brain as the executive organ of the mind, it is impossible in these cases to escape the conviction that mind and brain are aspects of the same functional unit.

The fourth illustration demonstrates how a grossly abnormal behavioral response to the environment may be generated not only by abnormal circumstances but also by an abnormality in the brain's interpretation of normal circumstances. The brain consequences and therefore the mental consequences of information flow are abnormal for autistic children, and their deviant behavior is the logical consequence of that abnormality.

Limits on Divided Attention

It can be very difficult to do two things at the same time (unless one of them is virtually automatic and demands little or no attention—e.g., walking, knitting, driving in easy circumstances). This finding has been thought to illustrate the "unity of consciousness," and psychologists have thought of it as representing a limitation on the moment-to-moment availability of some crucial resource, such as "attention" or "mental capacity" (Allport, Antonis, & Reynolds, 1972). But if attention is divided between two concurrent tasks, it does not follow that each can concurrently be done at half the efficiency at which they can be performed one at a time. The total performance falls short of that, by an amount that has been thought to represent the attentional demands of some "executive" or "clerical" system (Kahneman, 1973) that serves to allocate attention separately to the two performances. However, there is no need to think in terms of a hypothetical construct such as flexibly disposable mental capacity.

Limitations on the ability to distribute attention follow logically from the highly linked organization of the brain. High-speed computers, whose active elements are fully insulated from each other, can act independently of each other at the same time. In contrast, the active elements of the central nervous system, the neurons, are highly interconnected, such that very few synapses are interposed between any one neuron and any other one in the brain. For any but the simplest and most automatic stimulus–response relationships, this would naturally lead to a widening of any locus of activation in the system, leading to loss of specificity and an adaptively useless diffuse behavioral response. Any such tendency is opposed by the insulation of loci of activity by inhibitory surrounds. If different loci subserve different functions, these functions could in principle be exercised simultaneously. And yet, such insulation tends to be imperfect. Leakage of excitation to adjacent (i.e., highly connected) control centers does occur, "priming" the latter for similar activity (Kinsbourne, 1970a) or even throwing them into unexpected action (see section on motor concomitants of states of mind in this chapter).

If this leakage of patterned activation were uniformly distributed across the brain, then differential effects related to functional localization would not be expected. But if we regard it as primarily affecting adjacent ("highly connected") loci ("functional cerebral distance principle"), then a number of observations become intelligible and a number of predictions can be made that would not follow from purely mental considerations (Kinsbourne & Hicks, 1978).

When subjects try to do two things at the same time, they find this hardest when the two tasks are categorically similar and yet unrelated. Brooks (1967) accomplished an elegant experimental demonstration of this intuitively obvious fact. He had subjects mentally represent visuospatial relationships according to verbal instructions. Subjects performed better when the instructions were spoken than when they were written. There appeared to be interference between the mental representations of the instruction and the representation of the spatial display to be acted on when both were visual. In relating these findings to the brain, one might hypothesize a central "field" available for visual representation, for which concurrent representations would compete. But if we apply the more general proposition of the "functional cerebral distance principle"—that unrelated attention-demanding activities interfere in proportion to the interconnectedness of their central control facilities—we can generate further predictions that would not be possible without knowing how the hemispheres are specialized for cognitive function and for manual control (left hemisphere for verbal thought, vocal utterance, and right-hand control; right hemisphere for spatial thought and left-hand control). On the assumption that areas within a hemisphere are in general more interconnected than areas in different hemispheres, one would predict more interference between verbalizing/vocalizing and right-hand performance and between spatial processes and left-hand performance than say, between verbalizing and left-hand performance. In non-right-handers, when cognitive specialization may diverge from this pattern, correspondingly different interference patterns would be predicted.

The way in which dual-task performance is determined by the relative loci of central processing is well illustrated by vocal-manual interference paradigms (Kinsbourne & Cook, 1971; Kinsbourne & Hicks, 1978). In these experiments, the hand is engaged in continual performance (dowel balancing—Kinsbourne & Cook, 1971; Hicks, 1975; sequential finger movements—Hicks, Provenzano, & Rybstein, 1975; Hicks, Bradshaw, Kinsbourne, & Feigin, 1978; finger tapping—Kinsbourne & McMurray, 1975; piano playing while concurrently the subject also performs a vocal task—Kinsbourne & Hicks, 1978). The effects of a concurrent activity are measurable in terms of a disruption of contralateral (right) manual performance. Reciprocally, the vocal performance is also apt to suffer when thrown into conflict with a functionally adjacent manual control center (for the right hand) (compare Hicks et al., 1978; Kinsbourne & Hicks, (1978), and it is not a necessary condition for the interference effect that the verbal activity be overt.

Hicks *et al.* (1975) had subjects prerehearse letter series silently or aloud before writing them. During rehearsal they taped a predetermined sequence. Rehearsal, both overt and silent, interfered with typing skill of both hands, but more with right- than left-hand performance. (Overt rehearsal was more interfering than covert rehearsal.) Again, interference is greatest between functionally adjacent control centers, that is, between the verbal processor and the right-hand control center (both represented in the left hemisphere) rather than the verbal processor and the left-hand control center (represented in different hemispheres).

The point that differences in the ability to distribute attention between different tasks could not be predicted on purely mental grounds is dramatized by observations on groups with a high incidence of anomalous cerebral organization—non-right-handers. Non-right-handers are a heterogeneous group with respect to their cerebral organization. Perhaps two-thirds are organized as are virtually all right-handers, that is, left-lateralized for language. But one-fourth are organized in mirror-image fashion (right-lateralized for language) and about one-sixth appear to have language representation extending over both hemispheres (Milner, 1974).

Were body–mind relationships other than precise and compelling, one would not necessarily expect to find different movement patterns when non-right-handers are confronted with the same cognitive tasks as had been used with right-handers. But, even if the mental sets adopted by the non-right-handed groups were identical to those of the right-handers in these experiments, the substantial incidence of anomalous cerebral organization among non-right-handers should have impact on the mean laterality biases of the movement patterns observed, and they do. Hicks (1975) found no asymmetry in interference by verbalization in nonfamilial left-handers, and in familial left-handers (who on other grounds are thought to include a high proportion of individuals with right-hemisphere dominance for language), interference was actually maximal for left-hand performance.

We conclude that people have difficulty attending to two categorically similar tasks (which however cannot be integrated), because categorically similar tasks are controlled from highly interconnected cerebral loci and they are exceptionally subject to mutual interference.

Motor Concomitants of States of Mind

In Intact People

Shifts in receptor orientation that seem purposeless, in terms of goal-oriented behavior, can be shown to derive directly from the manner in which particular states of mind engage (or arise from) particular neural control centers in normal or abnormal brains. The illustration that follows demonstrates the inseparability of the mental processes in question from their substrate in the brain. Such an effect is observed when activation within the left-hemisphere language area overflows into the left-lateralized facility for rightward turning, the left frontal "eye field."

When people think in words, it does not necessarily serve any adaptive purpose for them simultaneously to move. Nevertheless, involuntary changes in position of which the subject is quite unaware can be observed during verbal thought. These movements are not directed toward any goal but rather are a behavioral spin-off of shift in the distribution of neural excitation within the brain due to the adoption of a verbal mental set. They depend on the left-lateralization of language in the cerebrum. Those relatively few individuals (usually non-right-handers) in whose brain language is other than left-lateralized also show an involuntary movement tendency, but in different directions (e.g., leftward, if language is right-lateralized).

It has long been known that when asked a question, people tend to avert their eyes while pondering the answer. However, it was only recently shown that the direction in which an individual turns his eyes while thinking varies systematically with cognitive mode (e.g., verbal versus spatial) and depends on details of cerebral organization (Kinsbourne, 1972).

Subjects sat facing a featureless wall. Unknown to them, their faces were monitored through a peephole. Behind them, an experimenter sat and read a series of questions aloud. Her voice and the subjects' responses were recorded on tape. Subsequently, direction of first head and first gaze deviation after each question were scored, and these judgments were then related to the categorical nature of the question.

The results showed that right-handed subjects tended to turn both head and eyes to the right when considering verbal questions, upward for numerical questions, and up and to the left for spatial questions. These findings were predicted from known features of brain organization. Left-hemisphere activation in the language area would tend to overflow more readily into the adjacent left frontal eye field rather than the relatively remote, contralateral right frontal eye field. This would bias the reciprocal balance between the two eye fields in such a way as to result in rightward turning. Numerical processes, presumably engaging both hemispheres, would lead to upward gaze (as does symmetrical electrical stimulation of both eye fields). More right-lateralized (though not exclusively asymmetrical) spatial processes would lead both to upward and to leftward turning. These findings have been confirmed (Gur, Gur, & Harris, 1975; Galin, Ornstein, & Merin, 1972; and see Kinsbourne, 1974a) and extended in relation to emotional state. When under the sway of emotion (Schwartz, Davidson, & Maer, 1975) and especially negative emotion (Schwartz, Davison, Ahern, & Pusar, in preparation) there results an increase in left gaze tendency (reflecting the greater involvement of the right hemisphere in the programming of these states). When non-right-handers were tested in the identical fashion, their eye movement patterns were quite different (Kinsbourne, 1972).

It is remarkable that these systematic gaze deviations had escaped notice during the centuries. And yet, lacking the necessary knowledge of brain organization and the necessary notion of mind–brain interrelations, it would be easy to write off the observed gaze shifts as motivated by the wish not to be distracted by external stimuli and fail to observe their systematic directional relation to the categorical nature of the mental set.

Another frequent accompaniment of speech, and of the hesitation pauses that precede connected utterance, is manual gesturing. Kimura (1973a) reported that right-handers gesture more with the right than the left hand while speaking (although not in a nonverbal control condition, Kimura, 1973b). Taken by itself, this finding could merely represent yet another preferred use for the preferred hand—gesturing while verbally active. But conjoint with an observation of Kinsbourne and Sewitch (unpublished), this observation assumes additional significance. They had subjects describe, or tell stories, about complex and mystical pictures. They observed copious gesturing (far more than did Kimura), often bilateral, and overall showing no asymmetry. Thus, when the task has a verbal, but not only a verbal component, then both hemispheres are engaged and not only the right hand (contralateral to the verbal hemisphere) is in action. (The speakers tend to be unaware of the laterality of their gestures and of how much gesturing they did.) The gesture is the motor marker of the laterality of the centrally active cognitive processes. Note that influence does not flow unidirectionally from thought to movement. Kinsbourne (1975) and Casey (1977) report studies that show that direction of movement (right versus left turning) measurably affects the efficiency of subsequent mental operations. In right-handers, right turning appears to be more compatible with verbal operations and left turning with spatial operations (compare principles discussed in the preceding section).

All the experiments discussed illustrate the predictive power of the functional cerebral distance principle (Kinsbourne & Hicks, 1978). When an asymmetrically represented control center is in action simultaneously with either of the bilateral control centers, it interferes ("cross-talks") more with the one closer to it and in the same hemisphere. Thus, the effect of the thought process on the quite unrelated bodily movement was not inherent in the thought content but arose simply and purely from the relative locations in the brain of their neural representation. Were the thought process not based on a specific and invariant pattern of brain activation, it would not have generated the particular pattern of movement activity and interference that was in fact observed.

When patterns of brain activation differ, holding mental state constant, motor concomitants differ. In Kinsbourne's (1972) study of cognitive effect on directionality of gaze, a non-right-handed group completely failed to show the gross systematic biases observed in the right-handers. In Kimura's (1976) study, non-right-handers did not show any gestural preference for the right hand while speaking. Thus, the motor spin-off from the mental state was different among the non-right-handers not because of difference in the relationships between the relevant cerebral processes in these partially anomalously lateralized individuals. In some left-handers, language is bilaterally represented and thus the functional distance between the verbal and the left-hand control center is less in them than in right-handers. Thus, different interference patterns are to be expected and were obtained.

We have recently uncovered another directional bias that could not have been anticipated on the basis of purely mental considerations. When people were asked to imagine how two-dimensional displays would look if they were rotated 90°, they answered more quickly and accurately when clockwise rotation was asked for than when they were instructed to rotate the display counterclockwise. This cannot be due to differential experience (e.g., with hands moving clockwise over clock faces), because non-right-handers, who have the same experiences, showed significantly less bias. Regarding mental rotation (Shepard & Metzler, 1971) as abstracted movement, we have found that its execution is affected by biased biological preprogramming (Lempert & Kinsbourne, submitted).

In Brain-Lesioned People

An interesting special situation arises when cerebral organization is disrupted in certain ways by brain damage. Again, holding mental state constant, will the motor consequences be different in these damaged cases in a manner predictably based on the location of the damage?

Patients with severe right-hemisphere lesions commonly manifest unilateral neglect of the left side of space. They fail to observe or respond to events arising from loci opposite the lesion. They show little tendency to explore the left side of space—be it by eye, head, or bodily movement. More precisely, it is not left space but the left extreme of any horizontal display toward which they fail to orient (Kinsbourne, 1977). Effectively, they are suffering from an imbalance between right- and left-side orienting tendencies, due to relative inactivation of the right-sided control center for left-side orienting (Kinsbourne, 1974b).

A problem arises when patients with comparable left-sided damage are considered. They do show neglect also, this time of the right, but far less frequently and less severely than do the patients with right-sided damage. A possible explanation for this fact was offered by Kinsbourne (1970b) on the basis of the functional cerebral distance principle.

Kinsbourne (1970b) assumed that, like anyone else, these patients frequently, if not constantly, think in words. When approached by the clinician as he comes to make his observations, they prepare to speak and do so spontaneously or when spoken to. They adopt a verbal mental set. Therefore, they activate a large sector of the left hemisphere.

The patient with right-hemisphere damage is already in imbalance, with an attentional bias to the right. Left-sided activation intensifies the bias, rendering the neglect gross and obvious. The patient with left-sided disease, to the contrary, is helped in reinstating an impaired left–right balance by adopting a verbal mental set. He thinks in words, the left hemisphere is activated, and its feeble influence bolstered. Attentional asymmetries are minimized and become hard to observe.

Heilman and Watson (1977) report a direct demonstration of the postulated effect. Patients with right-hemisphere lesions were asked to count either scattered letters or scattered segments of line. They showed significantly more neglect of the left side of the display when scanning the verbal material. The verbal set proper to the display of letters had deepened their orientational imbalance. Bowers and Heilman (1977) demonstrated a similar bias, but to the left, in normal adults given a spatial (tactile line bisection) task.

The phenomena of neglect thus also illustrate the physical repercussions of mental state. The direction or orienting movement across a display is biased by verbal mental set in patients with a particular neuropsychological syndrome in a manner not deducible from the mental state but readily deducible from knowledge of the location and condition of its neural substrate.

Another neuropsychological demonstration utilized subjects whose corpus callosum had been sectioned for therapeutic reasons. The great commissure connecting the two cerebral hemispheres is cut, and, with respect to much of their informational traffic, the two hemispheres are effectively isolated from one another.

Kinsbourne and Trevarthen (in Kinsbourne, 1975) asked such "split-brain" subjects to respond with a finger lift to the presence of a predesignated target letter when it appeared as one of the two letters briefly exposed on either side of a central fixation point. They found that these patients often completely failed to notice the target letter when it appeared to the left of fixation, whereas it was almost invariably detected when it happened to appear on the right. In contrast, when subjects were asked to respond to simultaneously exposed simple shapes to either side of fixation, no such asymmetry was evident.

The findings can be explained as follows. Section of the forebrain commissure renders the reciprocal balance between right- and left-hand orienting tendencies unstable. Given hemispherically neutral material (simple shapes), a balance can still be maintained. But given a task that calls for verbal mental set, a gross rightward biasing of attention results (well in excess of any such observed in intact subjects), and the observed "neglect" of the left-sided stimuli occurs. The patients' mental state led to a motor consequence irrelevant to the thought content but readily attributable to the interaction of hemisphere specialization and the disconnection of the cerebral hemisphere.

In a study of a single split-brain patient, Kreuter, Kinsbourne, and Trevarthen (1972) demonstrated an analogous amplification of the normally obtained effect of vocal–manual interference. The patient tapped simultaneously with both index fingers while performing verbal tasks. With simple tasks (e.g., adding one digit numbers), no effects on finger tapping were observed. But when the task was somewhat complicated (e.g., adding fractions), differential interference with right-sided tapping became grossly evident. Only when the patient actually made a mistake, collected herself and reattempted the item, was there bimanual arrest of tapping. Callosal section increases the effective functional distance between the left-sided verbal processor and the right-sided control center for left index finger tapping.

The patients' hemispheric disconnection led to a shift in the relative effect of verbal operations on the movements of the right and the left hand. A study of laterality of gesture in split-brain patients should cast further light on this issue.

Contribution of Cortical Analyzers
to Content of Consciousness

Following Pavlov, we can distinguish between the channels of information flow to the cortex and the cortical analyzers that process the information so as to render it available to help guide the behavior of the organism. No one cortical analyzer, nor any one other part of the brain, is the "seat" of consciousness. Rather, the sum total of the activity of the cortical analyzers determines the content of awareness at that moment. The sum total possible states of the analyzers determines the individual's potential for conscious experience.

When a particular information channel is deprived of input, or severed, particular signals are precluded from reaching the brain, but the range of possible conscious experiences is not diminished. An area of skin deprived of innervation feels numb. That sensation is the subjective concomitant of a signal from the relevant cortical analyzer stating "no message received." The individual is fully aware of the sensory deficit and can imagine (imaginatively represent) various possible sensations from the numb area based on his previous experience. Similarly, a person who is blinded by damage to the peripheral optical apparatus experiences a homogeneous visual greyness, blackness, shimmer, and so on; is fully aware of loss of that information source; and can continue to visualize although he can no longer see. We regard awareness of the sensory deficit as indicating output from an intact cortical analyzer and the ability imaginatively to represent as corresponding to throwing the analyzer into a state of patterned output comparable to that which it would have emitted had it received corresponding information from physical sources external to the body.

Quite different is the state of affairs when certain central lesions impair perception. If blindness results from bilateral parieto-occipital disease, the patient may be quite unaware of his deficit, even deny it, and continue to use terms that have purely visual reference (such as light and dark) in a seemingly senseless and capricious manner. More commonly, the deficit involves only half of the visual field ("hemianopia"). When the hemianopia is due to a communication channel lesion, of the optic tract or even the first cortical relay of the visual system in area 17 of the occipital cortex, the patient is aware of the absence of input from that side of his visual field, which instead may seem homogeneously white or black, and so adjusts the posture of his head and eyes to compensate as best he can for the deficit (i.e., he turns them toward the defective side so as to encompass points to either side of "straight ahead" in his functional visual field). But when it is due to more central lesions involving the parietal lobe, the patient makes no attempt to compensate for the visual defect, because he is quite unaware of it. He is literally unaware that he cannot see across half the visual field. If told so, he is incredulous, perhaps irritated. His direct experience does not include such a deficit; the assertion conflicts with experience. The cerebral lesion has destroyed the relevant analyzer. As there is no output from an analyzer indicating absence of visual input in the half field, the individual is unaware of its absence; in other words, information (or lack of it) in his affected visual field can no longer control behavior. Awareness of this source of information has been lost to consciousness. The individual can now neither experience nor represent experience in that visual field.

The incredulity of the patient about his central hemianopia is an instance of a range of phenomena involving denial of disability (Weinstein & Kahn, 1955). The classical case is that of unilateral neglect of person and of space. (Compare the discussion in the preceding section).

Not uncommonly after a right-sided stroke, the patient, though paralyzed and numb on the whole left side of the body, makes no complaint about this catastrophe, shows little concern about his state, or focuses on minor concerns (e.g., "my arthritis"). Questioned about the left side of his body, he vehemently denies disability and rationalizes wildly—shown his powerless arm, he might say, "It's your arm" or "It's a monkey." In self-care, he ignores the left side, from unbrushed hair on the left to slipperless left foot. The severe neglect can occur in the presense of otherwise demonstrably lucid mental processes.

Often concurrent with neglect of left side of the person is neglect of the left extrapersonal space (mentioned earlier in this chapter). The patient rarely glances to the left. He does not respond to instruction from left-situated observers. Conversely, he is attentive to a degree to right-sided input, granting it precedence even to information from straight ahead and shows considerable compliance with persons who issue orders from that side of space. Given a display to scan, such as a fully opened newspaper, his gaze swings to the rightmost margin, and, arrested there, he reads a few words at the end of lines, makes no sense of them, and complains of his "poor eyesight." He is totally unaware of his biased attention in space (which holds also for the auditory and tactile modalities) and at a loss to account for defective performance resulting from it (such as omitting the left side of drawings that he attempts to copy). Interestingly, the deficit applies not only to processing of immediate input but also seemingly to mental representation. Spontaneous drawings (of a person, or bicycle, or clock) show the same concern with right-located features and omission of features on the left. Or left-sided features, when distinctive, such as the 7–11 on a clock face, are crowded in on the right side of the drawing. A direct study of lateral bias in visualization has recently been done, and it found left-sided neglect in imagery similar to that in direct perception (Bisiach & Luzzatti, 1978).

The present model accounts for this striking phenomenology. Having lost the cortical analyzers for input from the left side of the body, the patient has lost consciousness of the left side of his body. No amount of logic can overcome direct experience, and so the patient resorts to a variety of psychodynamic devices to rationalize his biased behavior. He has names for the left side of his body, but they now lack reference. His awareness of his body has shrunk.

The right attentional bias for external events can be understood, not as a loss of attention to one-half of space, but as an orienting bias to one side of space. As is suggested by our description of the phenomena, there is an imbalance between opposing (leftward and rightward) orienting tendencies such that, given any signal at all, rightward orienting supervenes. It is as if left orienting (and also the left approach that might normally follow) are eradicated from the patient's repertoire of possible activity. Yet, leftward movement is by no means lost: When menaced from the right, the patient will retreat leftward. Then, it is not so much a particular movement pattern, as it is the action with reference to left-located events, that has ceased to feature among the behavioral options.

How can one fit the notion of cortical analyzers, ostensibly concerned with decoding input rather than with encoding output, into a model to explain a deficiency that is as much motor as it is perceptual? One can do so on the basis of ideomotor theory (Greenwald, 1970). This conceives of movement as being programmed in terms of the sensory feedback to be expected once it has occurred. If one cannot mentally represent the sensory situation as it would be changed once the movement has occurred, one cannot move. This notion, though speculative, is attractive from the cybernetic point of view. One cannot, after all, plan a movement type once and for all. It is well known that in order to achieve a goal, one's movement patterns will necessarily differ from occasion to occasion instead; one conceptualizes the goal, and, given skill in (automatization of) the performance in question, one's movements home in on the desired outcome by virtue of complex but lawful unconscious adjustments of several levels of motor representation (e.g., Bernstein, 1967). Thus, at the highest (conscious) level, one represents the goal in terms of a changed relationship between the body and its surrounds. This involves the cortical analyzers and cannot be implemented if the cortical analyzers are unavailable for the representation that is needed. This then is why the stroke victim complains so little of his inability to move the left side of his body or to feel it. He cannot represent action on the left.

A more complex case is denial of aphasia. Whereas many aphasics are acutely conscious of their language problems, and avoid speaking whenever they are able to communicate in some other fashion, other aphasics chatter on, oblivious of the fact that they are failing to communicate. It is typically the patients whose difficulties are concentrated on output (expressive or nonfluent aphasics) who inhibit their speech, whereas patients with "central" (input and output) difficulties continue to chatter on "fluently," although their speech lacks intelligibility (a fact they are unaware of). An extreme case is jargon aphasia, in which the patient, once conversation is initiated, seems able only with difficulty to stem his own flow of largely incomprehensible speech (Kinsbourne & Warrington, 1963). These people can be shown to be implicitly denying their disability and will deny it explicitly if asked. Attempts to account for denial by mental clouding, by psychological factors (Weinstein & Kahn, 1955), or as implicating some "denial" area in the brain are unconvincing with respect to this unusual but very characteristic syndrome, in which consciousness and lucid intellect can often be demonstrated. Instead, we regard this as a further instance of the effect of loss of a cortical analyzer, in this case a language-related analyzer. The patient has lost the communicative aspect of speech; he remains conversant with the social circumstances that elicit speech but is insensitive to the cues we use to determine whether what we say is understood. Speech for those people becomes a rote ritual, as opposed to an activity used deliberately for the purpose of communication.

Further illustrations could be cited from many other so-called parietal syndromes, that is, clinical expressions of parietal damage that selectively impair the patient with respect to cognitive functions, the diagnosis of which is complicated by the patient's own incomprehension of the nature of the recent limitation on his ability. An instance is visuospatial agnosia. The patient has lost his ability to perceive individual features in their spatial relationship to one another. He is lost in visual space—the more so because he has no comprehension of what that means (Paterson & Zangwill, 1944).

We conclude that awareness is the outcome of cortical analyzer function in decoding input, representing the outcome of planned movements, and representing imagined possibilities. The process or mechanism of analyzer function is "preattentive" and not usually consciously experienced.

Abnormal Processing of Normal Input

When people suffer abnormal experiences, they react abnormally. If the abnormal experience results from sudden malfunction of the brain's input-decoding capability, the patient will usually recognize the abnormality and complain of it, for instance, when hallucinating under the influence of a psychedelic drug. This is because the patient can use his previous experience as a standard of reference. But a problem arises when the brain abnormality is congenital. The abnormal experience is then the only one the individual has ever known. Lacking any standard of reference, the child is unaware of anything to complain about. He behaves in ways appropriate to the way he feels.

Autistic children behave in strange ways (Kanner, 1943). They keep to themselves, avoid exposure to change or rich stimulation, and when excited or overaroused, initiate repetitive spinning, whirling, or head-banging movement routines. In addition, they have cognitive difficulties varying in extent, with emphasis on language abnormality (Rutter, 1968). Evidence from several sources converges on an explanation for these children's "stereotypic" behavior and "need for sameness" (Kinsbourne, in press).

In normal life, people process information and respond sequentially to whatever part of the content is judged as relevant for adaptive purposes. If information is decoded that calls for response, but the response is blocked by circumstances out of the organism's control, then an abnormal movement pattern substitutes for the desired response. In everyday life this applies to the familiar concomitants of nervousness and frustration—repetitive twitching, drumming of fingers, pacing, hair stroking, clothes adjusting, and fingernail biting. In ethological terms, these are "displacement behaviors" (Delius, 1969; Zeigler, 1964).

When an animal is shown a rewarding stimulus, such as food when it is hungry, but thwarted (by physical restraint, fear of punishment, or response conflict) from approaching, it goes into a species-specific motor routine. The exact nature of the movement varies with the species—pecking for birds, grooming for cats, etc.—but it is always a familiar (high-frequency) behavior, carried out repetitively, in spite of its total irrelevance to the existing situation. The exact mechanism is not known, but there is evidence that displacement behaviors occur when the organism is overaroused, that is, when there is a high degree of central activation. In the course of displacement, arousal decreases, even to the point that the animal sometimes becomes so underaroused as to fall asleep. We conclude that when an animal is in a state of indecision, central activation (arousal) cumulates. The activation can be discharged by repetitive automatic activity. Nervous mannerisms in humans presumably serve the same purpose.

Normally, overarousal is situational in origin. But it can also be chemically induced. Amphetamine, apomorphine, methylphenidate, and laevodopa are agents that, given in excess, cause animals to go into "amphetamine stereotypies." Rats, for instance, locomote intensely and repetitively, then gnaw on the steel wire of the cage. The stereotypy may last as long as the drug effect, with remorseless mechanical regularity (Wallach, 1974).

Compared to the effect of these chemicals, all of which have in common the effect of increasing dopaminergic neurotransmission, displacement activity is relatively brief and less dramatic. But when arousal occurs physiologically, the displacement activity can modify it and need not continue indefinitely. When the arousal is chemical, the stereotypic movements are probably ineffective. The resemblance is more significant; In both cases, overarousal triggers repetitive motion.

How, then, can we understand the notorious stereotypies of autistic children? Presumably, as a device to combat overarousal. In fact, much of the typical behavior of autists becomes intelligible if regarded as having the purpose of protecting the child from overarousal (Hutt, Hutt, & Ounsted, 1965). Gaze avoidance, and the concern to keep things as they are, limit information flow and the activating effects of novel experience. The stereotypies themselves preoccupy the child and deter interaction. Even when those autists who can, converse, they often produce conversation stoppers in the form of echolalic responses, which merely repeat what the interlocuter said. These children's coldness and detachment deter intimacy, and it has been observed that the most effective teaching technique with these children is neither to blame and punish, nor to warmly praise them, but to approach them in a neutral matter-of-fact fashion (Richer & Nicoll, 1971).

It appears, then, that autistic children are unduly susceptible to overarousal. Stereotypes also occur in two other conditions that lend themselves to the same explanation. Mentally retarded children are often subject to stereotypies. This could be understood if it applies to those retardates who try to process (rather than ignore) input and, because of their processing limitations, are easily overwhelmed by what, to others, would not amount to excessive information flow. Congenitally blind children indulge in "blindisms," which are typical repetitive movement patterns. In the absence of visual information, these children have a severely depleted world to which to respond. Accumulated pressure to respond may break through as stereotypies.

For mind–body relationships, the salient consideration is that subjective experience is determined by the way the brain extracts information from sensory stimulation as well as by what the environment has to offer. When the central calibration is awry, experience is distorted, and the individual responds with behavior that seems abnormal and arbitrary to the bystander but is perfectly intelligible in adaptive terms.

We conclude that neuropsychological studies show us that mental contents are reflected in postural adjustment, and postural adjustment influences mental processes. A malfunctioning brain restricts or distorts experience, and behavior becomes abnormal accordingly.

Do Split-Brain Patients Have Two Minds?

People whose corpus callosum has been surgically divided and whose cerebral hemispheres are therefore disconnected, have repeatedly been credited with dual consciousness (Bogen, 1969; Gazzaniga, 1972; Puccetti, 1977; Sperry, 1966). Using the concepts that we have discussed, we can now be specific about the realities that underlie this catchy but ambiguous attribution.

At any moment in time, the neural basis of any attention-demanding activity of a split-brain person is likely to be limited to one hemisphere. Spread of activation to the other hemisphere is blocked. Thus, the patient's available functional cerebral space is essentially halved (as if he had suffered hemispherectomy, but varying in side from moment to moment). This situation should maximize interference and cause extreme performance deficit when two tasks based on the same hemisphere are undertaken simultaneously. By the same token, two tasks based on different hemispheres should interfere minimally with each other. The callosal section has effectively rendered locations in opposite hemispheres infinitely distant from each other in functional cerebral space.

The same constriction of functional cerebral space should cause exaggeration of overflow from lateralized cognitive activity to the ipsilateral orienting control center. So, stimulating or activating a hemisphere should bias attention contralaterally, to a degree approaching that found in unilateral neglect of space. This effect was demonstrated by Kinsbourne and Trevarthen (Kinsbourne, 1974b). The callosal section uncoupled the two lateral orienting centers from their customary reciprocal interaction (Kinsbourne, 1974b). Whereas in intact humans attention can only be focused on one area at a time (Posner, 1977), split-brain subjects can simultaneously attend to discrete locations on either side. Trevarthen and Kinsbourne (in Trevarthen, 1974) demonstrated this, using the "completion" phenomenon (see section entitled, "Contribution of Cortical Analyzers to Content of Consciousness"). Subjects simultaneously viewed two briefly exposed incomplete geometric shapes. The one projected to the right half field was incomplete on its left side; the one projected to the left field was incomplete on its right side. By failing to notice the absence of the medial aspect of the figure, the subjects were exhibiting a disinhibited natural tendency toward a contralateral orienting bias.

Theoretically, one could rear a split-brain child in such a way as to have him amass completely different, and even contradictory, funds of knowledge, based on opposite hemispheres. But not only does this not occur—head and eye movements disperse information across both hemispheres even when their central communication channel is cut—but, even if it did, it would not constitute two separate consciousnesses, but one consciousness utilizing a variable data base.

A less ambitious claim is that each hemisphere exhibits a characteristically different cognitive style and applies different cognitive operations to the same input (Galin & Ornstein, 1973; Ornstein, 1973). The available evidence contradicts this. When one hemisphere is damaged, the person does not suddenly use what is for him a novel cognitive style. Left-damaged individuals do not achieve instant intuitive power and creativity, nor do right-damaged individuals attain a hitherto inapparent analytic style of operation. Instead the person is as he was, only less efficient in relevant skills. There is, of course, a wide range of individual differences in cognitive style, and this has been dichotomized into the right and left hemispheric (Bogen, 1969), but any such style characterizes the individual as a whole, rather than an ascendent hemisphere. The individual perhaps inherited his style as a temperament, or maybe he learned to act in particular ways that amount to a holistic or an analytic problem-solving approach, but there is no compelling need to attribute stability (trait characteristic) to this. Presumably, if contingencies change, so will style. The disconnected hemisphere does not indulge in a newly liberated cognitive style. It adopts the same mental set as the person did before, only less efficiently if the mental set of the moment is one for which the other hemisphere is more specialized.

Finally, how is space represented in the isolated hemisphere? The evidence suggests that each hemisphere is capable of representing both sides of the body and of space. It constructs its schematic representation of contralateral space from direct sensory information but its representation of ipsilateral space by inference from such relevant data as it has derived from the other side. For example, if a shape abuts the midline, by inference there is a part of it extending into the other (ipsilateral) field, and this is apparently "perceived" with the same feeling of reality as invests percepts that are veridical. Thus in this respect, the range of consciousness is not depleted, though its contents are.

We conclude that a split-brain subject operates in a limited cerebral space and manifests exaggerated functional cerebral proximity effects intrahemispherically and diminished ones between hemispheres. At times he applies the customary mental operations with differential effectiveness on different data bases. None of this amounts to dual consciousness.

Implications for the Mind–Body Problem

Intact behavior cannot be reduced to the sum of its components. A behavioral deficit does not merely deplete the behavioral repertoire. Instead, the unity and coherence of behavior is maintained, but it is a different unity (more limited, adaptive to fewer contingencies but with its own internal logic nevertheless). But the detailed nature of this readjustment of the organism's efforts to adapt cannot be deduced from behavioral information alone. A reorganization of the brain underlies the reorganization of behavior. How this is accomplished depends on the ways in which particular parts of the brain are capable of interacting. Those in turn depend both on the nature of the interference with normal function and on the individual characteristics of the afflicted person's brain organization. The findings discussed here illustrate the principle of emergence; mind as an emergent property of the brain (Bunge, 1977). It is not an emergent entity, in the sense of a novel and unique level of functioning, because it has no independent existence. Instead, mental states form a subset of brain states, as shown by the fact that when the mental states change, the brain states follow suit.

References

Allport, D. A., Antonis, B., & Reynolds, F. On the division of attention: A disproof of the single channel hypothesis. *Quarterly Journal of Experimental Psychology*, 1972, *26*, 225–235.

Bernstein, N. The coordination and regulation of movements. Oxford: Pergamon, 1967.

Bisiach, E., & Luzzatti, C. Unilateral neglect of representational space. *Cortex*, 1978, *14*, 129–133.

Bogen, J. E. The other side of the brain II. An appositional mind. *Bulletin Los Angeles Neurological Society*, 1969, *34*, 135–162.

Bowers, D., & Heilman, K. Pseudoneglect in normals using a tactile line bisection task. Paper presented to the International Neuropsychological Society, 1978.

Brooks, L. R. The suppression of visualization by reading. *Quarterly Journal of Experimental Psychology*, 1967, *19*, 289–299.

Bunge, M. Emergence and the mind. *Neuroscience*, 1977, *2*, 501–509.

Casey, S. M. *The effect of lateral eye positioning on information processing efficiency. Ergonomics program report.* Raleigh: North Carolina State University, 1977.

Delius, J. D. Irrelevant behavior, information processing and arousal homeostasis. *Psychologische Forschung* 1969, *33*, 165–185.

Easterbrook, J. A. The effect of emotion on cue utilization and the organization of behavior. *Psychological Review*, 1959, *66*, 183–201.

Galin, D., & Ornstein, R. E. Hemispheric specialization and the duality of consciousness. In M. Widroe (Ed.), *Human behavior and brain function.* Springfield, Ill.: Thomas, 1973.

Gazzaniga, M. S. One brain-two minds. *American Scientist*, 1972, *60*, 311–317.

Geschwind N. Disconnexion syndromes in animals and man. *Brain*, 1965, *88*, 237–294, 585–644.

Greenwald, A. G. Sensory feedback mechanisms in performance control: with special reference to the ideo-motor mechanism. *Psychological Review*, 1970, *77*, 73–99.

Gur, R. E., Gur, R. C., & Harris, L. J. Cerebral activation as measured by subjects' lateral eye movements is influenced by experimenter location. *Neuropsychologia*, 1975, *13*, 35–44.

Heilman, K., & Watson, R. Mechanisms underlying the unilateral neglect syndrome. In E. Weinstein & R. Friedland (Eds.), *Hemi-inattention and hemispheric specialization: Advances in Neurology.* New York: Raven Press, 1977.

Hicks, R. E. Interhemispheric response competition between vocal and unimanual performance in normal adult males. *Journal of Comparative and Physiological Psychology*, 1975, *80*, 50–60.

Hicks, R. E., Provenzano, F. J., & Rybstein, E. D. Generalized and lateralized effects of concurrent verbal rehearsal upon performance of sequential movements of the fingers of the left and right hands. *Acta Psychologica*, 1975, *39*, 119–130.

Hicks, R. E., Bradshaw, G. J., Kinsbourne, M., & Feigin, D. S. Vocal-manual trade-offs in hemispheric sharing of human performance control. *Journal of Motor Behavior*, 1978, *10*, 1–6.

Hutt, C., Hutt, S. J., Lee, D., & Ounsted, C. A behavioral and electroencephalographic study of autistic children. *Journal of Psychiatric Research*, 1965, *3*, 181–198.

Kahneman, D. *Attention and effort.* Englewood-Cliffs, N. J.: Prentice-Hall, 1973.

Kanner, I. Autistic disturbances and affective contact. *Nerv. Child.* 1943, *2*, 217–250.

Kimura, D. Manual activity during speaking I Right Handers. *Neuropsychologia*, 1973, *11*, 45–50. (a)

Kimura, D. Manual activity during speaking II Left Handers. *Neuropsychologia*, 1973, *11*, 51–55. (b)

Kinsbourne, M. The cerebral basis of lateral asymmetries in attention. In A. F. Sanders (Ed.), *Attention and performance III.* Amsterdam: North-Holland Publishing Co., 1970. (a)

Kinsbourne, M. A model for the mechanism of unilateral neglect. *Transactions of the American Neurological Association*, 1970, *95*, 143–145. (b)

Kinsbourne, M. Eye and head turning indicate cerebral lateralization. *Science*, 1972, *176*, 539–541.

Kinsbourne, M. Direction of gaze and distribution of cerebral thought process. *Neuropsychologia*, 1974, *12*, 279–281. (a)

Kinsbourne, M. Mechanisms of hemispheric interaction in man. In M. Kinsbourne & W. L. Smith (Eds.), *Hemispheric disconnection and cerebral function.* Springfield: Thomas, 1974. (b)

Kinsbourne, M. The mechanism of hemispheric control of the lateral gradient of attention. In P. M. A. Rabbitt & S. Dornic (Eds.), *Attention and performance* V. London: Academic Press, 1975.

Kinsbourne, M. The neuropsychological analysis of cognitive deficit. In R. G. Grenell & S. Gabay (Eds.), *Biological foundations of psychiatry.* New York: Raven Press, 1976.

Kinsbourne, M. Hemi-neglect and hemispheric rivalry. In E. A. Weinstein & R. P. Friedland (Eds.), *Hemi-inattention and hemisphere specialization. Advances in neurology.* New York: Raven Press, 1977 (a).

Kinsbourne, M. The mechanism of hyperactivity. In M. Blau, I. Rapin, & M. Kinsbourne (Eds.), *Topics in child neurology.* New York: Spectrum, 1977.

Kinsbourne, M. The neuropsychology of infantile autism. In L. A. Lockman, K. F. Swaiman, J. S. Drage, K. B. Nelson, & H. M. Marsden (Eds.), NINCDS Monograph No. 23. Bethesda, Md: U. S. Department of Health, Education, and Welfare, 1979.

Kinsbourne, M. Do repetitive movement patterns in children and adults serve a dearousing function? *Journal of Developmental and Behavioral Pediactrics*, in press.

Kinsbourne, M., & Cook, J. Generalized and lateralized effect of concurrent verbalization on a unimanual skill. *Quarterly Journal of Experimental Psychology.* 1971, *23*, 347–351.

Kinsbourne, M., & Hicks, R. E. Functional cerebral space: A model for overflow, transfer and interference effects in human performance. In J. Requin (Ed.), *Attention & performance VII.* Hillsdale, N.J.: Lawrence Erlbaum Assoc., 1978.

Kinsbourne, M., & McMurray, J. The effect of cerebral dominance on time sharing between speaking and tapping by preschool children. *Child Development*, 1975, *46*, 240–242.

Kinsbourne, M., & Warrington, E. K. Jargon aphasia. *Neuropsychologia*, 1963, *1*, 27–37.

Kocel, K., Galin, D., Ornstein, R., & Merin, E. L. Lateral eye movement and cognitive mode. *Psychonomic Science.*, 1972, *27*, 223–224.

Kreuter, C., Kinsbourne, M., & Trevarthen, C. Are deconnected cerebral hemispheres independent channels? A preliminary study of the effect of unilateral loading on bilateral finger tapping. *Neuropsychologia*, 1972, *10*, 453–461.

Lempert, H., & Kinsbourne, M. Clockwise bias in angular mental displacement. Submitted.

Milner, B. Hemispheric specialization: Scope and limits. In F. O. Schmitt & F. G. Worden (Eds.), *The neurosciences.* Third Study Program. Cambridge, Mass.: MIT Press, 1974.

Ornstein, R. E. Right and left thinking. *Psychology Today*, June 1973, pp..86–92.

Paterson, A., & Zangwill, O. L. Disorders of visual space perception associated with lesions of the right cerebral hemisphere. *Brain*, 1944, *67*, 331–358.

Penfield, W., & Roberts, L. *Speech and brain mechanisms*. Princeton: Princeton University Press, 1959.

Pribram, K. H., & McGuinness, D. Arousal, activation and effort in the control of attention. *Psychological Review, 82*, 1975, 116–149.

Puccetti, R. Bilateral organization of consciousness in man. In S. Dimond & D. A. Blizard (Eds.), *Evolution and lateralization of the brain. Annals of the New York Academy of Sciences 1977, 299*, 448–458.

Richer, J., & Nicol L. S. The physical environment of the mentally handicapped: IV. A playroom for autistic children and its companion therapy project. *British Journal of Mental Subnormality*, 1971, *17*, 132–143.

Rutter, M. Concepts of autism: A review of research. *Journal of Child Psychology & Psychiatry*, 1968, *9*, 1–25.

Schwartz, G. E., Davidson, R. J., & Maer, R. Right hemisphere lateralization for emotion in the human brain: Interactions with cognition. *Science*, 1975, *190*, 286–288.

Schwartz, G. E., Davidson, R. J., Ahern & Pusar. Manuscript in preparation, 1979.

Shepard, R. N., & Metzler, J. Mental rotation of three-dimensional objects. *Science*, 1971, *171*, 701–703.

Sperry, R. W. Brain bisection and consciousness. In J. C. Eccles, (Ed.), *Brain and conscious experience*. New York: Springer, 1966.

Trevarthen, C. Functional relations of disconnected hemispheres in the brain stem and with each other: Monkey and man. In M. Kinsbourne & W. L. Smith (Eds.), *Hemispheric disconnection and cerebral function*. Springfield, Ill.: Thomas, 1974.

Wallach, M. B. Drug-induced stereotypic behavior: Similarities and differences. In E. Usdin (Ed.), *Neuropsychopharmacology of monamines and their regulatory enzymes*. New York: Raven Press, 1974.

Weinstein, E. A., & Kahn, R. L. *Denial of illness*. Springfield, Ill.: Thomas, 1955.

Zeigler, P. Displacement activity and motivational theory. *Psychological Bulletin*, 1964, *61*, 362–376.

Chapter 8

Genetic Metaphysics: The Developmental Psychology of Mind-Body Concepts

JOHN M. BROUGHTON

> John, my roommate was taking this philosophy course. And he got me going round in circles one evening. Kept catching me out. And eventually I talked myself into a corner where the only thing that I could be sure about is myself, is that I exist, and that I am not even sure about that.
>
> —Peter, an undergraduate, interviewed by the author

> It is essential to destroy the widespread prejudice that philosophy is a strange and difficult thing just because it is the specific intellectual activity of a particular category of specialists or of professional and systematic philosophers. It must first be shown that all men are "philosophers," by defining the limits and characteristics of the "spontaneous philosophy" which is proper to everybody.
>
> —A. Gramsci, *Selections from the Prison Notebooks*, 1971, p. 323

Common Sense and Philosophy

Common sense and philosophy are intimately connected. This statement is itself rejected within the framework of our common sense knowledge. The popular belief is that philosophy is by nature the esoteric preserve of a small and quaint professional clique, that it is totally irrelevant to everyday life, and that it is a mystifying act of idle speculation with no empirical basis in experience. Admittedly, philosophy actually *has* become institutionalized and distorted so that it does in fact conform to this description to an embarrassing degree. However, it need not do so. It is not in the *nature* of philosophy to fit such a caricature.

The purpose of this chapter is to squarely dispute common sense beliefs about both philosophy and common sense itself. Those beliefs have made popular the assumption that philosophy is quite discontinuous with common sense and is in fact opposed to it. Instead, a "continuity thesis" will be main-

177

BODY AND MIND
Past, Present, and Future

tained: that common sense thinking is already philosophical in a certain way and that it has a tendency to develop into philosophy. Philosophy is not just a separate, abstract reflection upon common sense assumptions. It is a furthering of the purpose of common sense to make sense out of our lived experience. Contrary to popular belief, philosophy puts us *more in touch* with our experience, rather than distancing us from it, while common sense in fact is relatively *less in touch* with everyday life.[1] Robert Pirsig, in the bestseller *Zen and the Art of Motorcycle Maintenance* (1974) has presented a persuasive argument for this kind of continuity thesis. The continuity graphically established in his novel is that between the day-by-day experience of a father and son on a motorcycle trip and a running commentary by the father taking the form of a series of philosophical discourses interwoven with the events of the story (Shuldenfrei, 1975).

Another common sense belief concerning common sense is that it embodies a more or less unitary understanding of the world that is "common" in the sense of being natural to everyone and coming easily to all through the simple lesson of their experience. On the contrary, here it will be maintained that common sense is a hard-won developmental achievement. This assumption leads to three corollaries. The first is that common sense is not "common" in the strict sense, meaning that it is not unitary. It exists at different qualitative levels of organization. Second, these levels comprise an ordered sequence of transformations that follow a developmental progression. Third, common sense does not constitute a "sense." What develops does not do so by the simple tuition of one's senses. Rather than being a straightforward induction or assimilation of brute facts of reality, common sense comprises a complex cognitive system of interpretation, of mental categories and relations.

Metaphysics

Common sense (if we may still call it that) is what Gramsci called "spontaneous philosophy." It resides in language, "good sense," popular religion, ideology, and folklore. It is a rationally structured system that attempts to account for the structure of reality. In this respect it comprises, among other things, an ontology, or, as it is perhaps better called, a *metaphysics*.

How can one characterize metaphysics? Again, the common sense view is skeptical, and the term is usually taken in a pejorative sense. When people

---

[1] As Nowell-Smith (1974), Adorno (1974), and others have pointed out, common sense in fact serves to mystify reality and conceal the truth. Its elevated status in social and even philosophical discourse is unwarranted. Any critical analysis can and must reject common sense as the final arbiter in questions of knowledge, value, or beauty. The overvaluation of common sense is part and parcel of its ideological function. The very idea of common sense is, in the modern world, a reflection of the liberal laissez faire belief in the "natural" individual, who left to his own devices spontaneously develops a correct understanding of the world. This correct understanding "naturally" coincides with the way we commonly see the world. Clearly, certain strata of society have more interest vested in such a conventional individualism than do others.

describe philosophy as "talking in circles," as Peter does in the quote at the head of this chapter, they are usually referring to the metaphysical side of the discipline. Carnap called it mere "poetry." It is commonly seen as dealing with the "suprasensory," the sphere most devoid of reference to observable fact. For this reason, it is seen as impossible to reach any agreement with others on metaphysical questions, let alone reach any certainty. Even phenomenologists, themselves philosophically oriented, have been eager to celebrate the death of metaphysics. The funeral they proclaimed was for metaphysics in Kant's sense of the term. Kant has unfortunately helped to spread the idea of metaphysics as a science transcending experience and to a great extent divorced from it. This vision was moreover an image of a science involved in a series of inevitable self-contradictions. Small wonder then that Hegel and others in the phenomenological tradition become the allies of hard scientists in tolling the death knell for such a metaphysics, comparing it to the spurious sophisms of traditional essentialist philosophy (Arendt, 1977).

Kant had also given rise to the notion that the analysis of knowledge is central to metaphysics. Under this description, "metaphysics" had come to mean the theory of the most general concepts employed for the determination of empirical data. However, as Külpe (1897, pp. 26-27) pointed out, this is really a description of *epistemology*, the pursuit of which is entirely confined within the limits of possible experience. On account of this "scientific" bent, epistemology is unable to lead to any general view of the universe. The task of metaphysics is, in Külpe's words "the development of a Weltanschauung." It is the very practical study of how we develop a systematic interpretation of experience, a synthetic statement in ultimate terms of the nature of the real. Metaphysics does not really transcend experience in any other sense than that in which the whole transcends its parts. While it responds to the demand for completion of a scientific knowledge that would be free from contradictions, the kind of verification and demonstration that metaphysics employs is not the same as that of the natural or social sciences. Rather, metaphysics extends beyond experience, per se, to harmonize and rationalize it, exhibiting it as a consistent system or interconnected whole. It critically judges the reasonableness of assumptions about, and interpretations of, the world and thereby arrives at a progressively more meaningful world view. It synthesizes rational cosmology (the philosophy of the world, its origin, nature, reality, and transformation), rational psychology (the philosophy of mind, self, soul, and body), and rational theology (the theory of supernatural being).

Genetic Metaphysics

Metaphysics as defined by Külpe is clearly continuous in function with common sense. Historically speaking, both metaphysics (Külpe, 1897, p. 27) and common sense (Nowell-Smith, 1974) were conceived in the struggle against the authority of religion in defining reality. Both have taken over that function of religion as a provider of a Weltanschauung (Berger & Luckmann, 1966). Both have attempted to "desacralize" religious worldviews, to remove the mysterious quality and replace it with a purely rational structure (Döbert, 1973, 1975). Each modern individual is a common sense metaphysician who combines ideology and ontology (Sharpe, 1974).

"*Genetic* metaphysics" therefore must involve a developmental analysis of the transformations of this common-sense or "spontaneous" metaphysical awareness. This genetic approach to worldviews can be compared and contrasted with Piaget's "genetic epistemology." The latter has been a powerful source of empirical evidence for the continuity thesis, establishing qualitative relationships between everyday thought and the conceptual forms of science and philosophy. Genetic epistemology makes use of a "cognitive-developmental" approach (Kohlberg, 1969), which embodies six kinds of propositions: (a) that knowledge is the central concern of a true psychology; (b) that knowledge is not a privileged acquisition but constitutes a psychological structure common to all individuals; (c) that this structure of conceptual relations underlying the cognitive processes of individuals shapes and limits the forms of their experience and understanding; (d) that this structure undergoes a progressive development through an interaction between self and world, much as a philosophic or scientific theory develops objectivity by evidence and contradiction; (e) that the course of development in its successive stages resembles in its form the cultural history of intellectual endeavor; and (f) that the end point of individual cognitive development in the layman corresponds approximately to the infrastructure of modern professional intellectual activity.

In common with genetic epistemology, genetic metaphysics has a double concern. It combines a study of the historical genesis of worldviews with a developmental psychology of worldviews. The psychological half of the picture has been the predominant concern in Piaget's work, and it will be here, too, in our approach to genetic metaphysics. Piaget (1931) used to do research on children's worldviews, but in his later work (1962) he has assimilated this into his stages of logical–scientific development, which he argues form the basis of genetic epistemology. Even though Piaget does not appear to acknowledge the possibility of a developmental psychology of worldviews, the latter does borrow from the Piagetian tradition. For example, it does make the same kinds of assumptions (a–f) just listed as characteristic of Piaget's cognitive–developmental approach.

However, much as metaphysics cannot be assimilated to epistemology in the Kantian manner, genetic metaphysics cannot be assimilated to genetic epistemology in the way that Piaget, a neo-Kantian, seems to presume. Genetic metaphysics, at least in its developmental moiety, deals with the progressive emergence of a theory of reality, not a theory of knowledge. A theory of reality may be related to a theory of knowledge, but there is no reason at all to suppose that the former would be subordinate to or derivative from the latter. Genetic metaphysics thus challenges the idealist's preconception that reality can only be considered indirectly via the prior study of the knowing process that reveals the real.

Common Sense Psychophysics and Its Genesis

It was suggested in the preceding discussion that metaphysics, in Külpe's sense, synthesizes a philosophical cosmology, a philosophical theology, and philosophical "psychology." A genetic metaphysics would therefore eventually have to account for the developmental emergence of such philosophies in common sense and their synthesis in a total world-view. In the present exercise, however, the focus will be narrowed to cover only the development, in the layman, of philosophical psychology. By this is intended a stage-by-stage developmental account of common sense mind–body concepts. For short, these concepts, and the structural or organizational form that they take, will be referred to as "psycho-physics." This term has unfortunately come to have a rather narrow methodological connotation within psychology during this century. The intended sense of the term here is that in which it was taken at the end of the last century, when psycho-physical concepts were any and all philosophic interpretations of mind, body, and their relationship.

In the spirit of genetic metaphysics in general, common sense notions of the body and mind (and its soul or self), are here assumed to have a rational organization, which undergoes a sequence of developmental reconstructions. At its upper end, this sequence of cognitive transformations is presumed to merge into the metaphysics proper of mind and body, as is seen, for example, in the conduct of inquiry by professional philosophers and some social scientists.

Thus, we could say that the activities of individual metaphysicians would depend on their prior psychological preparation by passage through a series of more and more adequate "naive" metaphysics and psycho-physics. This would also be the case for psychologists and others whose metaphysical views are less explicit, though nonetheless influential. In addition, differences in the metaphysical positions held among philosophers, psychologists, etc. could in principle be explained in terms of the higher levels of such a developmental sequence, some positions being genetically more advanced than, and derived from, other positions. Such a prospect would have considerable significance for a cognitive–developmental psychology, since there is reason to infer that if metaphysical thinking is the basis of philosophy, as its creator Aristotle claimed, it would also form the base of an individual's naive cognition.

However, Kohlberg (1963) cast some gloom over the prospect of a developmental psychology specifically concerned with mind–body concepts 15 years ago when he said, "No definitive logical analysis of sequence at these higher levels can be made, since the position of educated adults (or psychologists) on the mind–body problem is at best confused, uncertain, and lacking in consensus [p. 41]." Contrary to this, and a half century earlier, the philosopher–psychologist James Mark Baldwin (the progenitor of both "symbolic interactionism" and the Piaget–Kohlberg "cognitive–developmental" approach) had presented a detailed logical analysis of how the structure of consciousness evolves through a series of levels or "modes," central to which is the progressive elaboration and transformation of the concepts of mind and body (Baldwin, 1904, 1906, 1908, 1911; Broughton & Freeman-Moir, in press). From an initial "adualistic" or animistic consciousness the psychic organization is transformed through a dualism of "inner" versus "outer" to a stage of "psychophysical dualism" proper: a Cartesian dichotomy of mutually exclusive mental and physical substances. Subsequently, this structure is transformed into an epistemological dualism of subject and object, culminating in logical, theoretical, or scientific thought (the contemplative consciousness of Kant's pure reason). This provides a basis for mature moral cogitation (practical reason), linking thought to action. According to Baldwin's scheme, the paradoxes of both pure and practical rationality are eventually resolved in the only possible way: development culminates in the immediate or "aesthetic" mode of experience. Throughout, developmental advance to a more adequate stage is motivated by the inconsistencies in individual and social experience generated by the present stage of thought (Baldwin, 1897, 1906, 1908, 1911, 1915). In this, Baldwin followed quite closely the tradition of Hegel's "Phenomenology" and "Logic."

For Baldwin, these stages are extremely general. As more recently for Bateson's work (1976), while the psycho-physical is a central and essential domain, it is only a strand in the skein of consciousness as a whole in its various phases of genesis. Mind–body concepts are, at each level, integrated with concepts of self, other, reality, and existence. In addition, at each level, this larger whole of metaphysics is integrated with a corresponding epistemology, a logic, a theory of symbols, and a sociology of knowledge. Thus, the different levels of existence are always integrally associated with compatible levels of truth and meaning. Baldwin's genetic framework was intended as a description also applicable schematically to intellectual history. Thus, it encompasses both professional philosophy and common ideology.

Baldwin's account is a theory drawn from anecdotal observation of his own children and on the analogy of intellectual history. Is there any systematic empirical evidence for his contentions, at least insofar as the development of psycho-physical concepts? Is there even reason to suppose that the cognitive–developmental version of the continuity thesis applies to the psychological domain of metaphysics in general or to the mind–body realm in particular? Or, should we rather accept Kohlberg's scepticism about currently extending the cognitive–developmental model into this new area? Certainly, there is a marked paucity of empirical evidence to date. That this situation is no different in Europe than in America is suggested by Horkheimer's (1974) lament, "I know of no penetrating study, for western Europe, which aims at determining the precise meaning and degree of vitality that the soul concept has at contemporary man's various levels of awareness [p. 31]."

Psychologists are not open to the study of metaphysical concepts for two reasons. First, metaphysical conceptions (such as "mind substance") fail to map onto the logical or physiological mechanisms that modern psychology, with its one-dimensional technical interpretation of minds and bodies, is used to analyzing (Merleau-Ponty, 1963). Second, psychologists adhere to the common sense notion of metaphysics as a disordered set of purely subjective speculations, upon which agreement can never be reached. Kohlberg reveals a tendency to think that way in the passage quoted above. In general, it seems likely that empirical research on metaphysical concepts has been inhibited by the assumption that metaphysical beliefs are unstable, vary from person to person, and are artifacts of culture that are not fit objects of serious study for a science of psychology.[2]

Life, Consciousness, and Nature in Genetic Metaphysics

For our purposes, it is helpful to go back to the type of research done by the young Piaget (1929, 1930, 1931). There are two reasons for this, both of which have to do with the fact that Baldwin exerted a much more profound influence upon Piaget's work at that time (Broughton & Freeman-Moir, in press). First, that work deals with naive cosmology and the child's conception of the natural world, both of which involve metaphysical thinking. Second, Piaget's genetic epistemology took seriously the parallelism between early philosophy in the life of the child and early philosophy in human history.

The ancient Greeks lived in a time prior to the ascendancy of epistemology as such. Their philosophy was primarily "ontological," concerned with the analysis of objective being. It was based on the presumption that things can be known as they are (Baldwin, 1902, 1905, 1913; Collingwood, 1940, 1945; Guthrie, 1950). Mind and its external referents were not differentiated. Nature was seen as permeated with a spiritual principle. This is what made it *alive*, *active*, and *intelligent*. Life, mind, and matter were still fused. There was not yet a mind–matter dualism, since both form and matter were seen as things existing apart from the self. The contents of mind were undifferentiated from their objects.

Following this, in the Eleatics and Sophists, and culminating in Socratic

---

[2] The philosophical precursors and the previous empirical research relevant to genetic metaphysics have been summarized in a longer version of this chapter (Broughton, 1978b). An important study, emerging at the time of going to press (and therefore not covered here) is that of Johnson and Wellman (1979; Compare Wellman & Johnson 1979).

thought, there was a shift of focus from nature to mind, although this was still mind-in-body. Body was not yet simply matter but alive and filled with desires.

Renaissance cosmology (from Copernicus to Descartes and Spinoza) reacted against this world view, seeing the natural world as devoid of intelligence and life. It was an ordered mechanism, activated by an external intelligence (God). Mind was not immanent in body; it transcended it. Sensation went over to the body side and was included in nature, where along with life it became confounded with material existence. Mental and physical substances were separate and functioned according to their own laws. Behind the apparent sensed world of secondary qualities, changing and therefore unknowable, was the constant and real object of science. This was from one point of view the *substance*, the matter which took various changing forms, and from another perspective the *laws* according to which these different arrangements of the same substance occurred.

Thereafter, a second shift from nature to mind occurred from Berkeley onward through Hegel (Cassirer, 1923; Collingwood, 1945; Mead, 1936). Here the question was raised of how mind can have contact with something so opposed to itself as this purely mechanical nature. The answer proposed (still assuming nature as essentially foreign) was that mind constructed a real and existent nature through its own independent activity of reason.

Much as the ancient and medieval cosmology exhibited a fusion of "mind," "matter," and "life," so children confound the physical, vital, and human orders in their early philosophies. This progressive emergence and differentiation has been charted in detail by Barbara Schecter (Table 8.1) in her work at Columbia.

Until age 6, "life" is infused with anthropomorphic characteristics. It is attributed to nature wherever nature appears to display activity like a person. Life is not fully distinguished as animate nature until age 10, when the first notions of form appear. At this third level, the temporal dimension of genesis becomes central to the definition of life. However, as in pre-nineteenth-century biology, so in early adolescence, the process of generation is seen as a mechanical cycle of exact self-reproduction.

Consciousness is initially confined to the "living," but since this includes inanimate nature, in effect consciousness is projected into reality. In this early phase, the consciousness attributed to humans is physicalistic mind-in-body, confounding knowing, feeling, and sensation. Consciousness begins to be associated with a distinguishable organ or instrument of knowing at around age 8, and feeling is differentiated from sensing. However, not until early adolescence can consciousness transcend sensation, and at that point, sensation may still be allowed to plants or even objects. A peculiarly human mind, a reflective subjective consciousness distinct from material brain, is rarely conceptualized prior to age 14. Even at this point, mind is not fully differentiated from life but comes back to haunt it. This is still a "pre-Renaissance"

TABLE 8.1
Schecter's Levels in the Development of Life–Mind Concepts (Evolution in Criteria Used to Attribute Animacy–Consciousness)

Life	Consciousness
1. (Age 5–6) *Zoomorphic–anthropomorphic.* No clear categorical boundaries. Human (and animal) orders confounded with inanimate nature. Attribution of life derives from global similarities to living beings, based on having bodily characteristics and appearance like a person, e.g., "has eyes," "has legs." Animacy of natural objects like sun, river or wind, derived from similarity of their movement to a person's activity.	1. (Age 6–8) *Sensorimotor.* Bodily organs of sense, or bodily activity. Consciousness reduced to *sentience* ("feeling it") as defined by zoomorphic–anthropomorphic criteria (having eyes, nose, talking, etc). *Action* and even *existence* automatically imply conscious knowledge, i.e., feeling (to do or be something is to know it). Must be "alive" to know.
2. (Age 6–8) *Quasi-animistic.* Level 1 criteria still apply, plus inner biological characteristics ("has brain," "thinks," "senses things"). *Borderline* category formed of manmade and natural things "alive in a different way." This type of thing is defined *functionally* by the fact that is works or does something useful. At the same time, real life may be denied to the mechanical and natural because they are not "things" (unitary objects).	2. (Age 8–10) *Quasi-mental.* Knowing and sensing. Cephalic *organ* (brain or mind) necessary for knowing. Partial differentiation of *knowledge* as contents of thought or memory, e.g., in puzzling things out (math-thinking). Yet most knowing still connected with sensorimotor activity (brain "uses senses," or "tells you how to swim"). Knowledge still automatic. Must be alive to know.
3. (Age 10–12) *Genetic–organic.* Concern with origins, natural form, and formation. Integration into a temporal or spatial order. Things that grow are *born* rather than made, and natural or spontaneous *wholes* resisting decomposition. Life as generative and irreversible, yet still cyclical (replication, self-substitution).	3. (Age 12–14) *Psychobiological.* Phylogenetically different ways of *experiencing,* responding to, or coming to know things (process becoming differentiated from product). (*a*) *Registering impact* (objects–plants): passive knowledge ("they can just tell what's happening to them") allowed to inanimate things; a nonsentient knowledge still like a "sixth sense." (*b*) *Instinct* (plants–animals): repetitive mechanical reaction: automatically know how to do things. (*c*) *Reason or understanding* (humans): poorly defined global notion. Know how to get things, using reason, choice, and decision.
4. (Age 12–14) *Volitional.* Voluntary and reflexive choice, control, or self-determination. Notion of immaterial cause (formal and/or final), purpose, tendency, or potential; "has a mind of its own." (No clear distinction between conscious and unconscious volition.)	4. (Age 14+) *Subjective.* Mental activity of humans: higher conscious functions or processes of imagining, interpreting, inferring. Mental further differentiated as novel, creative, and unique; able to extrapolate beyond empirical experience. Thus mind is both conscious will and subjectivity, relative to individual. Nonconscious biological activity.

stage, where life now conceived in terms of growth and development remains to be distinguished from volition, and so animate nature is construed vitalistically.

Mind and Body in Genetic Metaphysics

Much as the mind-body concepts and problems of modern philosophy are grounded historically in the matrix of ancient and medieval notions about life and nature (compare M. Bakan's chapter in this book), so my own work on psycho-physical concepts takes off from the empirical studies of "animism" carried out by Piaget, Laurendeau and Pinard, and Schecter. These researchers had fleshed out the empirical details around the theoretical skeleton that Baldwin provided, indicating how the animism of his "adualistic" stage gave way to a differentiation of the living and then to the inner and outer being of animate things.

A question that captured my interest was exactly how the distinction of mental and physical arose in Baldwin's next stage of "substantive dualism." In order to further empirically clothe Baldwin's theoretical skeleton, an attempt was made (Broughton, 1974) to trace in adolescence and early adulthood that "definitive logical analysis of sequence" in metaphysical concepts, the absence of which Kohlberg and Horkheimer had lamented. The theoretical formulations of Baldwin (and to some extent his heirs) suggested that metaphysical concepts might develop psychologically, as they did in the history of ideas, within a complex network of conscious modes that also included logical, moral, religious, epistemological, aesthetic, and sociological perspectives. My empirical research, only part of which will be reported here, took such a putative evolving network or structure as an object of study. Since cognitive–developmental researchers had already covered most of these domains,[3] I confined my study to the areas that had not received attention: metaphysics and epistemology. This choice perhaps seems less arbitrary when we note that philosophers often see these two areas as comprising a larger conceptual unity of "theoretical reason," or what I have called, in the domain of common sense psychology, "natural philosophy."

My own study, originally of cross-sectional design, employed interview methods, and the subjects were 18 female and 18 male middle-class urban and suburban Bostonians between the ages of 10 and 26. The aim was to track the progressive emergence of Baldwin's substantive dualism, with hopes of also finding evidence of the two subsequent stages of "subject–object" dualism and "logical" or "theoretical" rationality. In order to increase the probability of

---

[3]These authors have been much less concerned than Piaget with propositions (e) and (f) of the cognitive–developmental approach mentioned earlier in this chapter and so cannot properly be called "genetic epistemologists."

sampling these higher levels, undergraduate and postgraduate subjects were selected from a variety of disciplines and professions.

An interview was devised, using particular content suggested by Baldwin's work, in conjunction with an exploratory pilot study. In order to obtain as complete a picture as possible, a broad range of philosophic questions was asked in the domain of theoretical reason, including epistemological as well as metaphysical ones. Subjects were asked directly such questions as "What kind of things are there in the world?" "What is a person?" "What is someone's self?" "What is 'real'?" "What is the mind?" "How do we 'know' things?" Specifically in the psycho-physical realm, subjects were asked: "What is the mind?" "What is the body?" "What are 'mental' things?" "What are 'physical' things?" "How are they related?" "What is the brain?" "What does it have to do with the mind?" "What happens to these things when someone dies?" "Could you have a mind without a body or a body without a mind?" "Is there a 'soul,' 'spirit,' or 'ghost'?" "How do you know you have a mind?" "Can one mind know another mind?" "Is the mind (or are mental things) real?" "What is thought?" The aim was not, as in ordinary language philosophy (Naess, 1953), to elicit common sense *definitions* of terms but rather to get to the general structural principles underlying the *reasoning process*, through the systematic probing of subjects' responses. Often, the interviewees spontaneously brought up the mind–body issue, frequently using their own preferred terms or language. The interviewers encouraged this, trying to elicit reasoning around the issues just mentioned as far as possible without introducing their own terminology.

Subjects were also administered a standard Kohlberg moral judgement questionnaire and Piaget's pendulum, chemicals and verbal seriation tasks. This was in order that any observed "progress" in philosophical concepts could be related to stages of logical and moral development.

Empirical Findings

On previous occasions (Broughton, 1975a, 1975b), I have presented the empirical findings of this cross-sectional study, which are in several respects compatible with a cognitive–developmental interpretation, that is, there is (a) correlational integrity to the domain of theoretical reason; (b) internal consistency indicating ideal types (or possibly stages); and (c) strong relationships to cognitive maturity, and to cognitive levels in the domains of logic and morality, already shown by Piaget and Kohlberg to possess structural characteristics of stage-by-stage development. This is unlikely to surprise most developmental psychologists, for whom structural levels of development probably approach the status of an assumption rather than an empirical generalization. So instead of belaboring these findings, or discussing methodology (compare Broughton, 1976), I prefer to devote the space here to a detailed qualitative analysis of the interview material. In particular, I wish to focus on that part which bears on the *psycho-physical* aspect of development. The total scheme of qualitative levels that was derived from intensive analysis of the interview material is presented in Table 8.2. This tabulation sets the emerging levels of psychophysical concepts in the context of other metaphysical and epistemological notions.

The psycho-physical category (labeled "Mental–Material" in Table 8.2) is conceptually distinct. Nevertheless, before proceeding to present examples from each level of the category's development, it should be pointed out that it is quite difficult to tease out mind–body concepts from others at an empirical level. Since philosophical distinctions, such as "philosophy versus psychology" or "metaphysics versus epistemology," are not explicitly made within the world views of typical adolescents or even normal adults, their thinking confounds and intermingles the issues from both sides. Much as psychological concepts pervade metaphysical ones, notions of self first pervade those of mind, so that the latter are thoroughly confounded with the former (Broughton, 1977; Mead, 1934; Selman, 1974). Initially, mind and thought are equated, and neither is distinguished clearly from knowledge or knowing (Cross, 1976; Piaget, 1929).

Compounding these difficulties is the fact that since the original cross-sectional study comprised a research on adolescence, our official sample started at age 10. As a result, the data for childhood metaphysics are confined to less formal interviews from age 4 up, carried out subsequently in collaboration with Cross and Schecter.

Level 1

Preliminary analysis of the interviews by Schecter, Cross, and myself suggests that developing ideas in the psycho-physical domain are compatible with, and often overlap with, concepts of life, consciousness, intelligence, dreams, thoughts, intentions, names, affects, motives, and personality. Corresponding to the earliest level of Schecter's life and consciousness concepts is the first level of ideas about mind and body. This can be seen as analogous to Baldwin's "adualistic" or animistic mode of consciousness. At Level 1 (approximately ages 4–7), the child's thinking entertains at best one type of control in the body. "Mind" is a difficult and nonspontaneous word for the child (see examples 1.1c and 1.3 in the following discussion), while "brain" tends to be used spontaneously to describe this entity. Despite the fact that the term "mind" is not part of the child's active repertoire, it is often partially *understood*, can be used once introduced into the interview, and is associated regularly with certain conceptual content. This tends to be the same content ascribed to "brain" (1.4b). It is arbitrary whether the child says mind is or is not the same thing as the brain. Whatever (s)he says, (s)he will often then proceed to contradict this (1.4), or acquiesce to whatever the interviewer sug-

TABLE 8.2
Levels of Natural Philosophy by Category

	Mental-material	Self-world	Physical-social	Reality-appearance	Knower-known
1. Objective (Age 4–7)	*Adualist:* Gross head-body distinction. Visible and invisible not differentiated. Mind and body mutually permeable.	*Presumptive:* Self-evident, bodily self. Not differentiated from reflexive "itself."	*Animistic:* Living and nonliving only partly distinguished. People distinguished from things only along quantitative physical dimensions.	*Objective:* Reality presumed. Simple and immediate existence of external things. Real undifferentiated from nonartificial.	*Dogmatic:* Thought and its objects undifferentiated. Direct, automatic knowing. Single extrinsic truth, known and handed down by authority.
2. Individual (age 8–11)	*Organic:* Mind differentiated from body as brainlike organ, controlling rest of body. Discrete, nonvisible mental contents.	*Individual:* Self is a specific person, me or you. Perceiving, acting person. Source or agent.	*Subjective:* People distinguished as conscious, sentient, or as self-active individuals. Body is (subordinate) part of person.	*Naive realist:* Certainty of reality directly sensed. Appearance is the way something "looks"—*is* reality. Real differentiated from imaginary as persistent.	*Empirical:* Partial differentiation of knower from known. Experience directly caused by object. Subjective not opposed to objective. Truth is absolute fact, is opposed to lie, and is individually apprehended and asserted.

(Continued)

TABLE 8.2 (Continued)

Mental–material	Self–world	Physical–social	Reality–appearance	Knower–known
3. Divided (Age 12+)				
Immature dualist: Abstract mental differentiated from concrete physical, as fluid and invisible medium. Mental and physical as shared classes, with interdependence (overlap).	*Divided:* Self is mind (mental self) more than body (physical self). Unique subjective traits, opinions, beliefs, or values. Authentic inner self differentiated from false outer appearance (social personality or role self).	*Interpersonal:* People have personality and show themselves to other people. Body is appearance, ambiguous. Physical as impersonal "scientific" world.	*Realist:* Appearance generally realistic, but mind may add "personal" distortion (opinion or value). Mental is belief rather than reality.	*Social:* Concrete facts known by individuals. Trust as interpersonal demonstration and plausibility (overlap). Nascent scepticism.
4. Dualist (Age 18+)				
Cartesian: Dualism between objective mechanistic system of scientific cause–effect, and subjective or spiritual world of belief, purpose, and reason. Unconscious differentiated from conscious.	*Substantial:* Self as system: soul, intellect, logic, identity or "cogito" (self-control). Self has mental and physical attributes. Self-concept, or "me," rather than "I." Generalized self or perspective.	*Individual:* Social as system of abstract individuals. People as spiritual, self-regulating, and purposeful (vitalist), instances of the general rule. Body now estranged as part of material world (mechanist).	*Dualist:* Reality assumed. Noumenon differentiated from phenomenon. Substantial reality is lawlike system generating appearances (data).	*Positivist:* Knowledge is inductive generalization of observation, constructive copy of world. Truth, which subordinates reality, is replicable and is achieved through social conventional testing of models. Impartial "generalized other" defines objective standpoint.

5. Subjective (Age 20+) *Reductionist:* Monistic materialism. Mind as epiphenomenon.	*Process:* Self as flux of experience, or process of self-realization. Breakdown of substantial soul or identity. Everything has self.	*Anarchist:* Fusion of natural and social. Either biologizing of social or panpsychism. Dialectic of organization and anarchic chaos.	*Subjectivist:* All reality phenomenal. Full determinism at level of data.	*Relativist:* All knowledge is individual and subjective, or arbitrary convention. Opposition to objectification. Scepticism and solipsism.
6. Rational (Age 25+) *Parallelist:* Functional "mental" and "physical," psychology versus physiology, as ideational systems of explanatory constructs.	*Epistemological:* Self as transcendental ego, or function of universal self-consciousness. Self-conceiver or subject-self differentiated from empirical or object-self.	*Rational:* Social as rational democratic organization, versus natural as nonrational but systematic sphere. Natural law. Physical and social sciences.	*Perspectivist:* Reality presupposed. Reality defined by coherence and utility of system within which it is interpreted.	*Methodological:* Objective relativism. Knowledge and truth defined by intersubjective use of paradigm, such as idealism, behaviorism, etc. Logical level distinguished from empirical.
7. Dialectical *Interpenetrative:* Dialectical materialism. Nature and culture penetrate each other through human activity (work).	*Historical:* Self as trans-individual subject (e.g., class subject), transforming natural-social reality.	*Dialectical:* Natural world transformed into cultural, or alienated from it through domination.	*Materialist:* Objective material reality dynamically evolving and appearing through human activity.	*Social:* Knowledge as active social transformation of reality through manmade historical categories.

gests. Perhaps this reflects general difficulties with understanding sameness and difference at this cognitive level. Even when a distinction between mind and brain is temporarily sustained, it is on the grounds of gross morphology rather than difference of function (1.3b).

"Mind" is construed as an anatomical principle of life (1.1). It is the source of bodily movement (1.1c) and at the most primitive level may therefore be attributed to other moving things (1.1d), especially if these are living things (1.1e).

1.1a. *R.F.* (Age 6.0, Female [F]) **How do you know the mind is real?** I know it's in the body. Everyone has a mind. **How do you know that?** Almost every living thing has a mind.

1.1b. *M.I.* (6.9, F) **What is someone's mind?** It makes them think. If they have no mind, they couldn't think and they won't be alive. Because everyone has a mind except dolls and tables. **How do you know it's there?** Because if you are alive then you know it is there. But if you are not alive, then you don't. If you have no mind then you can't be alive. Because your mind helps you. And if you have an empty head with no mind, you can't be alive, because no one can have an empty head.

1.1c. *J.V.* (5.9, Male [M]) **What is your mind?** The mind is your head, isn't it? **What does it do? What's it for?** I don't know . . . . Because I don't know what minds are. **Do people have minds?** Yes. **Anything besides people have minds?** No. **Your dog?** He has a mind. **How do you know?** Everything that moves. Or walks.

1.1d. *M.F.* (7.2, F) **What kinds of things don't have minds?** Table, bike. **What do they have in common?** Things to do things with . . . . **Tell me some things that think. Does a car think?** No, because it's run by a motor. **A tree?** When it's a baby, a seed, it thinks whether it's going to grow up. **The sun?** Yeah. It has to think about things before it does it. **How do you know the sun thinks?** Because it just can't do something. It has to think about it first . . . . **Does the sun (have a mind or a brain)?** It thinks, but it doesn't have a brain. **Does it have a mind?** Yes. **Why?** Because the mind can think too.

1.1e. *A.H.* (5.4, M) **Do chairs have minds?** No, they have legs. **Why don't they have minds?** They're not a person. **Do trees have minds?** Yeah. They can move. **How?** When they saw it down.

1.2a. *M.I.* (6.9, F) **What does someone's mind do?** It helps them think. . . . **What is the brain?** It is a thing that helps you think and helps you do stuff.

1.2b. *I.M.* (6.0, M) **What does the mind do?** It goes through the body. And it helps other things. **How does it do that?** It flows through the body, like two ghosts flying.

1.3a. *I.M.* (6.0, M) **What is the mind?** The mind of my head? **Yes.** What is my mind? Let's see. That's a hard question. Well, I think about it. **What do you think about it?** Because I feel like it. **When you think about the mind, what do you think about?** What do I mind? **No. When you think about it, what do you think about?** I think about you. A., myself, L., C., A., and me. And J.—she's my girl friend. **Can you tell me anything else about the mind?** Well, I think about your bed, my bed, boats. Everything in the whole world. **Is the mind what you're thinking?** Yes.

1.3b. *A.H.* (5.4, M) **What is the mind?** (No response) **Have you heard that word?** (No response) **What is your mind like?** I don't know. **Are brain and mind different?** Yeah. **How?** Because they're not the same shape.

Mentality is reified and limited to the form of individual minds. It may be specifically limited to one's *own* mind (1.3). Either mind or brain "help you"; they are used like tools (1.2). Thus, while internal to the corporeal person, they are nevertheless somewhat external to the self (1.1), whose purposes they serve.

Insofar as the child comes to make "mind" something distinct during the course of the interview, subjectively it is confused with thoughts (1.3a). These are reified (1.4b), even personified (1.5), as therefore is the mind (1.2b).

1.4a. *I.M.* (6.0, M) **Is the mind the same as the brain?** Yes. **How's that?** Because, thinking is the brain? **Is that what you said? No. I said, is the mind the same as the brain?** No. **What's the difference?** Because the mind is in the brain. The mind isn't the *same* as the brain.

1.4b. *I.M.* (6.0, M) **Is the mind the same as the brain?** No. **What's the difference with the mind?** It's something that you think in. **How?** Blood vessels help you. By giving the blood. **Are the thoughts in the blood?** Yes. **Is the mind the same as the brain?** Yes, yes, yes, yes. **So why two words?** I don't know. **Anything else the mind does?** It thinks. It helps the blood. . . . **What does the brain do?** It helps the blood go through the vessels.

1.5. *G.S.* (5.3, M) **Where is thinking?** In there (points to head). . . .**In your head?** Yeah. **All over your head?** In there (points to middle of forehead). Right up in the middle. **Why?** Right in your nose. **Why?** Because they want to do. . . . They are learning their lessons. That's their school. Thinks go in there to learn thinks. (Chuckles).

The mind is given a spatial interpretation. It, or its spatial extension, may be equated with the head (1.1b, 1.1c, 1.3). Its location is specific (1.6). It is a physical property of the body (1.1e). As a physical property of people, mind may even transcend life (1.7).

"Body" is conceptually more central at Level 1 than "mind" (1.8). The body is not yet a whole corporeal person but is confined to the torso (1.9b). The morphology of the person is restricted to a bodily inside and outside, where the inside is the realm of the organs, blood, etc. (compare the Munari, Filippini, Regazzoni, & Visseur [1976] study of children's anatomical representations).

1.6a. *G.S.* (5.3, M) **Can you tell me where the mind is?** I don't know. **Can you guess?** In your head. **Where in your head?** I think so. *Where* **in your head?** By your hair.

1.6b. *M.I.* (6.9, F) **Where is the mind?** It is in your head. **Where is it in the head?** In the middle. **In the middle?** Yes, in the middle.

1.7. *S.S.* (4.10, F.) **Do tables think?** No, because they're not people. **What about trees?** They don't think. Only thing trees can do is grow. **Do dead people think?** Yeah. **About what?** Things that they do. . . . **Does a dead person have a mind?** Yeah, because it's a person.

1.8. *I.M.* (6.0, M) **Anything else the mind does?** It can think. **How does it think?** I've had enough of this mind stuff. . . . I don't want to talk about this. I want more about my body.

When we turn to mind–body relations at this level, we are confronted with a kind of "head–body dualism," defined in terms of gross physical features of the person (1.9). While the cephalic and central location of the mind gives it a measure of power (it "thinks what to do"), the body is still able to make its own contribution. It "helps" in moving (1.9) and acts to some degree autonomously (1.10).

1.9a. *M.I.* (6.9, F) **What is the body?** The body is something that does stuff. Like, if there was no body on me, I would only have a head. And my head would be bouncing around with no arms, and it won't be able to do anything. My body helps me walk, touches, and helps me pick up stuff. If I had no arms like this (she shows her arms), and no body, all that will be left is the head.

1.9b. *M.I.* (6.9, F) **How are the mind and the brain related to the body?** Well, they are in the head, and the head is on the body. The head is on the neck, and the neck is on the body. And the body can walk on the floor, or it stays in bed or something.

1.10a. *D.P.* (4.4, F) **Did that man without a head have a mind?** No. **So what could he do?** He could move, cook, steal, walk. **Could he think?** No.

1.10b. *S.S.* (4.10, F) **What do you dream with?** My arm. With everything. I just do. . . . **What do you think with?** Anything. **Your hands?** Yeah. . . . **What's the mind?** (No response) **What's it used for?** (No response) **Do you use it when you run?** No. **Could you run without a mind?** Couldn't. You'd run around in a circle. **Do you need a mind to run?** No.

1.10c. *M.F.* (7.2, F) **What could I do if I had no mind or brain?** You'd just be walking around. **Could I walk to the store?** Yes. Anywhere.

Without anything specifically corresponding to a mind–body dualism, it is scarcely surprising that thought is not necessarily confined to the head. It exerts its influence in a quasi-physicalistic fashion, so that it may spread throughout the body. (1.2b, 1.11a, 1.11b, partially 1.11c) and can even pass out of the body (1.12). Thinking does not even necessarily originate in a brain (1.1e).

Finally, correlative with these other properties, thinking tends to be reified as "thoughts," as feeling is reduced to molecular "feelings." The child is open to the spatial quality (1.11c) and visibility of these elements, or at least their potential visibility (1.13).

1.11a. *I.M.* (6.0, M) **Can your thoughts be in your body?** Yeah. The blood takes them. **Can your thoughts be outside the body?** No. **Why not?** Because they're all locked up. They can't get through my mouth. My breath is crowded with germs.

1.11b. *A.H.* (5.4, M) **Are thoughts just in our brain, or do they go anywhere else?** They go everywhere else. **Where?** Everywhere.

1.11c. *K.Y.* (9.9, F) **(After you had a thought) is that thought there?** I don't think so. That'd probably take up all the space, and you'd probably think of something else. . . . It just pops out of your brain. I don't know exactly where it goes. It probably goes down in your body. But it wouldn't be out of your body because then you'd forget the whole thing. . . . **Could it be in your body?** No, only the mind. . . . Because all the places are took up. . . . Well, I don't know why it can't go into the body.

1.11d. *E.E.* (8.8, M) **Where does the sad feeling come from?** Your brain. And it goes down to your stomach. **It does?** I don't know. It might not. **How could it get from the brain to the stomach?** It goes through your sinuses. . . . **Where does it start?** In your ears, because you have to hear someone tease you or something. . . . **What happens if someone makes you mad?** You hit her. **And then what happens to the feeling?** Goes away, through your fist. **Is it all gone then?** Well, the feeling may go to somebody else. Maybe some of it to her.

1.12. *M.F.* (7.2, F) **What are thoughts made of?** Dreaming. Dreams are just like thoughts. But they go out of your head. **Do thoughts go out of your head?** Yeah, sometimes. When you're thinking really very hard. **Why?** Because when you're thinking light, it's in your head, because it's light air. But when you're thinking really hard, it's heavy, heavy, heavy. So your brain can't hold any more, because it's getting bigger, and bigger, and bigger. Blast your head off. It's little when you're thinking light.

1.13a. *A.H.* (5.4, M) **Where are thoughts?** In our brain. **If I cut open your head, could I see your thoughts?** (No response) **What if I had special X-ray glasses, could I see your thoughts?** Yes. **What would they look like?** I don't know.

1.13b. *G.A.* (5.3, M) **Could I see thinking?** No. **What if I were a surgeon, and I opened up your head. Could I see it?** No. **Why is that?** We'll have a try then. My sister has a torch. You could see down there.

1.13c. *S.S.* (4.10, F) **What are thoughts?** They're in my head. Can't see them—they would hide. They live is a special place no one can find them.

1.13d. *I.M.* (6.0, M) **What is a feeling?** . . . **What is a happy feeling?** When you're happy you go: (hums and smiles). **What is it?** You go "I like you!" **Where is the feeling?** In my brain. Here. In here. **Can you see it?** No. **Why not?** Because your brain is locked up. And I don't have X-ray vision. **If you did, could you see it?** Yep. **What would it look like?** It would look like little blood vessels twisting around, and feelings going "hmmm, hmmm!" **How are feelings different from thoughts?** They're the same thing . . . **Could you see thoughts with X-ray vision?** Same thing. Blood vessels winding around, and the thought goes, "Grrr, I'll punch you in the mouth!" The thoughts and the feelings: the thoughts and the feelings go "hmmm, hmmm," and then "I'll punch you in the mouth!"

1.13e. *J.B.* (7.6, F) I have a rash there, sometimes when I rub, it hurts, and that's a feeling. **Yeah . . . If I was a surgeon, and I looked inside you, could I see this feeling of hurt or pain?** Sometimes you could and sometimes you couldn't. **What would it look like?** It would look like, I don't know, bumps. You look inside and there's germs.

Level 2

Like Level 1, Level 2 (approximately ages 8–12) is still predualistic, in that there is as yet no division of reality into "mental" and "physical" things. However, all the psychological advances recorded in previous research (Broughton, 1978b) contribute to the progressive segregation of "inner" from "outer" worlds, despite the fact that this differentiation remains far from complete. In brief, Level 2 can be seen as taking the issues and problems raised at Level 1 to their logical conclusions, thus preparing and clarifying conceptual conflicts or "embarrassments" that can only be resolved by a major shift of emphasis (Levels 3 and 4). Level 2 deals with the nature of the "mind–brain," develops the first differentiation of mind from body, and establishes a hierarchical relationship between these. The inner world's visibility and persistence come under further question, and the reification of thinking declines.

The term "mind" enters the spontaneous vocabulary. It is distinguished from "life," as in Schecter's second level of consciousness (Table 8.1) and is confined to human beings (or animals). The notion of mentality is still limited to the mind of an individual person as related to the individual body. However, this relationship tends to be construed as universal. In addition, the prominence of an *anatomical* interpretation of mind as a physical property (e.g., in terms of "head") is replaced by a *biological* conception of a cephalic *organ*. It is just another body part but "a lot smarter than the other parts of your body," (*C.S.*, 10.2, M).

One of the questions most perplexing to the Level 2 thinker is how "mind" is related to "brain." Unlike Level 1, Level 2 offers a specific and complex organization for conceptualizing this psychophysical problem. There are three alternative ways to "organify" mind: (*a*) by positing it as a separate organ with an integrity of its own (2.1); or (*b*) by denying the distinction and identifying it with the brain (2.2); or (*c*) a combination of (*a*) and (*b*) (2.3).

The second position (*b*) is an apparently ambiguous one. On the one hand, it seems to amount to a failure to differentiate mind from brain. On the other hand, it reflects the cognitive maturity of being able to differentiate between things and symbols. An understanding has emerged that just because there are two words does not mean that there are necessarily two referents; the terms may be synonymous.

2.1. *L.B.* (9.11, F) Mind and brain are like together in the same place. They like work together, because your brain also gives you signals to do something . . . You could work with just a brain, but you wouldn't be thinking much things. Well, the brain thinks, but it doesn't have much feelings. . . . **Could a brain surgeon see the brain?** He could see the brain. Not the mind I don't think. I don't know. Like I guess you could see the mind. **What would it look like?** Oh messed up and curled together with the brain. **The mind is harder to see?** Yeah, because the brain's bigger. **How small is the mind?** It's got to be small enough to fit in your head, so it would probably be 3 or 4 inches.

2.2a. *J.W.* (10.0, F) **What is the mind?** The brain. **The same thing?** Yeah. **Is it different from the brain at all?** I don't think so. **Why are there two words then?** So people can use two different words. So if they don't understand the other word, they can talk about the other word.

2.2b. *M.I.* (6.9, F) **With what do you think? With the brain or the mind?** They mean the same thing. **Are the brain and the mind the same?** Yes. **Exactly the same?** N—, yes. Like they mean the same thing. **Do we have a brain and a mind?** No. Brain is a mind. **Brain is a mind?** Brain is a mind, and mind is a brain. They mean the same. **When the surgeon operates on the head, what does he see?** He sees the brain. The brain is also the mind. They are same thing. They are not two things stuck together, but they are one whole thing. They mean the same thing. And both those words are the same. They just sound different. Like "mind," "the brain," are different words, but they mean the same.

2.3. *C.S.* (10.2, M) **What is your mind?** It's just the thing that keeps me living, helps me to know things. Keeps me living. **What kind of thing is it? Can you describe it?** You mean touch and look? **OK. Anyway you can describe it.** Well, it's kind of membrane that has veins and cells and nerves to help you feel things and see. **How does it help you feel things?** Because it's a lot smarter than the other parts of your body . . . . The brain is making you do all those things. It makes you think, it makes you move, play. **The *brain* does that?** Yeah. **Same thing as mind?** Really a different thing. The mind is the part of the brain, the mind is where you think, where you have all your knowledge. The brain sort of takes it all in. OK. **Where is the brain?** The brain is the mind. It's all joined together, like a double exposure.

Solutions that compromise between alternatives (*a*) and (*b*) (2.4, 2.5) are to argue that the mind is a more or less demarcated area *within* the brain or that "mind" and "brain" are the names for the *two sides* of a single organ. The latter position (which could be seen as a kind of concrete precursor of the "double aspect" theory) need not necessarily be exclusive of the former (2.5).

2.4. *P.S.* (9.7, M) **What is the mind?** It's something that thinks and transmits messages, and that's about it. **What is the brain?** The mind. The mind is part of it. **Which part?** The part that thinks, makes you decide. **What does the rest of the** brain do? It helps the body, sets the pulse. **Are the mind and the brain the same thing?** They aren't the same thing. **Is the brain part of the body?** Yes. **Is the mind part of the body?** Yes . . . . **What is the self?** My body. **Is your mind part of your self?** Yes. **They're not the same thing?** No. Because my mind is much uglier than myself . . . . It is like your brain.

2.5. *K. W.* (9.5, M) **Could you see the mind?** If you took away the skin you can. **What would it look like?** Like whatever the guy imagines or thinks. **What would it look like?** Probably like the brain . . . . The mind is part of the brain because the brain is very strong, and pretty big, so it can hold both. The mind is big and the brain is big. There are two separate parts with a line down the middle. They are both attached, so one part is for seeing, and a big part is for thinking . . . . Parts of the brain could be on one side, and the imagination in the mind could be over here . . . . If the brain wasn't there, the mind couldn't figure out a math problem. All you could do is imagine the rain—you couldn't know where to go.

At Level 1, where mind was confused with brain, any distinction between them was on the basis of gross morphology. At Level 2, if mind is not equated with brain (whether it is seen as a separate organ or not) there are attempts at differentiating the *functions* of the two (2.1 and 2.4). While it is difficult to draw black and white conclusions, there appears to be something like a general consensus on what mind and brain can do. There is a tendency to see mind as images (imagining and dreaming), whereas brain has a more executive function. Regarding the legislative function, there is no consensus on which of the two does the thinking and deciding, a sign of the fact that mind and brain are still only incompletely differentiated at Level 2. However, the brain appears to take the initiative, keeping the mind informed, and exerting authority over it. Only the brain can figure out things like math problems. (It is hard to resist the speculation that this nascent division of labor reflects the stereotypic one of men and women, dads and moms, or boys and girls!)

Either mind or "mind–brain" is an organ. The fact that it does not yet have mental and physical aspects is evident from a 10-year-old, M.U., who was asked to distinguish the two terms "mental" and "physical" and replied, "Mental like has to do with your brain, and physical has to do with the parts of your body." This corroborates Schecter's and Asch and Nerlove's (1960) findings that children in this age range are unable to understand metaphorical (psychological) uses of physical terms, as in expressions like "hardheaded" or "softhearted." The mind–body does not yet really have a mental aspect differentiated from the physical. It is just another body part (2.3, 2.4), and as a part, it is less complex than the whole (2.6). It is, however, a regulating part, an organ that "organ-izes," whose relation to the rest of the body is reminiscent of the brain's relation to the mind (2.7). It is personalized, like a relation between master and slave. This hierarchical organization is expedient, since without it the wayward enslaved body might stray (2.8).

2.6. *K.Y.* (9.9, F) Bodies are more difficult than minds. Because a body has lots of difficult things, but a mind is only one thing. It doesn't have a heart or anything. But it's alive.

2.7a. *L.B.* (9.11, F) The mind tells the whole body what to do. It's the controller. . . . It uses all of your body for doing things.

2.7b. *J.W.* (10.0, F) The mind tells the body . . . . It says "Go over there," and it tells you what to do.

2.8a. *C.S.* (10.2, M) **How do we know that the mind is there?** Because if you didn't have a mind, you wouldn't be sane. You wouldn't have anything to control yourself.

2.8b. *G.S.* (9.4, M) **Does the mind control the self or the self control the mind?** . . . A little. Like if the mind didn't control the self, you would jump right out the window any day . . . . The mind controls you, tells you not to jump out the window.

While the mind–brain is being distinguished as a specific, visible bodily organ within the head, its contents undergo differentiation from their container and are construed as invisible (2.9). While we could say that "mind" was still reified, the reification of mental contents diminishes as they are differentiated from mind. One result is that they are no longer able to move freely outside the mind (2.10).

2.9. *G.S.* (9.4, M) Only thoughts can disappear . . . It's not the same thought. You can't have it again. It's gone by. **Why does it disappear?** Well a thought isn't really a thing. It's just an invisible thing sort of. Well no, it's just not there like. Well yeah, it's there. It's just not like a solid thing. It's not a real thing . . . They don't really disappear; they just go away. You just don't think any more. Just like you burn a leaf, then it's gone. But it isn't gone—it's ashes . . . . It's just going to a different place.

2.10. *G.S.* (9.4, M) **Where are thoughts?** Brain. **Anywhere else?** Anywhere. Come out in words and stuff. **Can a thought go into your body?** It can go into your body too. **How does it do that?** Your brain makes it. **Can it go into your leg?** I guess so. You think you're going to the candy store, and it goes into your legs, and you walk. Well it can't go into your leg, because your leg can't think. It just tells the leg to walk to the candy store. **Why can't the leg think?** It doesn't have a brain.

The "invisible" is not an easy conceptual acquisition. A crude idea of *events*—things happening—is opposed to the concept of solid *things* and allows for some understanding of the reality of thought despite its transitory nature. "You can't pick it up because a thought isn't solid," said *K.W.* (9.5, M), "but it's solid in your mind—it stays there." Yet disappearance is hard to comprehend. Images of transformation elide with notions of thoughts as special things that "go some place" (*J.F.*, 9.9, F) "to a different place" (2.9), an idea that is now problematic since the conceptualization of thoughts at Level 2 limits them to remaining inside the mind. Thoughts are still *things* happening. Thoughts are the "thing-event." As yet there is no *process* distinguishable from the discrete thought entities, and so there is no persistence attaching to some faculty of *thinking*. By Level 2, psychological things are beginning to be segregated from physical ones. However, as yet there is no domain of the "psychological" per se that is the object of contemplation. Presumably, this is the reason that there is no need for a concept of a mind that is something really different from the brain.

Level 3

Level 3 (age 13 up) is qualitatively very different from Level 2, since it is the first truly dualistic level. The concepts of the "mental" and the "physical" start to emerge as something shared, extending beyond the individual mind and body. They are more like general classes of things. The terms are used spontaneously (3.1).

> 3.1a. *J.F.* (13.11, M) **What is the self?** The self as a person? I guess it is just what you are. **The self as a person, what does it include?** Probably his mind. He has certain things—his mind, his way—and that is his self. He is different as far as I know . . . . **Is your mind and self the same thing?** Yeah. That is talking mentally, not physically. **What is the difference?** Mental—the self would be how you think. And physically would be mostly if you got a broken leg. And that is your self because not too many other people might have that . . . . The physical self is sort of just the way you are—biologically.

> 3.1b. *C.H.* (13.8, F) The brain is the part of me where the mind is. Mind is part of the brain, *is* the brain. I don't know if you could cut it out. Maybe the mind isn't the instinctive things. I would consider it the whole brain . . . . I have never thought of the mind as a solid thing. I think of it as like a cover round the brain, taking out messages and stuff. You can't say "There is the mind," because it is the whole brain I think. **It isn't solid?** No. Spiritual maybe? That means not solid, not gas, not something you can grab. It's not there! Well, it is not *bodily* there. You couldn't prove it either, because it is not there. You could not prove that we have a spirit. You could not do tests on it or anything because it isn't physically there. Because all our tests are made to test something solid . . . . Maybe the mind is something you *can* hold on to. We have to say that it is something.

This common-sensical quality tends to bring the general classes of mental and material back to the individual level again. However, the concepts of individual mind–brain and mind–body relationships have also undergone change. The mind is no longer seen as a body part or organ. It *is* the brain, but in a new and more differentiated sense (3.1b). It is distinguished from the brain as an invisible faculty, presence, or activity: what the whole brain is *doing* (3.2a).

This notion extends the thing–happening distinction of Level 2. There is now a *general* notion of activity not just a set of particular functions as in the "division of labor" model at the last level. This activity can therefore be construed generally as *energy* (3.2b).

> 3.2a. *A.B.* (14.1, M) **How do you know you have a mind?** Did we clarify the mind is the same thing as the brain? I mean the brain is an actual thing, but the mind is what goes on in the brain . . . . The mind is what the brain does.
>
> 3.2b. *J.F.* (13.11, M.) Put the mind in the verbal form, the brain in the noun form . . . . The brain is your mind. Your mind is what you do in your brain. Like your mind, you think. The brain is the matter itself. The mind is more the energy thing. You can't see energy, but you can see matter. Energy is in matter, but matter isn't in energy. Like there is no such thing as a solid mass of energy, but there is a solid mass of matter. **How is the energy in the matter?** The energy is what makes it work, right? Gasoline makes a car engine work. **But gas is matter.** Right. But put the two matters together creates energy.

Commensurate with the description of mind as activity is the emphasis on the volitional and intentional qualities of mind (cf. Schecter's Level 4 of consciousness in Table 8.1). Primarily, mind intends and initiates action. "It is everything you do," in the words of *M.G.* (14.0, F). "And like voluntary control of the body, the mind controls everything the body does," says *C.H.* (13.8, F). While the predominant motif is still the unilateral control of mind over body as at Level 2, mind is not just brain—it involves a willful evaluative component. "With our mind we can make our own judgments, and do what we feel is right" (*M.G.*). *A.B.* says, "Everything you do is controlled by your mind. It decides between alternative ways of doing it, on the basis of their consequences." *M.L.* (17.6, F) says, "Your mind tells you, is it right for me to walk right now, or should I just stay here?" Mind is conscious thoughts, opinions, ideas, decisions, and ideals, pragmatically oriented, which prescribe the right and wrong things to *do*. It is deliberate, and it deliberates.

Since there is as yet no independent mental substance in its own right, mind is often negatively defined as "not-body." To borrow a phrase from a precocious 10-year-old (*A.J.*, M), it is "the something which is nothing." When asked what the mind is, *S.R.* (13.9, F), for example, says, "The mind is made up of everything you do that isn't physical." *A.B.* says, while pondering the ontology of thinking, "Thoughts are not physical as far as you're not telling a part of your body to do anything. That's what I consider physical." While the reality of mind is often less secure than the reality of the visible body, the mental as will has a power over the physical that for the first time makes it central in defining the person, and the world. "The mental outwits the physical," says *A.B.* *M.L.* even goes so far as to say that the "real body *is* the mind," and *M.G.* echoes the sentiment by saying "the body is just an outer layer of the mind." Mind represents unlimited potential, whereas the body represents limitation (3.3).

3.3a. *M.C.* (18.4, F) The mind does whatever it feels like doing. It can think whatever it wants . . . . I guess people are afraid to use all of their mind . . . . If people used all of it, forget it! . . . . Like you know, all these walking geniuses, they come walking around, be kind of afraid to go against each other, a battle of the minds.

3.3b. *J.F.* (13.11, M) **Can the body control the self?** I don't think so. It can restrict it if you have a handicap. No, not really. I think it can restrict itself. When you are talking about the body you are talking about the physical self. And I think the physical self can't stop the mental self from doing anything.

Mind as the voluntary, or as an expression of individual will, is essentially variable. "Mind things can change a lot more easily than body things" (*S.R.*, 13.9). The physical is "how it works," the "scientific," the "mechanical thing" that does the "functioning." Matter, in the body as elsewhere, has a universal standardized quality. It is the involuntary. "Your body is just something your self is telling you to do" (*M.C.*, 18.4, F). As such, it is less unique to the individual and therefore less the *self* (3.4).

3.4. *J.F.* (13.11, M) Everybody that is living has a beating heart. **Is that part of your self?** It is, but it is mandatory. It had better be beating. **Does that make it less your self?** Yes, it does, because it is the way you *have* to exist . . . . **What parts of the body are most your self then?** I guess it is the part that you use whenever you make what you do. Like an Olympic runner runs if he likes to run. It is what makes him do what he wants to do.

This dualism of the voluntary and involuntary does not work very well, because it is admitted that there are parts of the mind that control the involuntary functions. These parts (probably conceptual precursors of the subconscious) "know by the habit of the body what to do," says *S.R.*, who later refers to them as "the self's body" (3.7). These parts are excluded from the self, or even from the mind (3.1b), since mind and self are first and foremost conscious will.

3.5. *A.B.* (14.1, M) **What is the self?** The self is an individualized person. Everyone has their own style. That's my idea of a personality . . . their own style of doing things. Maybe the way they think about people, the way they become socialized, the way they work. If they don't want to work, they don't work, you know . . . . It's a section of your mind. **What's the rest of your mind?** Coordinating movements and all kinds of stuff—heart-pumping and so on . . . . Your functions . . . I don't think they are part of your self. They're part of your physical self, not part of your mental self.

With the emergence of the conceptual dichotomy of the voluntary and the involuntary (choice and matter, the spontaneous and the predictable) and the admission of the self's mental–physical duality (3.1a) comes a preferential identification of the self with the voluntary parts of its mental moiety. The mind is naturally variable and resists uniformity. It reacts, opines, values, etc., thereby creating mental contents that are *unique* to the individual (3.1a, 3.5). Also unique and individual is the overall "style" (*A.B.*), "way" (*J.F.*), "way the mind works" (*C.G.*), "mental state" (*S.R.*) These terms betoken a new conceptualization of mind as dispositional, a possibility created in parallel with the concept of thinking as part of an invisible mental medium, a process irreducible to discrete thoughts.

The mental stands out from the material by virtue of its inherent variability. It is the concrete embodiment of metaphysical individuality. "Everyone has to have a mind to be different. To know what you're doing, to think about what you're going to do. I mean a person has . . . got to have a mind to be different" (*A.B.*). It is not enough that the mental stand out from the material. The individual mind qua mental self must also stand out from the uniform mentality of the crowd. "Mental means applying the thinking cap to decide for yourself," said a 20-year-old student interviewed in Ghana. Otherwise, the self becomes mere habit, a copy, a pale imitation, a not-self. The individuality and uniqueness of what *I* think, and the active demonstration of *my* beliefs, is the major criterion that separates the real inner self from the phony, conforming outer self. Much as the standardized quality of the material world threatens the identity of the parts of the mind that control the physical self, so too the standardized human world of fads and customs threatens the authenticity of that part of the self that engages others (3.6). The new "dispositional" self includes a dangerous disposition to be disposed toward others. The self "for-itself" is segregated as sacred and private from the profane, public self "for-others". The latter "outer" self is usually called "personality". Through the separation of true self from personality, the nascent dualism of mental and physical intersects with a simultaneously emerging morphology of inner and outer *and* the dualism of noumenal and phenomenal—essence and appearance. The outer appearance is seen as vulnerable to manipulation and, in this respect, is like inert matter, merely "the shell for the mind" (*M.G.*). Here then, the physical pole and the apparent pole converge. These three metaphysical dualisms of mind–body, inner–outer, and reality–appearance are therefore inextricably embroiled in an epistemological conundrum: How can I know the other, and how can I be known? At this level, knowledge starts to involve a notion of interpersonal sharing, but it is precisely this kind of objectivity that when applied to knowledge of persons threatens to violate the sanctity of the self. The objective and public is the not-self.

3.6a. *J.M.* (16.00, F) I think that religious people feel that you're given a soul, by God or something . . . . There's an outside force that's controlling your personality or your mind or whatever . . . . **Personality or mind? Are those the same things?** Um, well your mind is something inside. Your personality is inside but, yet it's what you show to the outside . . . . There are certain things we can't show to the outside, whether we're aware of it or not . . . because they don't want other people to find out certain things about them . . . . It just happens that certain things you keep inside and certain things you don't. **Can you ever know what someone is like on the inside?** No, not completely . . . . We have no way of judging on the inside . . . . So the only thing we have to go by is what's on the outside, which is personality.

3.6b. *M.C.* (18.4, F) **What is the self?** Being yourself, acting natural . . . not phony . . . . The self is something you want people to see. It's natural in one way and phony in another. I mean I think everybody is really phony, but you're try- ing to act natural. The mind . . . is what you really think inside of you . . . and sometimes you're scared to say. And the self is something you kind of like im- itate.

How is the adolescent dualism of mind and body mediated? In this first level of dualism, which Baldwin calls "immature dualism," there is a certain slippage between mind and body (3.7), a continuation of the idea of power and freedom of the mind. This entails, in compensation, a form of attachment or dependency between mind and body (3.8).

3.7. *S.R.* (13.9, F) Some people can take themselves out of their body. They can still feel it—it is your self's body, not your physical body. **How can the self do that?** Maybe if the conscious and the self-conscious got together and really con- centrated on it . . . . The self sort of goes like the thoughts of the body. It's not tied down by a physical body, so it sort of wanders around.

3.8. *C.H.* (13.8, F) The mind is not connected with the body. I imagine it as a halo-type thing. It can't be connected with the body, because it's not really there. It's not physical or anything. It could be reincarnated or something. **Why doesn't it move about when you're alive?** It has a responsibility. Without the mind, there wouldn't be anything here. I guess it keeps the blood flowing. It stays as long as it is supposed to. And the body probably has some set limit, you know, as to how long it's got to stay.

Unity may also be achieved in use, where mind and body need each other (3.9), and you *have* to "get it together."

3.9a. *S.R.* (13.9, F) **So there are mental and physical?** Yeah. They sort of go together . . . . People are made up of minds and bodies. But when you put them together, you get a so-called person, that can use them together, and not a separate thing apart . . . . You are around other people and other things. You have to put together your actions from your body and mind to make them work, and make them do things that you want to do, using both.

3.9b. *C.H.* (13.8, F) It is hard to get it together, so you have everything com- bined, where you can't have a distinction. When you are doing things, I guess, is getting your mind together, body together.

There is a contingent quality to the connection, reflecting an incompleteness in the differentiation of one from the other. Mental and physical are still seen as two different things at roughly the same level of existence. This is perhaps the reason that *J.F.* (3.2b) still sees "energy" as a kind of rarefied matter. There is a physical "something" and a mental "something which is nothing," a rather mysterious state of affairs that predisposes one to a speculative and mystical outlook (3.7, 3.8). This could be related perhaps to the "pre-Renaissance" vitalism mentioned at the beginning of this chapter, which is apparent in Schecter's fourth level of life concepts (ages 12–14).

In sum, there are parts of the body that have a mental quality (the "private body," including feeling and psychosomatic phenomena) and, conversely, there are bodily aspects to mind (e.g., its primary function of imitating voluntary action, its nonconscious and involuntary parts, and its relative unreality until expressed in action). One needs the concept of "mind" to fill out the concept of "body" and vice versa. As a result, their common characteristics make separating them difficult. The overlap is reified in terms of a loose dependency between actual minds and bodies. Thus when *J.F.* said, "I need my mind for my body and my body for my mind," he might just as well have been talking about his own problems in concept-formation, rather than the objective realities themselves.

Level 4

As we have seen, the relatively stable and consistent network of mind–body concepts at Level 3 leaves a variety of profound contradictions and paradoxes. The core of these is the incomplete differentiation of mental from physical, an "immature dualism" that intersects with equally indecisive dualisms of reality and appearance, and subjectivity and objectivity. At Level 4 (late adolescence, early adulthood), these dualisms mature, bringing to a head the nascent problematic of early adolescence.

A full-blown Cartesian dualism arises, positing two completely separate and mutually exclusive systems or categories of substance, through which the world is to be exhaustively interpreted. The body, including the personal body of feeling and sensation, passes over to the material side. This physical world now gains an internal structure and a certain autonomy, by virtue of being regulated by a fixed scientific order of mechanical cause–effect relations spoken about in a language of force (4.1).

4.1. *V.F.* (26, F) I believe in action–reaction. Something happens, something caused it. And that is a whole world view.

Level 4 attempts to find an orderly connection between the two halves of reality, but this is made problematic by their mutually exclusive relationship. The mental half remains a source of puzzlement (4.2).

4.2a. *V.F.* (26, F) There is something that goes on in your mind that is real, at the basic level of electron flows, something that is happening and is real. Now I don't know how to trace from an electron flow to an idea in my mind. The conclusion is that the one is the cause of the other, and therefore I think it is real . . . . The electron thing is real. It is measurable, and it is a reaction, a thing. I believe if I can do calculus in my mind, that it is associated, it is a reaction to that electron flow, and therefore it is real. It is a belief. I believe it, but I can't prove it . . . . Maybe the mind is part of the brain we don't understand.

Elsewhere she distinguishes from the "physical reality of the self," the "metaphysical" or "intellectual reality." Another young woman, describing thoughts, also finds that the intellect resists physical interpretations (3.2b).

3.2b. *M.L.* (22, F) There are chemical things. And a mental thing, too, which is the actual picking over of the thought, the memory. The dissections and putting back together again. The idea of thoughts is more romantic than just chemicals.

Knowledge is defined as a scientific kind of understanding, which means that the spiritual, nonscientific mental world is hard to know and has a mysterious, vitalistic, noumenal, and religious quality. However, unlike Level 3, Level 4 does construe mind as qualitatively different—as a reality in itself, requiring a separate kind of explanation (4.3).

4.3. *W.W.* (22, M) From my point of view, the brain is the physical machine that makes the mind go. If you believe in life after death, if you believe in a soul, then the brain is kind of like a physical explanation to satisfy people about the definition of the mind. And the mind is something above that. I don't know if I believe that . . . . No one quite understands how it works. I don't think we'll ever find out. It's something to do with electric charges in the brain. It's incomprehensible to me that electric charges could do that, but it seems more logical than the mind just being because God made it so. **The mind is electricity?** It's something beyond that . . . . It's far beyond electricity . . . . They are just such opposite things: electrons on the one side, and mental images on the other. No one knows how they're joined. There are scientific explanations for it, mechanical explanations. They can tell you how it happens but not why.

While *W.W.* and others engage in attempts to explain the mind in quasi-mechanistic terms, talking of sensory "information" and "coding," their psychological empiricism runs into contradictions, since sensation falls on the *physical* side not the mental (compare M. Bakan's chapter in this volume). The mental is still something bigger or more real, "above" the mundane physical reality, which is bound by certain earthly limits. This is reflected in part of a discourse about truth (4.4).

4.4. *E.L.* (22, F) Certain chemicals always in the same proportions do the same things. And you know that's so, and there's just no way to refute it. That is somehow a physical truth I guess. A chemical physical truth . . . . When you get into big things, things aren't always one way or the other. Mental things you can't always say black or white . . . . You can know every aspect of the chemical. Whereas to me you just can't know every aspect of a person.

What is this additional quality? The common response at Level 4 is that it is logical order (4.5).

4.5a. *V.F.* (26, F) Type of thinking is, probably. The way a person uses or doesn't use logic. A type of planning. A way of running your life or not running it.

4.5b. *B.C.* (22, M) The way your mind puts things in a logical progression—thought patterns . . . . I think the self is the life force in a logical progression. **Is that the same thing?** Well, no. Life force is the thing that motivates you, but the logical progression is just the intellect, the thought processes of the self.

This inner cognitive self is quite separate from the bodily self (4.6a). It is the soul, the noumenal essence or being of someone (4.6b).

4.6a. *B.C.* (22, M) I mean the body for me is just an appearance, is just a shadow. It's the living force inside you know, the ideas that emanate that are the self.

4.6b. *J.F.* (18, M) **What is the self?** I don't know. The self, you can describe it as the *soul* of one, the inner thing that makes him go . . . . giving you a reason for being . . . . The soul is completely separate. It is so much higher up than any of them.

The self as soul has been differentiated from the mind and is a purer more abstract or more logical part of mentality:

4.6c. *J.F.* (18, M) It is something more than the mind, is all I can say. It goes deeper. Say it is the psyche . . . . The mind seems to be straightforward; a person has to have depth to him . . . I think there is a soul, mental, and physical self . . . . The soul does seem to be separated from the mental and physical . . . . The soul is completely separate. It is so much higher up than any of them, because the mind cannot comprehend the soul . . . . If you believe in God, it is closer to God . . . . Then every thought that every person in the world has, no matter how much of a genius he is, God is always higher than him because he gives him the genius thoughts.

The notion of "soul" is a two-edged sword. While each soul individuates someone as a separate monad, all people have souls, and the spiritual substance thus defines a common, fused "personhood." *J.F.* says, "Because you are part of mankind, your thoughts are always related to someone else's thoughts." There is a potential here for absorption into some reified "group mind," a pre-established harmony uniting the "windowless monads" (4.7a).

4.7a. *M.L.* (22, F) The mind, you talk about philosophies of the mind. You don't talk about philosophies of the brain. Because the mind refers to something that in addition to the brain has a larger, has the thoughts of people past . . . . We are prone to attribute large movements to a Mind of man. Hitler's Mind . . . a philosophy that can be attributed to the whole . . . . The opinions of his mind along with the opinions of other like-minded individuals to produce the Hitler Mind . . . . The mind is a larger thing that may encompass more than just one or two people.

This calls for some segregation of you as self, as identity, as she goes on to point out:

4.7b. *M.L.* (22, F) Especially in today's world, people tend to think of mankind as being a mass. Mass society, mass communications, mass media. There has to be a part that takes it apart from that huge mass, that can bring you alone with yourself. To be able to do that is confirmation that there is indeed individuality in the world and that there is still a self.

What keeps the soul or self independent is *B.C.*'s "logical progression" of "thought patterns" (4.5b). The purity of mentality is associated with formal, abstract, or logical intelligence, a quality achieved by segregating mind from the concrete sensory world and from feeling. This organization of the subjective world in terms of rules gives it a reality of its own, and internalized within the self, it lends an individuating quality of will or self-control. As rules embrace their instances, so will tends to unite the self. "The whole controlling the parts is the natural order of things," says *M.L.*, although she admits that "the self being so many parts is ungovernable by itself, and it may be very difficult if one has a very strong will." Thus, in internal structure, self is characterized by the same kind of systematic interrelatedness that typifies mind–body at this level, where the metaphysical problem underlying thought is the relation of whole to parts, mediated through the two poles of "force" (or control) and "law" (logic, or form). By this level, therefore, we have reached the psychological equivalent of the Renaissance cosmology outlined earlier in the chapter.

Level 5

At Level 5, in the early twenties, the acute embarrassments of the Cartesian dualism are temporarily resolved through a monistic materialism that breaks down the dichotomy of substances (5.1).

5.1a. *L.R.* (22, F) **What is the mind?** The mind is the brain, the actual physical brain . . . **It's the same as the brain?** Yeah. **Any difference between mind and brain?** No . . . . Mind is matter that knows how to do tricky things. It is special kinds of cells or something, special chemicals . . . . I would have blamed it on

Plato. Early philosophers invented the division of body from soul . . . . The person is just the physical thing. Nothing metaphysical. There isn't any disembodied life-force, as in Star Trek . . . . Mind is a part, a sort of category of the body. It is one of the parts of the body, like feet.

5.1b. *D.O.* (22, F) I guess there is no such thing as immaterial things . . . . **There are no mental things that are immaterial?** No . . . . The mind is just an extension of the brain.

Self suffers the same fate, being dismissed as a reification:

5.2. *L.R.* (22, F) **What is the self?** I think it is wrong to say you have a self. You are what you see, what the body can do . . . . So I don't really believe in the self. It's a philosophical invention . . . somebody made up to sell deodorant.

With this materialistic turn comes a thoroughgoing determinism. This is well illustrated by a quotation from a young woman who was on a Laker Airways flight en route from London to Kansas for the annual Guru Maharaji festival when I interviewed her and feverishly scribbled down her answers on airsickness bags.

5.3. *D.L.* (22, F) Each person is a puppet of the universe . . . . My total freedom is when I see I am completely a puppet, helpless.

Part of the determinism is biological—one's "higher" activities are reducible to needs and instincts, to "a motivating force . . . where a person is trying to get the most out of his environment" (*J.N.*, 18, M).

Left over as a residue from the individualism of Level 4 is the problem that Schrödinger (1958) has called the "arithmetical paradox"—the fact that the *one* world is concocted from *many* conscious egos or souls (compare Broughton, 1978b). As Schrödinger suggests, the single most obvious solution to the paradox is the unification of minds or consciousnesses, as in the mystical doctrine of the Upanishads. *D.L.* refers to "*the* mind, the eternal mind everyone taps into . . . your whole world being . . . the real totality of love . . . pure form . . . unmanifest energy."

In addition, objects of awareness, previously assumed to be different in nature from the mind aware of them, are now found to have a natural identity with consciousness. "The mind is part of the world," says the Guru's devotee. Thus consciousness and the world are united. Conversely, all being is now consciousness. "Environment and reality are part of your thought processes, which is part of your mind" (*J.N.*, 18, M). Everything becomes one at "that point that is indescribable, where there is no logic" (*D.L.*), which means that mind and matter are united in experience, and knowing is directly contained *in* the very experiencing itself. This means that mind and body, previously sundered and assigned to opposed spheres of existence, the "ghost" and the "machine," are restored to an immediate unity, as are thought and feeling.

"For myself, I experience them linked up," says *D.L.*; "Experience I have with the body is the same as the experience I have with my mind." *J.N.* says, "All experience is a combination of the physical and mental." However, in uniting mental and physical in the moment-to-moment flux of experience, all reality becomes subjective. In this way, the materialistic worldview is supplemented with a subjective idealism [5.4].

> 5.4a. *L.R.* (22, F) I think that everything is totally subjective . . . . Everything you perceive comes from you, is colored by you.
>
> 5.4b. *J.N.* (18, M) Reality is my own belief . . . . It's an expression of self, revealing your truth, an element of yourself.

Since the only reality is in individual, particular, and unique experience, mind may be dismissed completely as too rational and reflective, making unjustified generalizations and falsely separating you from your body, from feeling, and from reality. "It's just a bunch of junk," was *D.L.*'s opinion. "It's just all those things that drive you crazy, 5 million times a minute."

> 5.5. *L.R.* (22, F) It is an extra step that complicates things . . . . [A person] should be able to exist without having to worry about everything he does falling on top of his head . . . . If you were really in tune, you would not need to ask those things.

Existence is a fusion of mind and matter, person and world. Existing thereby comes to completely subordinate knowing, which can only be self-knowledge. This kind of reflectivity implies a self, and therefore even self-knowledge is illusory.

Level 6

As Cassirer (1923, p. 388 f.) points out, the scepticism that we have just seen in Level 5 dissolves reality in appearance and despairs of reaching the absolute "things" because the world requires those things to be put into relation with minds or perceivers for them to be known. The despair felt, however, reflects a tacit belief that there *might* have been essences or substances and that they would have been the only alternatives to "mere abstractions." *L.R.* had said, for example, "There could be an unsubjective reality, [but] that would not matter to anyone because no one would be able to see it." What Level 6 realizes is that nature does not consist of things, but of *laws*. While physical reality was "lawful" at Level 4, at Level 6 there is a reflective *concept* of law, which can then be applied to the mental realm as well, legitimating social sciences in addition to natural sciences. Rather than reducing everything to relations, Level 6 adults see that these laws codify the relations that make up reality. Thus, psychology and physiology as realms of study replace mind and body as substances (6.1).

6.1a. *N.S.* (26, F) Mental and physical are two different systems of description describing me, or my brain. Each have their own laws. They are parallel descriptions of what is happening . . . . Two different ways of describing what's going on in me—neurons firing, or thoughts.

6.1b. *N.B.* (26, M) We come to find out about this one thing in two different ways . . . one by experiencing them, and the other by doing physiology. The laws that apply to mental states are not the same as apply to brain states. You're cutting it up in two different ways.

This position combines the flavors of "double aspect" theory, "psychophysical parallelism," and "predicate dualism." While Level 6 does not imply any one specific philosophic position, and may combine analytic, pragmatic, and idealist assumptions, there are certain recurrent characteristics worthy of note. Like the previous, skeptical level, there is a strong resistance to reifying mind (6.2). However, the mind is no longer equated with the brain (6.3). Instead, it is seen as an emergent level of organization in its own right, for which a physiological level is admittedly necessary but not sufficient.

6.2a. *N.S.* (26, F) Mind is not a thing. It just brings together descriptions of mental processes . . . . There are mental ways of talking, mental explanations, and mental descriptions.

6.2b. *N.B.* (26, M) **What is the mind?** I think the term "mind" is often misused. In fact, I think it is misused when people ask what it is! I think it is correctly used to refer to aspects of mentality or mental states.

6.3a. *J.W.* (26, M) Mind is not material in the same way as the brain is material . . . . It is something else. Psychic. Mind is a phenomenon.

6.3b. *R.B.* (26, M) Mental things have physical determinants. They're dependent upon physical and physiological processes. But they go beyond them . . . they have an existence that is more than truly physical . . . . Henry Miller says the brain is a collander, sifting the vegetables of the mind. The brain is the physical corpus of the mind. The mind is embellished way beyond that.

This is described picturesquely by *J.W.* (26, M), who, combining the strengths of both Levels 6 and 2, said, "The brain is, as we know, the biological seat of the mind—the mind sits on the brain and smokes cigars."

There is a return from the monistic materialism of Level 5 to a dualistic position, but now with an added dimension: the awareness of the problems of dualism itself. Part of this awareness is the wisdom that a purely reductionist solution will not wash (6.4).

6.4a. *R.B.* (26, M) If you want to eliminate everything but physico-chemical processes, you could call that the functions of the brain. That's why there's a problem in reducing the mind to the set of those functions, because there's something beyond.

6.4b. *H.M.* (18, M) You could reduce the human being to body, saying it's all in

the mind, which is something controlled by the body. Or you could start from
the divine, encompassing all of human nature, and say the self is the realm of the
divine . . . . For the time being, I would accept the religious viewpoint.

As a result of nonreductionism, there are more or less complex attempts to
deal with how the psychological and physiological domains are related (6.5).

> 6.5a. *J.W.* (26, M) Every psychological statement has a physiological correlate,
> but what is the chicken and what is the egg there I don't know . . . . There are a
> whole lot of psychological states that make up the physiological
> correlate . . . . Also the reverse: many to one.
>
> 6.5b. *N.B.* (26, M) Things that are mental are also physical and affect other
> physical states, have causal relations with other states which are physical and
> also other states which are mental. Each of these of course is both. It is correct to
> say that mental states affect causally physical states and vice versa, although the
> mental states are also physical states.
>
> 6.5c. *N.S.* (26, F) There is some correspondence of some mind things and some
> brain things . . . . You can't generalize from one system of laws to another.
> Nothing particular is happening in the brain every time I think of Vienna. But if
> you take the different times I think of Vienna, they form an explanatory kind. If
> you took the corresponding brain states, they would not show any neurological
> similarity. There are no explanations going from one level to the other.

Mind and body, rather than mental and physical, are related also through the
notion of "self-consciousness" that emerges at Level 6. This parallels the second historical shift from nature to mind mentioned early in this chapter. Mind
is seen as interpretive, reflecting on experience, part of which is self-experience
and experience of the body (6.6).

> 6.6a. *J.W.* (26, M) Mind opens on to and interprets the world. It is the leading
> edge of the self . . . . It is the effective element of life, the self-conscious part of
> the self.
>
> 6.6b. *H.M.* (18, M) Self is to a degree the way a person thinks of himself. Not in
> physical terms, and not the way he looks at himself in the mirror . . . . Thought
> is always changing, and yet there is something that is very constant about
> it . . . . I am angry at myself means not I am angry at my body, but I am angry
> at the total thing that happened to my body and my thoughts.
>
> 6.6c. *R.B.* (26, M) The flesh and bones—the stuff that your body is made up
> of . . . . The difference between them and the mind and the self is that they are
> not constructed by the self. The body does create itself by the process by which
> the cells divide. Maybe what distinguishes it is that it is not a self-conscious
> process.

Much as mental and physical are seen as psychology and physiology, reflective or conceptual domains, mind and body are construed as reflectively experienced by the constructive, interpreting mind.

Level 7

While Level 6 is the last one for which there is sufficient interview material for an empirical definition, there are reasons to search for a second truly adult level of mind–body metaphysics. If Hegel, Baldwin, Cassirer, and Piaget are to be believed, the history of ideas runs sufficiently parallel to cognitive development that we can generate potential stages of thought from what we know of sequential intellectual periods. Now, the world-view just described, Level 6, has a strong flavor of Kant and Hegel, indicating the possibility that, much as their ideas fell prey to the profound critiques by Feuerbach, Husserl, Marx, and others, Level 6 might suffer a similar fate.

That development might move beyond Level 6 is also suggested by unresolved tensions in the thinking of the subjects we just examined. Those individuals did not succeed in escaping the problems of all dualisms; they simply replaced a dualism of substances with a more comprehensive and powerful dualism of "psychology versus physiology," a methodological dualism. Although moving to this more reflective level permits an account of how mental and physical are related, it leaves open a gulf, yet to be bridged, between psychological and physiological forms of explanation themselves. Moving to the methodological level also raises the possibility of a variety of psychological and biological theories, and yet it affords us no criteria by which to decide between the alternative candidates. Finally, there are problems of an idealistic nature implied by the following characteristics of Level 6: (a) ontology in general is subordinated to epistemology; (b) in the flight from reification, mind and body become aspects of experience, whose concrete existence thereby seems to be cast into question; (c) mind is reduced to a cognitive activity, leaving prereflective emotion, perception, language, and action in some limbo between mind and body; (d) mind, as "meaning-maker," tends to swallow up body, since the latter takes its meaning within mind's interpretation; (e) the very self-consciousness that defines mind's relation to body cannot itself be known and remains unexplained, as does the connection between the self as knower and the self as known.

If it is permissible to indulge in some speculation at the end of this empirical odyssey, it is that ontogeny recapitulates phylogeny and that a seventh level of naive metaphysics, with dialectical, social, and historical emphases, supersedes Level 6. It achieves this by simultaneously criticizing the assumptions behind Level 6 thinking and indicating possible avenues for resolving the contradictions which that thinking embodies. A sketch of Level 7 can be illuminated by excerpts from two rather different interviews with unusually sophisticated individuals, one (P.P., 30, F) a student of Chinese and philosophy, the other (B.B., 38, M) a psychiatrist. An extended section from each interview follows.

> (P.P.) I'm interested in the connection that language has to the stuff that can't be named—tone of voice, gesture and so on. I don't feel that languages do justice to those sorts of experience. Beyond words is the embodied stuff, or the perceptual

stuff. It's like a music . . . . Language doesn't make any sense unless it's embodied. When you interpret words on a page, what you bring to that interpretation is primarily embodied. It's your perspective at the moment, your literal situation . . . one's whole location in a certain time and a certain place . . . a sort of here and now which is felt . . . . If you ask me whether my feelings are more physical or mental, I'd have trouble telling you (laughs). **Can you say something about those kinds of terms, "physical" and "mental"?** Yeah, lots. None of them very good! . . . I think it's quite clear that "mental" is a label for what's conceived of as private or secret. "Physical" is a label for what's conceived of as obvious and public. And I think that's silly, because most of the time I don't think we have trouble knowing when people are having certain feelings . . . people are never blunt objects, they are always in a sort of interpretational context . . . that to me is the crux of the "mind–body problem"—it makes communication between human beings impossible . . . . I don't think it's possible to have a "mental state" without some bodily reaction. **Why is that?** Because I don't think there's such a thing as *the* mind and such a thing as *the* body . . . . I don't believe that there are two separate entities which interrelate. Just because I'm so hostile to idealism I'll say there's "embodiment"—what we call a person's consciousness is embodied . . . . To have a "mental state" is precisely to be embodied. People not as *having* bodies, but as *being* bodies. As I define the mind–body problem, it's primarily a social problem, in this culture.

(*B.B.*) **Where would you want to start?** When I was younger, I used to think about starting with *matter* . . . . As the years have worn on, I think I start more with some kind of critical perspective on the *knowing subject*, the person. It seems to me we only begin with knowledge, and our knowledge of the world is always contingent, not so much upon the world out there, as upon the human world. This is fundamentally a social project, that we are able to abstract from to certain propositions about physical, and indeed metaphysical, qualities . . . . I think the notions of matter etc. are social categories . . . . constructions that we make . . . Space–time coordinates are not social constructions, but they're socially processed, they're historically processed. We think of time and space in terms of how we *occupy* it, how we do things. Those categories of space and time are imposed upon reality, but they also *participate* in it . . . . [These] social constructions in fact represent a certain way in which nature has been *deadened.*

The world is only the world that we know, and this knowledge is arrived at through our senses. But it seemed to me that one had to therefore make a critical analysis of this data . . . a critique from a historical perspective. One that does not assume the distinction of the knower from the known . . . . You can show through a social–historical critique that ordinary discourse is repressed. It's less than what we're capable of . . . . If you're truly in the spirit of critique, you have to be endlessly self-reflective . . . . My psychoanalytic head allows me to make a sort of metacritique of critiques through language. Because after all these are linguistic categories. That's why I think poets have to respect it. I mean when Blake writes something metaphysical he's not only perceiving something, but he's also sort of using that perception to tear through the veil of language.

Marx had a wonderful statement, "The five senses are the work of the whole history of mankind." . . . So that the human world that we have to be critical about is the world that is based upon the emergence of the human from nature, and the transformation of nature. A mutual determination of man and nature, as a result of a direct human activity upon nature . . . . Then the historical critique is based upon the expropriation of that power, because of which nature appears to be much deader than it is . . . . Matter is that part of the world that is worked on. The whole world is invested with human energy, and all that we call human is invested with the history of that energy . . . . The fundamental unit of human discourse is the appropriation of the material reality as is known through sensuousness. And when you introduce that, you introduce a whole conception of consciousness.

While *P.P.* and *B.B.* approach the metaphysics of mind and body in very different ways, their complementarity is indicated by their shared critique of the kind of idealistic thought that we saw in Level 6. Both emphasize the reality and primacy of prereflective experience (the "embodied," the "sensuous") and the secondary and constructive quality of reflective cognition. Both focus upon language and yet stress the importance of a critique that moves beyond its powers of analysis. Both start from a point that does not *assume* the segregation of knower from known but arrives at it. Both depart from individualism toward a view of the person as essentially communicative, as situated in an "interpretational context." As *B.B.* later says, "the reality of the self is the boundary between the sensuous experience of the physical nonhuman world and the linguistically given human world." Both undercut the "mind–body problem" by transforming the initial relation of the person to the world, such that it becomes impossible to talk about isolated individual bodies containing discrete minds, as "ghosts" in "machines." Both understand the relation of mental and physical, as well as our concepts of that relation, to be historically situated within certain social and cultural contexts. These do not lie outside the person, as the relativist would have it, but actually "participate" in the person, who in turn is invested with the whole social history of that embodied mentality. From this position, the idealist claims that the mind's cognitive experience of the world is primary and that body is known only mediately via mind, are undermined, and are exposed as a deadening of nature due to particular historical difficulties encountered by a society that operates through a segregation of private from public. Rather, matter and consciousness are related in those peculiarly human activities of work and communication that transform nature and human nature.

While these two self-reflective interviews indicate possible directions that Level 7 adults might pursue in the interests of an adequate and meaningful psychophysics, their dialectical and historical quality does not resolve all problems. For example, there is the danger at this level of erecting a more subtle dichotomy, one between the "superstructure" of ideas and the cultural "infrastructure" responsible for their form. Much as dialectical materialism and phenomenology have been questioned, and to some extent superseded in the history of Western thought, further empirical examination of Level 7 and its own contradictions may lead us to an extension of the present developmental psychology of metaphysics. This task is made difficult by the convergence it implies between the *telos* of individual development and the frontiers of all human knowledge and experience. The task also demands of psychologists two further qualities: (*a*) an expanded awareness of their own situation in the social and historical and (*b*) a willingness to be "infinitely self-reflective" in a way that will permit their own thoughts, theories, and lives to come under as intense scrutiny as those of their subjects. Under those conditions, it seems possible that the purely cognitive and structural account presented here could be integrated with the concrete life history of the developing individual and with those other spheres of reality—the social and historical—that at one and the same time lie outside and inside the strictly psychological domain.

Conclusion—Psychology and Philosophy

The aim of this chapter has been to empirically demonstrate the existence and development of what Gramsci called "spontaneous philosophy" and to show that the mind–body question is a problem for the layman as well as for the professional philosopher. At the same time, it is hoped that this encourages critical reflection upon the common sense notion of "metaphysics."

While we have attempted to show how concepts of mind, body, self, and soul impinge upon cosmological and theological beliefs at various levels, we have concentrated on that part of genetic metaphysics that has to do with the evolution of psychophysical concepts ("rational psychology") per se. This may appear to involve some inconsistency. On the one hand, we have assumed the validity of an empirical psychological approach in order to illustrate the feasibility of the "continuity thesis." We have "naturalized" metaphysics. On the other hand, we have steadfastly maintained that rational psychology must be distinguished from empirical psychology at the level of the layman's consciousness. We have held to the view that the "ought" of a reasoned worldview that makes philosophical sense cannot be derived entirely from the "is" of psychological facts. This was implied in our initial attempt to contrast metaphysics with epistemology, and genetic metaphysics with genetic epistemology.

Hopefully, the reader who feels the pressure of an inconsistency here can also see that any sleight of hand involved takes place in the above account of how and why individuals move into Levels 5, 6, and 7. Rather than directly reduce the "ought" to the "is," we have argued that the "ought" is an emergent stage of rational organization that develops naturalistically out of the "is" (compare Kohlberg, 1971). While even ancient Greek philosophy *was* philosophy, and had a normative or "ought" component, its purely objective attitude toward existence can still be compared to the purely realistic metaphysics of early childhood. Similarly, Renaissance philosophy's dualistic mixture of mechanism and religion is at least partly homologous with the achievements of adolescent metaphysics. Finally, our adult levels reflect some of the advances of idealistic and materialistic philosophy in the Enlightenment and post-Enlightenment periods.

In the spirit of the Darwinian era, we have "temporalized" the relationship of descriptive and normative. However, we have tried to avoid the fallacy of "later is better" by arguing that higher levels have a progressively greater philosophical adequacy. They are more rational, meaning that they offer a more systematic, comprehensive, and consistent interpretation of the universe within which our experience attains a unity that it cannot reach through undeveloped common sense (the lower levels). These claims would require detailed justification in a separate, more philosophical paper. However, the purpose of presenting interview material and interpretation in such abundance here has been in the interests of showing that such a justification may not be so far off. Thus, using these excerpts, we have tried to show ways in which each level (a) reflects upon the previous one; (b) clarifies distinctions and relations and resolves issues in a way not possible at the previous level; and (c) raises important new questions that become the object of reflective analysis at subsequent levels. Indeed, if we had not demonstrated this, we could hardly claim that what is presented constitutes a "development." We would be open to the accusation that we had dogmatically asserted a hierarchy of philosophical positions legitimated solely by our own preferences, themselves perhaps the mere product of ideological enculturation.

The real structural transformations—the progress hidden amongst the to and fro between nature and mind, objective and subjective—are easier for a *genetic metaphysical* psychology to elucidate insofar as the genesis is claimed to parallel the history of Western thought. The movements of this history have already been the object of intense scrutiny, aimed at deciding (a) what ideas and practices form a whole (Foucault's "epistemé"); and (b) what is to be interpreted as progress (development) and what as repetition or even regress (Döbert, 1973).

In conjuring up such parallels between development and history, a genetic metaphysics may appear to perpetrate a further sleight of hand. When we allude to *formal homologies* between history and development, however partial and tentative, we subtly shirk the responsibility of demonstrating the real structural and functional roots of thought *in* history (Broughton & Riegel, 1977). We run the risk of contradicting our own seventh level, regressing to the ahistorical idealism of Level 6. Remember our Level 7 subjects concurred in interpreting the mind–body problem as primarily a historical phenomenon. They construed it as the product of social categories emerging in a determinate social situation in the context of specific historical events. From their perspective, surely the naturalization of the mind–body problem, by converting it into a set of self-generating cognitive structures, constitutes an unwarranted psychologism.

In our view of time, however, the present does not supplant the past but develops it. Thus, Level 7 should advance beyond Level 6 while preserving its peculiar contributions to truth (its improvements upon Level 5). It is true that our genetic metaphysics employs the "internal dialectic" of Hegelian psychology. By "Hegelian psychology," we mean a developmental rationalism that seems to equate reality with reason and in which new structures seem to emerge entirely out of the logical contradictions of old ones. This is the legacy of Baldwin, and perhaps his Achilles' heel. However, just because stage theories in Baldwin, Piaget, and Kohlberg have failed to integrate psychology with sociology and history does not imply that normative sequences of structural levels necessarily preclude an "external dialectic"—a social and historical context. For example, in the work of Jürgen Habermas (1975, 1976; McCarthy, 1978), we have a dialectical materialist philosophy incorporating Hegelian psychological dialectics as an intrinsic part.

Without normative psychology, Habermas correctly points out, a historical theory of social evolution is itself incomplete. It runs the risk of degenerating into a kind of double relativism—both social and historical—thereby threatening to subvert itself as yet another instrument of ideology (Broughton, 1978c). In fulfilling the Frankfurt School's promise to wed psychology to sociology, Habermas's (1976) revision of social theory has provided firmer grounds for the original intent of Hegel's and Baldwin's developmental–historical project:

> The ontogenetic models are certainly better analyzed and better incorporated than their social–evolutionary counterparts. But it should not surprise us that there are homologous structures of consciousness in the history of the species, if we consider that linguistically established intersubjectivity of understanding marks the innovation in the history of the species which first made possible the level of socio-cultural learning. At this level, the reproduction of society and the socialization of its members are two aspects of the same process; they are dependent on the same structures [p. 5, translated by T. McCarthy].

Our empirical psychological claims about ontogenesis clearly need to be "better corroborated," particularly with longitudinal evidence. However, in addition to this task, it remains to be shown how levels of development such as those outlined here simultaneously generate and reflect the way in which our society's pedagogical and child-rearing practices bring about "the socialization of its members." Even were a real rapprochement between psychology and philosophy achieved, it would be no laurel to rest upon. What is needed is a theoretical integration of metaphysical judgment with its practical origins and consequences. This is something that would require the synthesis of genetic psychology with a historical theory of social evolution and cultural transmission.

At the level of such a synthetic worldview, cognitive structuring of mental and material blends into the sphere of ideology, where false dualisms set up a domination of physical by intellectual labor, female by male, and emotion by rationalization. In this wider ideological context, sustained by family, school, and the political economy of society, theories about normative cognitive structures per se may seem like pale intellectualizations. Nevertheless, it is only through determining what the higher levels of such normatively ordered interpretations are that we could ever identify, encourage, and systematically propagate more reasonable, true, and just ways of relating our minds to our bodies.

Acknowledgments

I would like to acknowledge the help of the following: Larry Kohlberg, who introduced me to Baldwin and the early Piaget; Nelson Goodman, who got me interested in metaphysics; Howie Gruber, who encouraged me to look more closely at the metaphysical content of my data; Bernie Kaplan and Jacques Vonèche, who reassured me that philosophy, intellectual history and psychology had something to do with each other; Barbara Schecter, Lisa Cross, Sara Zarem, and Stephanie Lafarge, who have generously shared their interviews and their ideas with me; Ellen Carni for a careful reading of the manuscript; Liz Gude, Irwin Blumer, Francis McKenzie, and the staff of the Driscoll School, Brookline, Massachusetts, who have made the research possible; and finally Jean Parsons and family, whose hospitality and friendship during 20 or so visits to interview my subjects in Boston has been a constant source of happiness and energy.

References

Adorno, T. W. The stars down to earth. *Telos*, 1974, *19*, 13–90.
Arendt, H. *The life of the mind, Vol. 1: Thinking.* New York: Harcourt, Brace & Jovanovich, 1977.
Asch, S., & Nerlove, H. The development of double function terms in children. In B. Kaplan & S. Wapner (Eds.), *Perspectives in psychological theory.* New York: International Universities Press, 1960.
Baldwin, J. M. *Social and ethical interpretations in mental development.* New York: Macmillan, 1897.
Baldwin, J. M. *Dictionary of philosophy and psychology* (4 vols.). New York: Macmillan, 1902.
Baldwin, J. M. Genetic progression of psychic objects. *Psychological Review*, 1904, 11, 216–221.
Baldwin, J. M. Sketch of the history of psychology. *Psychological Review*, 1905, *12*, 2–3, 144–165.
Baldwin, J. M. *Thought and things, Vol. 1: Functional logic.* London: Swan Sonnenschein, 1906.
Baldwin, J. M. *Thought and things, Vol. 2: Experimental logic or genetic theory of thought.* London: Swan Sonnenschein, 1908.
Baldwin, J. M. *Thought and things, Vol. 3: Interest and art.* London: Swan Sonnenschein, 1911.
Baldwin, J. M. *History of psychology* (2 vols.). New York: G. P. Putnam, 1913.
Baldwin, J. M. *Genetic theory of reality.* New York: G. P. Putnam, 1915.
Bateson, G. Comments on mind and body. *Coevolution Quarterly*, Fall 1976, 56–57.
Berger, P., & Luckmann, T. *The social construction of reality.* New York: Doubleday & Co., 1966.
Broughton, J. M. The development of natural epistemology in adolescence and early adulthood. Unpublished doctoral dissertation, Harvard University, 1974.

Broughton, J. M. The cognitive-developmental model of epistemology and its relation to logical and moral development. Paper presented at biennial meeting of Society for Research in Child Development, Denver, April 1975. (ERIC Document Reproduction Service No. ED 122–923) (a)

Broughton, J. M. Toward a developmental psychology of subject/object concepts. Paper presented at third annual Dialectical Psychology Conference. Toronto, August 1975. (b)

Broughton, J. M. Naive epistemologies. Paper presented at Washington University, St. Louis, February 1976.

Broughton, J. M. The conceptual development of metaphysical and epistemological self. Paper presented at Jean Piaget Society, Philadelphia, April 1977.

Broughton, J. M. The development of concepts of self, mind, reality and knowledge. In W. Damon (Ed.), *New directions in psychology: Social cognition.* San Francisco: Jossey-Bass, 1978. (a)

Broughton, J. M. The developmental psychology of mind/body concepts. Unpublished manuscript, Teachers College, 1978. (b)

Broughton, J. M. Structuralism and critical developmental theory. Paper presented at a Conference on Recent Advances in the Social Sciences, University of Calgary, October 1978. (c)

Broughton, J. M. The divided self in adolescence: "The me nobody knows." *Human Development*, 1980, 4.

Broughton, J. M., & Freeman-Moir, D. J. *The foundations of cognitive-developmental psychology.* Norwood, N.J.: Ablex Publishing Corp., in press.

Broughton, J. M., & Riegel, K. F. Developmental psychology and the self. *Annals of the New York Academy of Science,* 1977, *291,* 149–167.

Cassirer, E. *Substance and function.* New York: Open Court, 1923.

Collingwood, R. C. *Essay on metaphysics.* Oxford, England: Oxford University Press, 1940.

Collingwood, R. C. *The idea of nature.* Oxford, England: Oxford University Press, 1945.

Cross, L. The development in childhood of reflective conceptions of knowledge and reality. Unpublished honors thesis, Harvard University, 1976.

Döbert, R. *Systemtheorie und die Entwicklung religioser Deutungssysteme.* Frankfurt: Suhrkamp Verlag, 1973.

Döbert, R. "Modern religion" and the relevance of religious movements: Pleadings for an evolutionary approach. Paper presented at the second International Symposium on Belief, Baden b. Wien, Germany, January 1975.

Gramsci, A. *Selections from the prison notebooks.* New York: International Publishers, 1971.

Guthrie, W. K. C. *The Greek philosophers: From Thales to Aristotle.* London: Methuen & Co., 1950.

Habermas, J. Moral development and ego-identity. *Telos,* 1975, *24,* 26–37.

Habermas, J. *Zur Rekonstruktion des Historischen Materialismus.* Frankfurt: Suhrkamp Verlag, 1976.

Horkheimer, M. *The eclipse of reason.* New York: Seabury, 1974.

Johnson C. N. & Wellman, H. M. Children's conception of the brain: A developmental study of children's knowledge about cognitive processes. Unpublished paper, University of Pittsburgh, 1979.

Kohlberg, L. Stages of development of physical and social concepts. Unpublished monograph, University of Chicago, 1963.

Kohlberg, L. Stage and sequence: The cognitive-developmental approach to socialization. In D. A. Goslin (Ed.), *Handbook of socialization theory and research.* Chicago: Rand McNally, 1969.

Kohlberg, L. From 'is' to 'ought.' In T. Mischel (Ed.), *Cognitive development and genetic epistemology.* New York: Academic Press, 1971.

Külpe, O. *Introduction to philosophy.* London: Swan Sonnenschein, 1897.

McCarthy, T. *The critical theory of Jurgen Habermas.* Cambridge, Mass.: M. I. T. Press, 1978.

Mead, G. H. *Mind, self and society.* Chicago: University of Chicago Press, 1934.

Mead, G. H. *Movements of thought in the nineteenth century.* Chicago: University of Chicago Press, 1936.

Merleau-Ponty, M. *The structure of behavior.* Boston: Beacon Press, 1963.

Munari, A., Filippini, G., Regazzoni, M., & Visseur, A. S. L'anatomie de l'enfant: Etude genetique des conceptions anatomiques spontanées. *Archives de Psychologie,* 1976, *44,* 45–55.

Naess, A. An empirical study of the expressions 'true,' 'perfectly certain,' and 'extremely probable.' *Avhandlinger Utgitt av det Norske Videnskaps-Akademi I Oslo, II. Historie-Philosophie Klasse,* 1953, *4,* 5–41.

Nowell-Smith, P. Common sense. *Radical Philosophy,* Spring 1974, *7,* 15–16.

Piaget, J. *The child's conception of the world.* New York: Harcourt, Brace, 1929.

Piaget, J. *The child's conception of physical causality.* London: Routledge and Kegan Paul, 1930.

Piaget, J. Children's philosophies. In C. Murchison (Ed.), *Handbook of child psychology.* Worcester, Mass.: Clark University Press, 1931.

Piaget, J. Introduction to M. Laurendeau & A. Pinard's *Causal thinking in the child.* New York: International Universities Press, 1962.

Pirsig, R. *Zen and the art of motorcycle maintenance.* New York: Bantam Books, 1974.

Schecter, B. Animism and metaphoric thinking in children. Unpublished doctoral dissertation, Teachers College, Columbia University, 1979.

Schrödinger, E. *What is life? and mind and matter.* London: Cambridge University Press, 1958.

Selman, R. *The development of conceptions of interpersonal relations.* Mimeo manual, Harvard/Judge Baker Social Reasoning Project, 1974.

Sharpe, R. A. Ideology and ontology. *Philosophy of the Social Sciences,* 1974, *4,* 55–64.

Shuldenfrei, R. Book review: Zen and the art of motorcycle maintenance. *Harvard Educational Review,* 1975, *45* (1), 95–103.

Wellman H. M., and Johnson, C. N. Children's conceptions of the mental world. Paper presented at the biennial meeting of the Society for Research in Child Development, San Francisco, March 1979.

Chapter 9

Contemporary Research and the Mind–Body Problem

HERBERT WEINER

This chapter will attempt to review some recent research findings that deal with the problem of the relationship of the mental and the bodily. The particular discipline in medicine that attempts to deal with this most complex empirical and philosophical problem is the cognate area, psychosomatic medicine. Despite the awkward name, workers in the area attempt to understand the impact of social and other external events on the mind and how such experiences may predispose to and initiate changes in the structure and function of the body.

Toward an Understanding of the Transduction of Experience by the Brain

Psychosomatic medicine has been the target of some criticism because it has failed to provide an answer to the question of how perceived social experiences and/or psychological conflicts and induced emotions could possibly be translated (transduced) into bodily physiology leading to illness. In other words the extremely complex problem of the translation of the psychological (the nonmaterial) into the physiological (the material) is unsolved. One may answer this criticism by saying that our failure to answer this particular question has both conceptual and empirical reasons. It is a question that

223

BODY AND MIND
Past, Present, and Future

philosophers have debated for ages, continue to debate, and that neuro-biologists are only now beginning to address. As a result of their efforts, the barest outlines of a theory are beginning to emerge. In the following section, I have reviewed the kinds of data that need to be addressed before a preliminary answer to this problem can be given.

One may begin by saying that one difficulty in the way of anyone trying to acquire an understanding of this problem is that the translation must occur twice. On the afferent side a form of energy such as light, as photons, must be translated into a visual perception with meaning—a psychological event—which may then lead to a change in heart rate, a change that also requires energy. The double translation from one form of energy will in the ensuing paragraphs be called "transduction."

The Problem of Transduction

Delbrück (1970) has described transduction as the central problem of neuro-biology. Since, explicitly or implicitly, it is a central problem in psychosomatic medicine as well, his comments are relevant in this context.

Delbrück has stated that transduction entails more than the entrainment of nerve impulses at a peripheral receptor, such as the precise manner by which a photon falling on the vertebrate retina gives rise to impulses in the optic nerve, a process about which we have learned something. We know that the photon changes rhodopsin from the *cis-* to the *trans-* form through four intermediate chemical steps (Wald, 1968). But the mechanism of this form of transduction from the chemical to the neural and the point in time of the chemical cycle at which excitation of the optic nerve terminals in the retina occurs are still unknown.

Yet receptors may act as "analyzers": Three different retinal cone pigments respond to different wavelengths of light and therefore to different colors. The pigment contained in retinal rods is responsive to yet another wavelength. Sounds are also analyzed according to their wavelengths in the organ of Corti, and the olfactory mucosa may separate different odorants according to the different migration rates of their constituent molecules (Mozell & Jagodowicz, 1973).

Once past the receptor and specific sensory pathways, the information carried as spike-trains—which measure the intensities of stimuli or the time derivatives of these intensities—are themselves transformed at each relay nucleus. For instance, the postsynaptic discharge at a relay nucleus may be less likely than the incoming (presynaptic) activity to occur at regular intervals (Viernstein & Grossman, 1961); it also depends on the ongoing spontaneous activity of the relay nucleus (Amassian, Macy, Waller, Leader, & Swift, 1964). In short, the dynamic changes that occur at the first relay nucleus depend on its current state.

Nerve impulses or spikes are, however, quantal phenomena: Impulses do not vary with stimulus intensity once the stimulus exceeds threshold. Further, the impulses lack specificity—they are propagated in all axons, regardless of origin, by the same mechanism but with different rates of transmission and with different timing. Further, the number of axons entrained may vary according to the intensity of the stimulus.

Yet on the input side, we are accustomed to believe that man responds to structured aspects of his environment—that is, to "wholes" or *Gestalten*. Yet even in this process, he usually abstracts and selects one whole from others—one configuration from the "ground"—in which it is embedded. He responds to this configuration at one time and to another at another: Both the structure and the context of the perceptual field are of crucial import.

The question is, therefore, how to proceed from the rate and timing of axonal transmission, and the number of axons entrained, to our perception of structures. Many of the leading thinkers of the past 2 millennia have stated that all we know of the external world, the objects and events in it, natural and human, is their structure.

Although the sound waves generated by a musical instrument or the light reflected from a painting are physically of a different kind than nerve impulses in the auditory or optic nerve, the relationships between the sound and light waves are largely preserved in the nervous system; that is, their intensity, timing, persistence, and duration, and the ratios among the frequencies of the simultaneous sounds and the sequences of sounds and their harmonics. A change in key in which the instrument is played or in the illumination of a picture still allows us to recognize the tune or the theme of the picture and even the artist who composed or painted them.

Although modifications of spike-trains may occur at relay nuclei, the essential relationships between components of complex stimuli, that is, their structure, must be preserved. Beyond that we can say little about the processes that allow us finally to decide or recognize the tune or picture or how it may acquire meaning for us. Presumably, there is an interaction of sensory input with memory stores that allows us to recognize the nature of the input. Thus, at the present time we are only able to speak about these matters in psychological generalities and with no great precision.

But even if we knew the answer to the question of how the nervous system perceives structures and assigns meaning to them, we would still not know how to relate such a perception and the emotional response it elicits to the output via autonomic, humoral, and neuromuscular channels. Implicit in this statement is the abiding belief that the perceived event and the emotional responses it occasions give rise in a causal, linear manner to physiological responses that are controlled by the brain. The problem thus stated is that fear and joy, for example, "cause" an increased heart rate.

Specifically, how is a psychologic experience translated by the brain into a physiologic event? Or, to put it another way, how does a nonmaterial process such as the emotional response to a "stressful" situation produce material changes, such as the elevation of urinary catecholamine levels or an increase in heart rate? This particular question has baffled philosophers and scientists for many centuries, of course. Yet it remains unanswered, which would seem to indicate that our basic approach to its solution may need to be reexamined. To begin with, I would draw attention to the manner in which this question is traditionally stated: It clearly implies that there is a causal link between non-material and material events. I would like to suggest two other possibilities: This causal link between psychologic events and physiologic changes may be much more complex than we have been led to believe. Or this assumed causal link may not exist at all: Concomitant events are not necessarily causally related.

We have continued to cling to the assumption that there is a causal link between these events, despite our inability to accumulate empirical data to show that in man psychologic response and physiologic change are highly correlated. Moreover, we have rationalized our failure to accumulate such data on the grounds that there are individual variations in response, or, more precisely, individual methods of coping with experience, and that these influence the physiologic response in some manner. Indeed, such individual coping responses can be identified. But this does not mean that they alone can be held responsible for the low correlation between psychologic and physiologic responses.

Three Classical Models of Transduction

It is the contention that one of the major reasons for our failure to solve this problem is that we have had only one hypothesis to guide us. This hypothesis is best exemplified by the fact that the emotional response is the mediator of the threatening stress and the physiological responses. This model is a linear one, although modified versions exist that suggest that the physiological responses can also attain conscious experience, presumably mediated by visceral afferents. However, the problem is again complicated by the fact that we do not know how impulses arriving over sympathetic or vagal afferent pathways can be perceived and acquire conscious meanings.

Thus, whether the line is straight or curves back on itself, we are faced repeatedly by the insuperable problem of how nerve impulses, changes in enzyme levels, or turnover rates of transmitter substances (putative or actual) can "produce" ideas, thoughts, images, feelings, moods, or vice versa.

There are naturally several ways of looking at this problem. I have already mentioned the traditional linear model that most psychobiologists have employed. It is best exemplified by Figure 9.1, taken from Knapp (1971). In it, the social event or situation is perceived (1), or not, acquires emotional meaning that may interact with inferred defense mechanisms, which if they are effective modify and temper the physiological responses (3), which may themselves be perceived (4) or effect the social event (5). For example, the child in an asthmatic attack may elicit a solicitous (or other) response from a parent, nurse, or a group of its peers. Further specification of this model entails the realization that acute changes in the environment may involve preparation to take action and anticipatory responses with their accompanying bodily changes, especially during novel experiences. Reactive and different responses also occur during both novel and routine experiences.

A modification of this point of view states that correlated psychological and physiological responses appear so different because they both are the product of the differences in the techniques whereby we study them. The mental experience—that is, the thought, mental image, or feeling—is the *inner* aspect of the subject's response to the event, as he perceives it. The neural and bodily events are the *outer*, and often measurable, aspects of his response to the event. The connection between the mental and the neural and/or bodily processes cannot be established by simple cross-identity. The difference between these processes (e.g., extension in space and time, in the case of bodily events, and nonextension, in the case of mental ones) lies in the way they are presented and accessible to us. They must, therefore, be studied by different techniques, of which they are a product. The problem with this line of reasoning is that because we have used different techniques, coextensive in terms of temporal boundaries, we have assumed that if two processes (e.g., the performance of a task and an increase in heart rate or a rise in blood pressure) occur concomitantly, they must be causally related.

In this second point of view, the psychological and the physiological are merely two different sides of a coin. However, the interpretation of how both come about is subject to misinterpretation, as stated. In addition, this point of view leaves open the question of how the two categories of events come about at all. Being two sides of the same coin, they might be the product of a third variable. For example, the behavioral and psychological changes seen in primary anorexia nervosa, and the correlated immaturity of circadian pattern of luteinizing hormone secretion, may simply be the "read out" of a defect in the anterior hypothalamus.

The third and classical point of view is that despite the coextensiveness of the psychological and physiological, the two belong to wholly unrelated realms of events. Although we may study the physiology and psychology of an ill person concomitantly, they really have nothing to do with each other and proceed independently. In this view, a bereavement may produce grief in the bereaved, but the physiological changes of weeping, or of rheumatoid arthritis, are independent of his loss. In this view, the physiological change arises in no understandable manner.

External Loop Model of Transduction

In a very serious way, then, our failure to solve this central and time-honored empirical and conceptual issue may be due to the fact that there is no solution to it because the problem is incorrectly assumed to be a real one.

There is a model that I have termed the "external loop" model. Briefly stated, it is that in some instances the initiating social event, perceived as a threat, is not coped with and produces emotional responses that are correlated with changes in behavior. It is well-known that some patients who become anxious may medicate themselves or obtain medication from physicians. Other patients who become depressed either gorge themselves, do not eat, or drink alcohol. In Weisman's series (1956) exacerbations of duodenal ulcer occurred in various settings, with various emotional and psychological reactions leading to the drinking of alcohol, a known antecedent of duodenal ulcer exacerbations. Similarly, Katz and his coworkers (Katz, Weiner, Gutman, & Yu, 1973) have observed that, in 60% of patients, attacks of gout followed situations in which predisposed patients had to prove themselves, and which lead them to eat and drink alcohol in excess.

In other words, given a particular predisposition, some persons when faced with a particular situation will respond not only psychologically but also behaviorally in terms of their diet and alcohol intake. More recently, also, it has been demonstrated that patients with hypertension seem to prefer diets high in salt if given a choice. We do not know whether this preference antecedes or is a consequence of hypertensive illness.

In any case, these examples suggest that in at least some cases the psychological responses to situations are mediated through changes in diet, in eating and drinking behavior in the predisposed. Heuristically, this hypothesis would be easily testable; the data could also be more reliably established and quantitated.

A variant of this model could also help us conceive of some cases of primary anorexia nervosa. It is known that about one-third to one-half (or more) of all cases of this illness begin with amenorrhea. Evidence is now beginning to accumulate that the amenorrhea is correlated with immature (age-inappropriate) secretory patterns of pituitary luteinizing hormone (LH) and follicle stimulating hormone (FSH), which in part may account for the amenorrhea (Boyar, Katz, Finkelstein, Kapen, Weiner, Weitzman, & Hellman, 1974). It is not known, however, whether these immature secretory patterns antecede the illness or why they occur at all.

In any case, the amenorrhea *antecedes* the remorseless dieting that the patient with anorexia nervosa engages in. Thus, it is possible that rather than oral impregnation fantasies being the antecedents of the illness in some cases, they are the way the patient explains the amenorrhea to herself. To be more explicit: The amenorrhea may be subject to (mis)interpretation by the patient as a pregnancy. The patient explains the cause of the pregnancy to herself as deriving from conflictful fantasies of oral impregnation, which in turn lead to not eating.

Thus, we have two variants of the external loop model, which are represented in Figures 9.1 and 9.2.

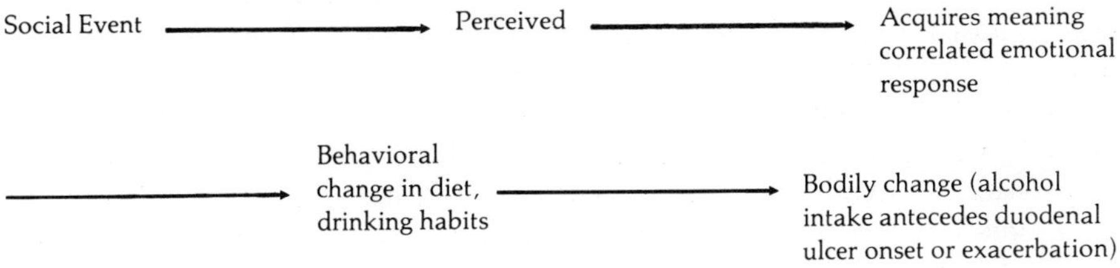

Social Event ⟶ Perceived ⟶ Acquires meaning correlated emotional response

⟶ Behavioral change in diet, drinking habits ⟶ Bodily change (alcohol intake antecedes duodenal ulcer onset or exacerbation)

FIGURE 9.1. External Loop Model A.

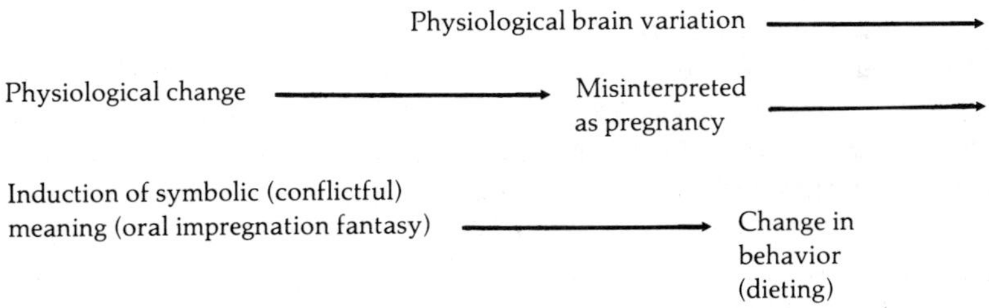

Physiological brain variation ⟶

Physiological change ⟶ Misinterpreted as pregnancy ⟶

Induction of symbolic (conflictful) meaning (oral impregnation fantasy) ⟶ Change in behavior (dieting)

FIGURE 9.2. External Loop Model B.

Clearly, the applicability of Model B to some forms of anorexia nervosa is subject to empirical test. It is not the sole explanatory model in all instances of this illness. For example, it would not apply to those instances in which amenorrhea is a late manifestation of the illness, which begins with not eating and weight loss.

Some authorities believe that "true" or "primary" anorexia nervosa is not initially a disturbance of eating but is characterized by a failure to recognize enteroreceptive hunger signals and to be able to discriminate these from other bodily sensations and feelings. In addition, the burden of this failure is placed on early experiences during the feeding of the infant, so that either the sensation of hunger or its meaning is never learned (Bruch, 1973). In addition, the child is a very compliant and model one and has at the onset of puberty a great fear of growing fat and therefore does not eat. Some experts do not believe that anorexia nervosa is primarily a disturbance of eating behavior, although other forms of such disturbances do occur with "secondary" anorexia.

Yet there is one striking fact that this account does not consider: "True" anorexia nervosa occurs about 10 times as frequently in girls as in boys. When it occurs in boys it *precedes* puberty; in girls it follows puberty. This fact suggests a "protective" role for male sex hormones and/or an initiating role for female hormones, both controlled by their respective gonadotrophic hormones. There is much to suggest that during puberty (the age at which the incidence of some forms of anorexia nervosa is highest) a reorganization of hypothalamic function and the hypothalamic-pituitary axis occurs. In normal adolescence, there may be bouts of asceticism and self-denial during which all gratification, including eating, is suppressed, followed by bouts of self-indulgence.

Should this hypothesis be proven, one could see that patients with anorexia nervosa are representative of one end of the distribution of adolescence. The behavioral, psychological, and physiological events in anorexia may be seen as a manifestation of the aberrant reorganization of hypothalamic function during adolescence, manifested by tonic inhibition of eating behavior, increased motoric activity, and failure of adult patterns of LH and FSH release to occur, although other pituitary hormones such as thyrotropin (TSH) and possibly human growth hormone (HGH) may be normally produced and or released. The antecedents of this disturbance may well be life experience that may alter hypothalamic function, specifically levels of neurotransmitter synthesis, release, re-uptake, or degradation. In this view, it is early experience that alters bodily function and the psychology of the child. The burden of the inception of the illness is not only placed on conflictful fantasies but on a complex interplay of experience, physiology, and psychology in which the conflictful fantasy may in some instances be induced or elicited by aberrant sexual functioning producing amenorrhea.

Collateral Models of Transduction

If we are to understand how the brain translates experience, the following factors must be taken into account: First, psychologic experiences may be associated with specific changes in a wide range of physiologic functions and also with exquisitely discrete and selective change at times. Second, when a variety of functions are studied during and after an experience, a pattern of change can be observed over time. Putting it another way, there is evidence that the brain has the capacity to amplify a signal, stimulus, or event in space and time. But the way this pattern is regulated and amplification occurs is not fully understood. Third, previous experiences produce changes in the nervous system that not only alter the response to later experience but also change this physiologic pattern. Finally, in view of the correlation between the steady-state activity of the nervous system with behavioral steady states, it is also essential to our understanding of the process of transduction to take into account the behavioral state of the animal or human subject at the time the experience occurs.

First, I would like to suggest that further insight into the events in the brain that link a psychologic experience with a series of physiologic events cannot be achieved until there has been careful analysis of the specific constellation of stimuli or events that impinge on the organism. For example, we need to know what it is about restraint–immobilization or crowding that is stressful. Is it the continuous sensory input from skin when the animal is closely confined, or the sensory input from muscle–tendon receptors when it struggles? Is it the deprivation of food, water, or a fall in body temperature, etc.? Second, we need to know whether each variable is equally capable of producing the same behavioral and physiologic effect. If so, are these effects mediated by the same or by different circuits in the brain? Is it possible that one aspect of the "stressful" configuration produces the behavioral effect and another aspect the physiologic one? Some test of this speculation might be made by systematically varying these aspects.

In many ways, this line of reasoning is without precedents. Mason (1968) sought the common element in his avoidance conditioning experiments, which he identified as the psychologic (emotional) responses of his animals to the experimental procedure. These responses were then translated into hormonal changes—somehow. But how?

In contrast, several experiments described in the following paragraphs were not only not predicated on this line of reasoning but have enhanced our understanding of the translational process. In so doing, they have provided us with models of this process that make it necessary to change our traditional view of some aspects of the mind–body relationship.

In the past, the authors of most studies of the effects on young animals of separation from their mother (Bronfenbrenner, 1968; Harlow, 1961; Hinde & Spencer-Booth, 1971; Kaufman & Rosenblum, 1969; Mason, Davenport, & Henzel, 1968) proceeded on the assumption that the removal of the mother was a complex psychologic experience for her offspring. No attempt was made in these experiments to determine the separate effects on the infant of the deprivation of nutritional, olfactory, tactile, auditory, visual, or thermal stimuli. The absence of such an analysis makes it impossible to determine whether changes in or deprivation of these simpler forms of stimulation do not produce, or at least contribute to, the observed sequelae of separation. Because prematurely separated young animals eat less and lose weight, their food intake may well be the most critical uncontrolled variable in these experiments. Deprivation of sensory inputs (Melzack, 1969) and litter size (Harlow, 1961) may also have noxious effects on the development of young animals. In Hofer's admirable studies (1971) the constellation of events that intervened in the cardiorespiratory and behavioral effects of separation of 14-day-old rats was composed of the lack of mother's milk, an unfamiliar environment, and the physical absence of the mother. The rats studied showed a 40% drop in heart and respiratory rates during the first 12–16 hours following separation (Hofer & Weiner, 1971a). Future investigations will probably reveal additional physiologic effects of separation.

But what needs to be emphasized is the fact that Hofer has identified the absence of mother's milk as the critical variable that produced the cardiovascular effect on the rats he studied. When these 14-day-old rats who had been without food for the first 16 hours following separation were fed milk by stomach tube, there was a complete (albeit transient) reversal of the decrease in heart rate that had occurred. Moreover, this reversal was rapid, produced by all three of the major components of milk (Hofer & Weiner, 1971b), and related to the amount given but not to gastric filling or distention. The fact that milk increases heart rate seems to depend on beta-adrenergic transmission on the effector side. But the afferent arc in the loop that mediates the nutritional effects on the heart remains unknown (Hofer & Weiner, 1974). If this were known, we would have a clue as to the brain sites that transduce the nutritional effects to produce increased heart rates on feeding. The obvious next step, as Hofer (1971) has pointed out, would be to investigate how milk sustains heart and respiratory rates; in other words, we could identify the afferent neural pathways or the substances in milk that sustain these rates.

There is still another possibility that merits investigation. Does the absence of milk produce changes in important neurochemical mediators in the brain (Himwich, Davis, & Agraval, 1968)? This question is not as farfetched as it might seem when one considers the known long-term effects of lowered protein intake on dopamine, norepinephrine, and tyrosine hydroxylase (TH) in the perinatal period (Shoemaker & Wurtman, 1971). What still remains to be done is to determine the short-term effects on brain amines of nutritional deprivation following separation. If nutritional deprivation is shown to produce such effects, different amounts of nutrition or different nutritional substances could be manipulated to determine dose-response relationships.

Research on the behavior of baby rats, studied individually, showed that after separation these animals showed an increase in activity and a greater tendency to rear up on their hind legs. When studied in groups of four, there was more self-grooming, increased defecation and urination, and a decreased tendency to enter REM sleep (Hofer & Weiner, 1971b).

Although gastric infusion of either milk or nonnutrient fluid inhibited the hyperactivity of these separated baby rats within 5 minutes after the infusion of fluid, it did not reliably affect their behavior an hour later. On the other hand, provision of a nonlactating foster mother prevented the behavioral effects manifested by separated and nutritionally deprived baby rats, except for changes in paradoxical sleep. In short, this work suggests that the cardiorespiratory changes that occurred in the separated baby rats were due to the absence of milk, while the behavioral changes (apart from the lowered probability of entering REM sleep) were due to the physical absence of the mother and the consequent absence of sucking activity. The point is that certain facets of the separation constellation affect the physiologic system, while others affect the behavioral system. Having specified which aspects of the organismic response to experience affect which system, analysis of the physiologic mechanisms that mediate the behavioral, cardiovascular, or sleep effects can proceed.

This work suggests that it is entirely possible that our concept that we perceive structures has led us to underestimate the brain's capacity to abstract elements of that structure and respond to them specifically. And indeed, there is considerable empirical work to substantiate this assertion, best exemplified in the visual system (Hubel, 1959; Hubel & Wiesel, 1959, 1960, 1962, 1964, 1968). Therefore, one may conclude that it is not necessarily so that a complex event such as separation that leads to bodily changes not only because of the absence of the mother but because her physical presence may "control" the pup's behavior, her bodily warmth may maintain its temperature, and her milk may regulate its heart rate. Her absence when the pup is prematurely weaned may immediately lead to its not eating for 24 hours and may make it later prone to gastric ulceration on not feeding, possibly because its body temperature falls (Ackerman, Hofer, & Weiner, 1975). Yet other behaviors, such as nonnutritional sucking, may be unaffected by separation (Hofer, 1974). These data suggest that some behaviors are directly under the control of the presence of the mother; others are independent of it and are autoregulatory, while some bodily functions (heart rate regulation) are under the control of a third variable—milk.

Once a psychobiologic analysis such as Hofer's has been accomplished and the critical variables producing specific but different effects have been isolated, important questions arise: Is the brain capable of actively abstracting one aspect of a stimulus or situation and responding to it? Can it also abstract and respond to another set?

As mentioned, the brain is capable of such activity in relation to the visual, auditory, and somesthetic systems. Some visual cortical cells respond only to the position (form or length) and orientation of a stimulus, that is, only to certain properties of a stimulus; other cells respond to specific combinations of these stimulus properties. It is logical to assume, therefore, that the brain is capable of abstracting certain aspects of a whole. If this process does occur and can be ascribed to the brain, then one might further conclude that early experiences bias the brain to respond to analogous or homologous aspects of experience later in time, specifically, by abstracting the analogue or homologue from that later constellation of events.

Hofer's analysis raises a second question as well. Once a specific aspect of a complex situation has been correlated with a specific physiologic effect, does the brain transduce this intervening variable by one or by several circuits? Or to rephrase the question, is it possible that even a single (simple) stimulus may produce different effects by different, that is, collateral, pathways?

One process in which the entire transduction of input and the resulting physiologic changes are known provides a clear-cut answer to this question. I refer to the manner in which light affects the functioning of the pineal gland. Fiske, Bryant, and Putnam (1960) have shown that the weight of the pineal gland decreases when rats are continuously exposed to light and that female rats remain in continuous vaginal estrus under such lighting conditions (Browman, 1937; Fiske *et al.*, 1960). These findings plus the observation that extracts of the pineal gland of cattle inhibit estrus led Wurtman, Axelrod, and Chu (1963) to conclude that melatonin reduces the incidence of estrus in the rat. We are further indebted to Axelrod and his group for working out the biosynthetic pathway of melatonin from tryptophan:

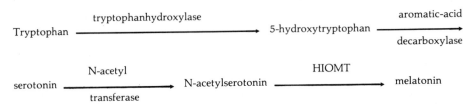

More specifically, Wurtman, Axelrod, and Phillips (1963) found that levels of hydroxy-indole-O-methyltransferase (HIOMT) in the pineal gland were elevated when rats were kept in the dark and reduced when they were exposed to continuous light. The fact that light inhibits the synthesis and release of melatonin would explain why continuous light produced persistent estrus.

If we were to adhere to the hypothetic psychophysiologic model traditionally used in our field, we would say that it is the *experience* of light that regulates the release of melatonin (Figure 9.1). But this is not what seems to happen. In fact, we are now presented with a most interesting model of how an external stimulus (i.e., light) is transduced by the nervous system. Moreover, it would be premature to minimize the significance of this model on the grounds it is the one and only model that can exist. It should be noted, however, that Axelrod's work on the pineal gland rests on his identification of light as the critical variable, which served as a point of departure for further analysis.

Axelrod and his associates have also worked out the rather complex and indirect pathway from the retina to the pineal gland and the manner in which the biosynthetic machinery of the gland is influenced (Moore, Heller, Wurtman, & Axelrod, 1967). In the mammal, environmental light passes via the retina to the inferior accessory optic tract to the preganglionic sympathetic fibers of the spinal cord to the superior cervical ganglion, from which postganglionic fibers pass upward to the parenchymal cells of the pineal gland, whose terminals release norepinephrine (Axelrod, Shein, & Wurtman, 1969; Axelrod, 1971).

Obviously, light also stimulates the retina to entrain impulses that pass via the classic visual pathways to the visual cortex, and, in a way that is not understood, produce the *experience* of light. It needs to be emphasized, however, that this experience is subserved by quite separate mechanisms from those that influence pineal gland functioning.

The release of norepinephrine in the pineal gland influences the formation of melatonin from tryptophan by inducing the enzyme N-acetyltransferase (Klein & Weller, 1970), which converts serotonin into N-acetylserotonin. Two additonal points about the transduction of experience and the regulation of pineal gland functioning need to be made: I would emphasize taking into account (a) the time during a biologic rhythm at which a stimulus is provided or an experience occurs and (b) the animal's age when the experience occurs.

The significance of the first variable relates to the fact that there is a biologic rhythm for the content of serotonin (Owman, 1965) and norepinephrine in the pineal gland. The content of serotonin is high during the day under normal lighting conditions and low at 11:00 p.m. (Quay, 1963). This rhythm is endogenous (Snyder, Zweig, Axelrod, & Fischer, 1965), although its driving oscillator is unknown; however, the oscillator can be entrained by light—for example, when day and night are reversed experimentally (Snyder, Zweig, & Axelrod, 1967). On the other hand, norepinephrine content, which reaches its highest levels at night, is not controlled by an endogenous oscillator but is under the direct environmental control of light. Thus, its high nocturnal content corresponds to the high nocturnal content of HIOMT and therefore of melatonin synthesis.

Of particular interest, however, is the fact that the oscillator for serotonin is not operative until the rat is 6 days old. This underscores the importance of the second variable, i.e., the animal's age at the time an experience occurs. In young rats not yet 27 days old, light travels via an extraretinal pathway to affect the serotonin level in the pineal gland (Axelrod, 1971; Zweig, Snyder, & Axelrod, 1966); once they have reached the age of 27 days, this earlier pathway is no longer operative and is apparently replaced by another one.

The principle illustrated by Axelrod's work is not unique. When the stimulus for a behavior has been clearly identified and the behavior has been carefully analyzed, one finds that even the components of the *behavior*, although they appear to form an integrated whole, are actually separate and distinct and, as such, merit individual analysis. Furthermore, these separate components may be subserved by different neural pathways. For example, a light touch of the dorsum of the paw of a cat produced the contact-placing reaction. However, careful analysis of this behavior discloses that the bending of hairs entrains impulses that travel by at least two routes. The early components of the biceps (EMG) and the first phase of the placing movement are activated by the ventroposterior nucleus (VP) of the thalamus. Later components are probably activated by a complex circuit that passes through the VP, sensorimotor cortex, pyramidal tract, red nucleus, interpositus nucleus of the cerebellum, ventrolateral–ventroanterior nucleus of the thalamus, and, once again, the sensorimotor cortex (Amassian, Ross, & Donat, 1971; Amassian, Weiner, & Rosenblum, 1972). What is more, these circuits are not fixed. A lesion in one circuit may cause the behavior to disappear for a time, only to return when, presumably, another circuit has taken over the function of the circuit that is incapable of activating the necessary behavioral components. Typically, circuit diagrams do not tell us that the information at each relay nucleus is transformed in a different manner— another aspect of the transduction process.

In summary, I think we can conclude from the available evidence that even a simple behavior, produced by a very simple stimulus, is the product of separate components that are regulated by different neural circuits. It would appear, therefore, that the critical element in the production of a behavior is the timing of the output of various components by different circuits—in the case of the contact-placing reaction, the sequential and orderly activation of different muscles of the forelimb, long after the stimulus that initiated the behavior has ceased.

Axelrod's work on the pineal gland, which gives a complete picture of the manner and mechanism by which an environmental influence on an organism is transduced into a highly relevant physiologic chain of events, appears to have broad implications for the mind–brain–body problem. It suggests that a specified input (light) may have physiologic and psychologic effects, which, though correlated and concomitant, are not causally related. In fact, the input to the receptor travels quite different neural routes to produce a complex phenomenon (the experience of light) and other behavioral and physiologic effects (a reduction in the synthesis and release of melatonin and estrus).

As pointed out earlier, those who subscribe to the traditional model of psychophysiologic relationships would contend, in this instance, that it is the experience of light that regulates the release of melatonin. For the assumption that mental experiences initiate physiologic events is, of course, a fundamental precept of psychosomatic medicine. In light of Axelrod's findings, however, one must question the accuracy of this view of the supremacy of the mental over the physiologic.

Data accumulated from other sources further detract from the validity of this concept of the prepotency of mental experiences. Specifically, there are only three known instances in which strict *isomorphism* exists between neural and behavioral events:

1. There is a linear correspondence between neuronal activity and muscular activity in the case of the spinal cord motoneuron and the skeletal muscle that it innervates.
2. In the case of receptors, an increase or reduction of an adequate stimulus gives rise to a homologous change in the discharge frequency of the axon leading away from the receptor. In neural coordinates, the frequency profile in a population of peripheral axons maps the contour, spatial position, and intensity of a stationary stimulus. The transform from receptor to the axonal population is isomorphic.
3. When the stimulus is applied to the brain rather than the receptors, the

strength-rate functions for electrically elicited overt behaviors are isomorphic with those that obtain for neurons. Thus, Kestenbaum, Deutsch and Coons (1970) showed that in the rat the mean percentage of lever-pressing responses to avoid aversive brain stimulation correlated with the known properties of neurons and axons—latent addition, the absolute refractory period and temporal summation decay.

As noted earlier, Axelrod's findings cannot be arbitrarily dismissed on the grounds that their application is limited to the functioning of the pineal gland. On the other hand, it is impossible to say how many instances of the model outlined occur in nature. One thing is clear, however: Axelrod's work provides us with a model that refutes the traditional linear theoretical model of mind–body interaction, which we have accepted without reservation in psychobiology and on which we have based our research efforts to date. Thus, at the very least, Axelrod's work raises the possibility that other models could be used.

With respect to the specific implications of Axelrod's findings for psychosomatic theory and research, his work on the pineal gland suggests that the mental experience of an external event is only one of several collateral processes to which that external event gives rise. In addition to the subject's consciousness of the event, they produce concomitant (but not actually related) neural and bodily processes.

The supremacy of the mental over the physiologic is not borne out by Axelrod's work, and the neurobiologic data delineated in the preceding section of this chapter cast further doubt on its validity.

Clearly, then, one can no longer automatically assume that psychosocial events and external stimuli alter bodily function in health and disease by their initial impact on the mind. Recent studies suggest alternative models of mind–body interaction by which the brain transduces experience to produce concomitant changes in behavior and bodily function, and they specify the manner in which this may occur by collateral neural pathways.

As outlined, therefore, a simple light or a touch–stimulus may entrain several collateral pathways in parallel. In addition, receptors and their central connections can be entrained by separate components of complex stimuli and events, as Hofer's and Weiner's work suggest. In turn, each receptor activated by these separate components may entrain two or more collateral pathways. By this means, psychological and physiological events might occur simultaneously and concomitantly and be correlated but could hardly be considered to "cause" each other. In the case of motor behaviors, the output is determined by temporal factors—by the number of synapses and hence synaptic delays in each circuit. When activated, each circuit serially activates muscles; it is the sequence of the muscles activated that determines the movement that comprise the motor behavior, depending in part also on the state of the autoregulatory activity of the afferent system.

Internal Loop Model

Another model has been proposed by Reiser (1975). In this model the inability to cope with the threat of the perceived "stress," the reactivation of the (unconscious) conflict that constitutes that person's psychological sensitivity, is associated with emotional arousal and a spectrum of autonomic and hormonal responses that in turn alter brain function and have been shown to affect psychological functioning. Reiser states that these physiological changes acting upon the brain are reflected in altered psychological functioning, expressed in ever more primitive ways of perceiving and thinking, evaluating danger, and coping with it and with the unconscious conflict. In this vicious cycle of events, a consequent series of more vigorous bodily changes would next occur. He goes on to say that as these continue, the function of the brain exposed to continuing changes in circulating hormones would become more plastic; inactive brain circuits would be brought into play and "make connection with appropriate efferent fibers to the viscera" to produce altered function. The psychological expression of the activation of these pathways, he believes, is expressed in the activation of new outflow pathways so as to alter visceral function that interacts with the predispositions mentioned earlier to activate illness.

This can be conceived of as a model that has much to commend it, since it puts into order many known facts, such as that exacerbations of many illnesses do occur during sleep and that rhythmic processes such as circadian rhythms must be taken into consideration in understanding the pathogenesis of illness.

However, the model does not explain how being alarmed occasions physiological mobilization or how altered brain physiology is expressed psychologically. The problem of translation of these two categories of events into each other remains unspecified, because at the present time we have no way of specifying it.

Reiser also postulated that once the outflow channels (e.g., autonomic, humoral, and neuromuscular) were activated, they would alter visceral function and would interact with the predisposing factors of that particular illness. The initiating psychoneuroendocrine sequence, which he has outlined, is not specific to the illness (in contrast to Alexander's hypotheses), but the predisposition to a particular illness is specific.

All models that have been discussed in this chapter attempt to bridge the gap between environmental events, mental processes, brain and physiological mechanisms, and illness. Their value is heuristic: For the sake of progress in psychosomatic medicine, it may be well to have alternative ways of organizing data until our knowledge is such that a correct model will emerge that will bridge the gap between mind, brain, and body in health and illness—a gap that remains a crucial one in biology and medicine.

References

Ackerman, S. H., Hofer, M. A., & Weiner, H. Age at maternal separation and gastric erosion susceptibility in the rat. *Psychosomatic Medicine*, 1975, *37*, 180.

Amassian, V. E., Macy, J., Jr., Waller, H. J., Leader, H. S., & Swift, J. Transformation of afferent activity at the cuneat nucleus. *Proceedings of the International Union of Physiological Scientists*, 1964, *3*, 235.

Amassian, V. E., Ross, R., & Donat, J. Development of contact placing and thalamocortical organization in kittens. *Federation Proceedings*, 1971, *30*, 434.

Amassian, V. E., Weiner, H., & Rosenblum, M. Neural systems subserving the tactile placing reaction: a model for the study of higher level control of movement. *Brain Research*, 1972, *40*, 171.

Axelrod, J. Noradrenaline: Fate and control of its biosynthesis. *Science*, 1971, *173*, 598.

Axelrod, J., Shein, H. M., & Wurtman, R. J. Stimulation of C^{14}-melatonin synthesis from C^{14}-tryptophan by noradrenaline in rat pineal in organ culture. *Proceedings of the National Academy of Science, U.S.A.*, 1969, *62*, 544.

Boyar, R. M., Katz, J. L., Finkelstein, J. W., Kapen, S., Weiner, H., Weitzman, E. D., & Hellman, L. Anorexia nervosa: Immaturity of the 24-hour luteinizing hormone secretory pattern. *New England Journal of Medicine*, 1974, *291*, 861.

Bronfenbrenner, U. Early deprivation in mammals: A cross species analysis. In G. Newton (Ed.), *Early experience and behavior*. Springfield, Ill.: Thomas, 1968.

Browman, L. P. Light in its relation to activity and estrous rhythm in the albino rat. *Journal of Experimental Zoology*, 1937, *75*, 375.

Bruch, H. *Eating disorders—Obesity, anorexia nervosa and the person within*. New York: Basic Books, 1973.

Delbrück, M. A physicist's renewed look at biology: Twenty years later. *Science*, 1970, *168*, 1312.

Fiske, V. M., Bryant, G. K., & Putnam, J. Effect of light on the weight of the pineal in the rat. *Endocrinology*, 1960, *66*, 489.

Harlow, H. F. The development of affectional patterns in infant monkeys. In B. M. Foss (Ed.), *Determinants of infant behavior*. London: Methuen, 1961.

Himwich, W., Davis, J. M., & Agraval, H. C. Effects of early weaning on some free amino acids and acetylcholinesterase activity of rat brain. In J. Wortis (Ed.), *Recent advances in biological psychiatry*. New York, Plenum Press, 1968.

Hinde, R. A., & Spencer-Booth, Y. Effects of brief separations from mother on rhesus monkeys. *Science*, 1971, *173*, 111.

Hofer, M. A. Regulation of cardiac rate by nutritional factor in young rats. *Science*, 1971, *172*, 1039.

Hofer, M. A. Studies on how early maternal separation produces behavioral change in young rats. *Psychosomatic Medicine*, 1975, *37*, 245.

Hofer, M. A., & Weiner, H. The development and mechanisms of cardiorespiratory responses to maternal deprivation in rat pups. *Psychosomatic Medicine*, 1971, *33*, 353. (a)

Hofer, M. A., & Weiner, H. Physiological and behavioral regulation by nutritional intake during early development of the laboratory rat *Psychosomatic Medicine*, 1971, 33, 468. (b)

Hofer, M. A., & Weiner, H. Physiological mechanisms for cardiac control by nutritional intake after early maternal separation in the young rat. *Psychosomatic Medicine*, 1975, *37*, 8.

Hubel, D. H. Single unit activity in striate cortex of unrestrained cats. *Journal of Physiology (London)*, 1959, *147*, 226.

Hubel, D. H., & Wiesel, T. N. Receptive fields of single neurons in the cat's striate cortex. *Journal of Physiology (London)*, 1959, *148*, 574.

Hubel, D. H., & Wiesel, T. N. Receptive fields of optic nerve fibers in the spider monkey. *Journal of Physiology (London)*, 1960, *154*, 572.

Hubel, D. H., & Wiesel, T. N. Receptive fields, binocular interaction and functional architecture in the cat's visual cortex. *Journal of Physiology (London)*, 1962, *160*, 106.

Hubel, D. H., & Wiesel, T. N. Responses of monkey geniculate cells to monochronic and white spots of light. *Physiologist*, 1964, *7*, 162.

Hubel, D. H., & Wiesel, T. N. The functional architecture of the striate cortex. In F. D. Carlson (Ed.), *Physiological and biochemical aspects of nervous integration*. Englewood Cliffs: Prentice-Hall, 1968.

Katz, J. L., Weiner, H., Gutman, A., & Yu, T.-F. Hyperuricemia, gout and the executive suite. *Journal of the American Medical Association*, 1973, *224*, 1251.

Kaufman, I. C., & Rosenblum, L. Effects of separation from mother on the emotional behavior of infant monkeys. *Annals of the New York Academy of Science*, 1969, *159*, 681.

Kestenbaum, R. S., Deutsch, J. A., & Coons, E. E. Behavioral measurement of neural post-stimulation excitability cycle: pain cells in the brain of the rat. *Science*, 1970, *167*, 393.

Klein, D. C., & Weller, J. Serotonin N-acetyl transferase activity is stimulated by norepinephrine and dibutyryl cyclic adenosine monophosphate. *Federation Proceedings*, 1970, *29*, 615.

Knapp, P. H. Revolution, relevance and psychosomatic medicine: Where the light is not. *Psychosomatic Medicine*, 1971, *33*, 363.

Mason, J. W. Organization of psychoendocrine mechanisms. *Psychosomatic Medicine*, 1968, *30*, 565.

Mason, W. A., Davenport, R. K., Jr., & Menzel, E. W., Jr. Early experiences and the social development of rhesus monkeys and chimpanzees. In G. Newton & S. Levine (Eds.), *Early experience and behavior*. Springfield, Ill.: Thomas, 1968.

Melzack, R. The role of early experience on emotional arousal. *Annals of the New York Academy of Science*, 1969, *159*, 721.

Moore, R. Y., Heller, A., Wurtman, R. J., & Axelrod, J. Visual pathway mediating pineal response to environmental light. *Science*, 1967, *155*, 220.

Mozell, M. M., & Jagodowicz, M. Chromatographic separation of odorants by the nose: Retention times measured across in vivo olfactory mucosa. *Science*, 1973, *181*, 1247.

Owman, C. H. Localization of neuronal and parenchymal monoamines under normal and experimental conditions in the mammalian pineal gland. *Progress of Brain Research*, 1965, *10*, 423.

Quay, W. B. Circadian rhythm in rat pineal serotonin and its modification by estrus cycle and photoperiod. *General and Comparative Endocrinology*, 1963, *3*, 473.

Reiser, M. F. Changing theoretical concepts in psychosomatic medicine. In M. F. Reiser (Ed.), *American Handbook of Psychiatry* (Vol. 4). New York: Basic Books, 1975.

Shoemaker, W. J., & Wurtman, R. J. Perinatal undernutrition: Accumulation of catecholamines in rat brain. *Science*, 1971, *171*, 1017.

Snyder, S. H., Zweig, M., Axelrod, J., & Fischer, J. F. Control of the circadian rhythm in serotonin content of the rat pineal gland. *Proceedings of the National Academy of Science, U.S.A.*, 1965, *53*, 301.

Snyder, S. H., Zweig, M., & Axelrod, J. Circadian rhythm in the serotonin content of the rat pineal gland: Regulating factors. *Journal of Pharmacology and Experimental Therapeutics*, 1967, *158*, 206.

Viernstein, L. J., & Grossman, R. G. Neural discharge patterns in the transmission of sensory information. In C. Cherry (Ed.), *Information theory*. Washington, D.C.: Butterworth, 1961.

Wald, G. Molecular basis of visual excitation. *Science*, 1968, *162*, 230.

Weisman, A. A study of the psychodynamics of duodenal ulcer exacerbations with special reference to treatment and the problem of specificity. *Psychosomatic Medicine*, 1956, *18*, 2.

Wurtman, R. J., Axelrod, J., & Chu, E. W. Melatonin, a pineal substance: Effect on rat ovary. *Science*, 1963, *141*, 277.

Wurtman, R. J., Axelrod, J., & Phillips, L. S. Melatonin synthesis in the pineal gland: Control by light. *Science*, 1963, *142*, 1071.

Zweig, M., Snyder, H. M., & Axelrod, J. Evidence for a non-retinal pathway of light to the pineal gland of newborn rats. *Proceedings of the National Academy of Science, U.S.A.*, 1966, *56*, 515.

Chapter 10

Mind and Body: A Dialogue.

GREGORY BATESON
ROBERT W. RIEBER

RIEBER: What is the so-called mind–body problem?

BATESON: Alright, for example, I have end organs in my fingers. And "I touch the tabletop." The question that we are up against is: What are we going to do with that pronoun "I." Do we need it? A dog may touch the tabletop with his nose. Does he have a pronoun? I would suspect that this split between "I" and the rest is rather late in evolutionary development. You don't have to start with a split between mind and body. The split between mind and body is something which occidental culture and perhaps other cultures have invented and played with and built up language around. And so on.

RIEBER: Then why did we develop the different words "body" and "mind" if the split is, as you implied, artificial, unnecessary?

BATESON: I think it is even counterproductive. It may also be productive, but it is very heavily counterproductive.

RIEBER: Then why did the two words emerge (in occidental culture) in the first place?

BATESON: Well, they were going fairly well by the time of the ancient Greeks.

RIEBER: I think there was certainly a distinction. In language, I am not sure about the words, because I don't know the original Greek language that well.

BATESON: Well, they had pronouns no doubt. But what they meant when they

241

BODY AND MIND
Past, Present, and Future

talked and used the pronouns, I wouldn't really know. The "body" for example? Yes, but what many peoples use for the self or the other person are not pronouns. They usually use names of relationships, outside themselves.

RIEBER: Perhaps the real breaking point was at the beginning of the seventeenth century. This probably comes out of some kind of a commitment to Baconian principles.

BATESON: Yes, and it comes out of Descartes, of course, too. I think that Descartes invented both the Cartesian graph and went screwy on the mind–body split or the mind–matter split. Those two inventions seem to be very closely related. It's the split of coordinates.

RIEBER: Well, why did he split mind from body? Wasn't it an arbitrary, capricious sort of thing? Or was he trying to achieve something? I suppose he was trying to shake somebody up.

BATESON: He was trying to shake somebody up, no doubt. And he was trying to do things unambiguously. And what he succeeds in saying, you see, is that the variables are to be handled separately.

RIEBER: Which variables? Or what were the variables?

BATESON: Oh, whatever. When you make a graph of temperature or of the rate of falling of a body, or whatever it is, you have time as a horizontal coordinate and whatever variable you want as a vertical. The temperature "rises," as we say, and "falls". It doesn't rise but that's the word for it.

RIEBER: Whenever you have matter on the one hand, you must then have its opposite.

BATESON: Yes, when you have matter, you have its opposite!

RIEBER: Apparently, whatever was opposite to matter was mind to Descartes.

BATESON: Yes.

RIEBER: And it was necessary to have something opposite to matter to account for something like one's intention.

BATESON: The question is, is body alive? You see, the split comes out of saying matter is not alive. And the moment you say organized matter is not alive then to handle purpose, humor, etc. you've got to invent a ghost of some kind.

RIEBER: The brain is matter, and the brain is alive.

BATESON: But the matter is not alive.

RIEBER: By alive, you mean what?

BATESON: Let's say you have a string, and you've got one end and I've got the other, and I give you a pull and you wake up or jump or whatever. Is the string alive?

RIEBER: No, it's not.

BATESON: But, does the string carry a message?

RIEBER: Perhaps!

BATESON: And similarly, neurons are a little bit more alive than a string in the sense that they carry messages. But the string is sort of a passageway to carry the messages but doesn't create the energy to transmit it. It depends on my pulling the string. The neuron responds from the energy of its breakfast.

RIEBER: So it's what these neurological mechanisms do that gives the organism's intention.

BATESON: But, you see, the subject of the verb was the neurons. To talk about the interface between the neuron and what the neuron does would be very awkward, wouldn't it?

RIEBER: Yes.

BATESON: That's the interface that I objected to at the beginning of our dialogue, when I objected to saying "I touch the table."

RIEBER: There's a distinction between what one means by body and what one means by mind that I would like to refer to, namely, the difference between such a distinction made about something in the past versus something in the present.

BATESON: Yes, but the thing doesn't change much from paramecium to man.

RIEBER: But, as you said before, it is rather late; that is, the distinction between mind and body is rather late in its appearance from an evolutionary point of view. It's late because man is late in the development on the phylogenetic scale.

BATESON: It's late because natural language is late in its development.

RIEBER: Is that dependent upon the development of consciousness in man?

BATESON: I don't know. Maybe I use the word "consciousness" differently from the way you do. For example, if I look at that artifact on the wall, I *consciously* see a dance shield. I am totally *un*conscious of the process by which I see that dance shield. I see only the product of that process.

RIEBER: But you're conscious of yourself seeing that dance shield.

BATESON: I'm conscious of the *product* of seeing that dance shield.

RIEBER: But you're conscious of you're being separate from the dance shield, and you are also conscious of yourself perceiving the dance shield in your own way.

BATESON: I don't know. Somehow, you see, I've got to make something in me. I have got to make an image of that thing. Right? Of that process, I'm totally unconscious.

RIEBER: You're probably better off if you're not conscious of it.

BATESON: Right. I wouldn't believe the shield was there if I were conscious of the process of making it. If you think about it, you discover there is a process between you and the shield that's making the thing—the image—that enables you to perceive the object. Three dimensions, color, etc., etc. This is a psychological product. That is to say, you really don't see the shield per se.

RIEBER: So, you don't see that shield. What do you see?

BATESON: What you see is your image of the shield.

RIEBER: In other words, the thing is not the same as your perception of the thing. Just like the word you use is not the thing that it stands for.

BATESON: That helps account for the fact that we don't all see it in the same way.

RIEBER: So, how does this tie in with the mind–body problem? The matter is what you're perceiving on the wall. Perception of the shield is the matter, then?

BATESON: The shield is matter by virtue of my perception of it.

RIEBER: You then seem to be extrapolating something from matter. It's giving life to matter.

BATESON: You can say that, but I'm not sure that you mean the same thing that I would mean by that.

RIEBER: What I mean is that you conceptualize it, therefore you give life to it.

BATESON: This is my hand, right? It is part of me? And I learned a lot from it.

RIEBER: Yes.

BATESON: How do I know it's a part of me? Did I teach it anything?

RIEBER: No, because it is a part of you. But that's animism isn't it?

BATESON: Ah ha. (Laughs.)

Now let's take a look at a much different way of approaching this What is the personality of the Balinese character in the middle of this illustration (Figure 10.1)? He is animated in every joint. Now, this gentleman, he lost his head (Figure 10.2). But his body is still animated.

RIEBER: In Figure 10.1, every joint has a head, right. What does that mean?

BATESON: It implies that each part is separately alive.

RIEBER: That's certainly animism, isn't it? But what does it tell us about the mind–body problem?

BATESON: It tells us that the Balinese don't have to think the way the occidentals think about bodies and minds. We're illustrating this with the Balinese, because we want to open up all of the ways of approaching this subject.

RIEBER: In other words, the dualism is unnecessary. You don't have to talk about bodies and minds at all in this context. Let's suppose that there were a few scholars who were really interested in discovering the truth about human existence and tackled the question of mind and matter mainly for that purpose. They felt, perhaps, that if they conceptualized a piece of matter like the body that they experience and a piece of something like antimatter called the mind that they could proceed to investigate them by elementalizing them and isolating their properties.

BATESON: But, now look, seriously, for instance, if you take a page of newsprint, the words are not there, you know.

RIEBER: What do you mean not there?

BATESON: On the page.

RIEBER: You mean you put the words there. Is that it?

BATESON: Yes. When I read, I, *in imagination*, put the words there. And so

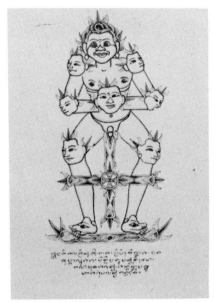

FIGURE 10.1. Illustration No. 4, p. 94, in the *Balinese Character* by Gregory Bateson and Margaret Mead (New York: New York Academy of Sciences, 1942).

FIGURE 10.2.

you see I wouldn't like to talk about the split between that ink and the word on the page, right?

RIEBER: I suppose we will have to, won't we? The distinction of body–mind implies there is something that has a space–time dimension relationship.

BATESON: Is there a relationship between the imagined word-on-the-page and the ink?

RIEBER: I suppose there was at one time, but I'm not sure there is one now.

BATESON: Where is the space between them, and where is the time?

RIEBER: Doesn't everything have to have some spacial and temporal dimension in the real world?

BATESON: I don't think so. Most things don't.

RIEBER: What does not have spacial and temporal factors associated with it?

BATESON: The difference between that shield and the wall.

RIEBER: That's a high level of abstraction, isn't it? I'm not referring to abstractions, I'm referring to real things. I can't perceive the word, "difference".

BATESON: You can't perceive anything but difference.

RIEBER: But difference is just a word, isn't it? I never bumped into a difference on the street, have you?

BATESON: Difference is a mental event. The only thing that can get into your retina is information about a difference. The lowest level of mental operation is the perception of a difference.

RIEBER: When I said that I couldn't understand how anything in the real world did not have some kind of temporal or spacial aspects to it, you disagreed, right? So, you claim that difference is something that has no temporal or spacial aspect to it, and I said difference is only an abstract idea and you agreed. So, it seems then that what we have been talking about is a state between ideas and ways of describing human thought processes or cognition.

BATESON: Right. But you cannot have an interface between matter, on the one hand, and mind, on the other.

RIEBER: Well, I suppose so, but it depends on your definitions.

BATESON: Well, when you pull them apart, that's already a step toward a definition. Having pulled them apart and given them a totally different nature, mind being an abstraction and matter being an abstraction, but arranged in such a way that they can't meet each other. And then when you attempt to understand how they are interfaced with each other, you are up against a blank wall.

RIEBER: So the split between body and mind is a fruitless affair, because you're trying to pull something apart which is already an integrated whole in order to see how it comes back together again. It's like Humpty-Dumpty not being able to be put back together again.

BATESON: Yes, it's like trying to take the print away from the words on the page.

RIEBER: Maybe that's the message intended in Humpty-Dumpty—at least one of the messages.

BATESON: Yes, perhaps it is one of the things that is meant in Humpty-Dumpty. Essentially, Humpty-Dumpty is negative entropy. He is a Gestalt pattern, and if you randomize him all the king's horses and all the king's men couldn't put him back together again.

RIEBER: Ergo, you can't split body and mind. Now, if we take it one step further and ask the following question: What gives us the power to know that we exist as an entity separate from anything else?

BATESON: I know that me touching a book is different from me touching your knee. Is that what you mean by "separate entity"?

RIEBER: Partially. But it goes further than that. For instance, suppose you wake up in the morning, and you feel that it's good to be alive and you're happy that you exist, and you feel your separate existence in a way that completely isolates you from anything else. On the other hand, you may wake up at another time and say that you're not happy to be alive, you do not value your life and do not wish to carry it on, and you wish you could self-destruct. Obviously, these two conditions are dependent upon the way you experience yourself both qualitatively and quantitatively at a given point in time and in a particular circumstance. In other words, what has given us the ability to experience this human condition? It seems to me that the human species is the only one that has the ability to experience this. And if that's true, how did this ability come about?

BATESON: I don't know. But I've given you the first step: the difference between the I that touched the book on the table and the I that touched your knee. Is that not the first step that one has to make toward what you want?

RIEBER: Yes, I suppose it is. Let me reword this by asking what it is about the development of the human organism that enables us to have this rather unique capacity.

BATESON: Obviously, it comes from the ability to distinguish the difference between the book and the knee.

RIEBER: Yes, but how does that capacity grow to the proportion that I described earlier?

BATESON: Are time and space useful abstractions when talking about mind? No.

RIEBER: Then what is a useful abstraction when you're talking about mind?

BATESON: Difference.

RIEBER: What do you mean by "difference"?

BATESON: Difference means an appeal to irritability. I can feel that edge of the table. This is an appeal to irritability. And short of that appeal to irritability, I do not receive information.

RIEBER: Difference has to make a difference, is that the idea?

BATESON: Yes. You can only receive news of those differences which can be made into events in time.

RIEBER: Then the temporal dimension is important when you talk about the mind–body problem because it helps you understand the term "difference."

BATESON: That's true.

RIEBER: But I'll go one step further and say that you also need the term "space" as well, because when you perceive the difference it all takes place in space.

BATESON: But difference is not in space and time.

RIEBER: Where is it then, all in your mind?

BATESON: Precisely. It is all in your mind. It is a mental operation, the perception of the difference. The behaviorists believe that the mind is flat, because they do not believe that perceptual categories are in the mind of organisms.

RIEBER: In other words, they reduce mind to a flat abstraction which they call behavior.

BATESON: It does not belong to the individual. It's not the individual's.

RIEBER: I'm not sure that all behaviorists would agree with that. Nevertheless, you might say that that position does lead them away from the whole individual, or any gestalt for that matter.

BATESON: Precisely. It leads them away from any whole, because the whole is a sum of its parts. In other words, in behaviorism, you don't have two arms, you have an arm and an arm. To have two arms you have to have a *class*.

RIEBER: What then is meant by *the problem* when one refers to the mind–body problem?

BATESON: We have invented or borrowed from Descartes an idea about a separation between something which is of one nature, mind, and something of another nature, body. From there on, I cannot make any sense of anything. But perhaps we were wrong to begin with—there ain't no thing called "mind" or a thing called "body." It's an idea that they made up. Why they made it up I have no idea.

RIEBER: There's an organism.

BATESON: There's an organism. Right!

RIEBER: The organism has a thing called mind and body.

BATESON: No. Well, if you call it mind and body, yes.

RIEBER: But the organism has to have different levels of existence. Does it not?

BATESON: Yes. The "difference" is different from "state."

RIEBER: And these levels of existence somehow got translated into terms like "body" and "mind."

BATESON: I think actually, the step from mind to body is the step from state to difference.

RIEBER: From state to difference?

BATESON: Yes.

RIEBER: "State" means a condition which is dead.

BATESON: But life can only exist in terms of difference. As long as you have difference, that is, the possibility of moving your states, by rubbing them on differences, then you have "mind". You see, it's like a frog in a saucepan of cold water. If its temperature is raised so slowly that at no moment is there a sufficient doc/dt to activate his neurons, he does not jump. There is no time marker to tell him *when* to jump. He gets boiled. He just wasn't that much alive. I hate to tell you what this reflects upon our society.

RIEBER: How does this problem relate to contemporary psychosocial distress?

BATESON: The problem is we think we can maintain a state which we call deterrence by increasing the pace that we make atom bombs. It's very strange and has something directly to do with the mind–body fallacy. They think about the body and mind in terms of one controlling the other. Thus, the phrase "mind over matter." "Mind over matter" or matter over mind"; whichever you say controls the other, the one that you say is not in control will take over.

RIEBER: Then in reality, neither is in control.

BATESON: Precisely, the word "control" is a fake anyway. It's one of those abstractions which is not represented by anything in the real world.

RIEBER: Now, perhaps we're approaching the heart of the matter. The more you look at it, the more it looks like it's all a hoax.

BATESON: A tour de force that didn't quite make it. And then whenever a materialistic phrasing doesn't quite make it, they invent a spiritualistic phrasing that's supposed to make it. And then you get a split between the mind and the body.

RIEBER: Today, on the other hand, we have the epiphenomenalistic position that sees the mind as a by-product of the brain.

BATESON: Yes, there are several "epiphenomenal" approaches around. The first one is spiritualism. Uri Geller is a good example of this. And the other is the one you referred to, namely the mind being a "by-product" of the brain. They're both off base in different ways. You see, the brain is only an idea of the mind. One is as good a statement as the other. And the mind is only a function of the brain.

RIEBER: They appear to be perfect examples of either end of the hoax that we were talking about a moment ago. And that traps you and forces you to choose between the devil and the deep blue sea.

BATESON: Yes. It's just like asking is your allergy mental or physical.

RIEBER: How, then, should the question be phrased so that it is actually answerable?

BATESON: But it isn't a question that's the problem. By making it a question, you make the division of mind and body. If you want to ask the question about the relationship between word and print, that's an interesting question that we're talking about. But once you split mind and body, you can't talk about anything sensibly.

RIEBER: OK then, let's not split mind and body and carry on from there and ask the question of how we study the unity of mind and body, that is, body within mind. Is the scientific method sufficient?

BATESON: Well, the scientific method as devised to study "bits of matter" is not a very good method for studying mental processes. Because you don't have any mental process until matter reaches certain degrees of organization, at which point you get mental processes. The characteristics of that organization, we can now lay down. Now, step one, it is not one chunk. That is, to have that organization, you've got to have multiple parts. The parts themselves are not capable of that organization. That is, you may have a brain that's made of protein, but the carbon atoms in the protein don't think. Second, thinking is a matter of first derivatives of some sort. If you want to talk the language of material matter, you have to jump to derivatives—to dx/dt. In other words, the process depends upon the differences. This is the essence of what Gustav Fechner was talking about with his "just noticeable difference." That is to say, what perception depends upon is essentially difference—contrast or ratio—not state. And it took a hundred years from Fechner to the 1940s to discover the Fechner law on the efferent side of the central nervous system. This was the discovery of Norbert Weiner, namely, that the tension of an isometric muscle is a function of the log of frequency of the stimuli reaching it. This is the same as Fechner's law and still depends upon the difference. This is the second criterion of the aggregate of matter that can show mental process. The third criterion is that in order for the organism to respond to difference, it must have energy stored up ahead of the presentation of the difference. There is no energy in the difference. In other words, there is only negative entropy in the difference. Therefore, you've got to have energy on your side of the counter if you're going to do anything about the difference. For example, if you kick a dog, the dog responds with *his* energy, not with energy from your kick. It goes right through the whole psychology and makes energy an irrelevant consideration. Because the cause does not energize the effect, the cause being a "stimulus." Many stimuli don't exist. For example, a letter which you do *not* get can trigger your responses.

A fourth criterion is that mental process occurs when the trains of causation are circular or more complex. In other words, the lineal system can't make a steady state.

And finally, there are the conceptual levels of abstraction. For example, the name is different from the thing it stands for. And there can be a difference between two differences. And you can combine differences into systems of differences and so on and so forth. The moment you've got all those criteria, you've got mental process.

RIEBER: Is that what you call body and mind relating?

BATESON: Yes, that's the solution to what used to be called the mind–body problem. Mind is no more separate from body than velocity is separate from matter. Or than acceleration is separate from velocity.

RIEBER: Now that we have come this far, what do you think the goal of scientific inquiry should be? Are we making science in our own image?

BATESON: Yes, except that our own image is so inaccurate, that's the problem. You see, I'm a Platonist; you know in the final analysis, I think we should make science in our own image. And our own image should be in the image of science.

RIEBER: But you better get the image right.

BATESON: Ah, that's the trick isn't it? You see, you can always wreck anything. If you have a stomachache, I can tell you "It's only mental." And if you fall in love, I can tell you "It's only physical." Either way, it would really do you no good.

RIEBER: And there are some who think that the whole business is just a delusionary system.

BATESON: Well, I believe it is much healthier on the whole to believe that the physical universe is an illusion and that the mind is real, than to believe that the mind is an illusion and the physical universe is real. But of course, on the whole neither is correct. But believing that the mind is real is one step better than believing that the physical universe is real.

RIEBER: When human beings engage in what we might call the meeting of minds, it seems that the major means of experiencing the phenomenon of differences is via language or communication.

BATESON: Yes, human beings talk.

RIEBER: Yes, they sure do; but they rarely really communicate, do they?

BATESON: I don't know; there was always a problem with two muddleheaded little old ladies. One was a good bridge player, and she managed to teach the other one to be a good bridge player. But no one knew how it happened, because they were both muddleheaded little old ladies.

RIEBER: Maybe the explanation lies in the possibility that one of the muddleheaded little old ladies had the same delusionary system as the other, and that enabled them to communicate and become good bridge players.

BATESON: Precisely, they shared delusionary systems and understood each other very well, but to everybody else, they looked like muddleheaded little old ladies.

BATESON: In order to illustrate a related point here, I conducted the following experiment with my students. I asked them to describe a drawing (Figure 10.3). Here's the object; what's your description of it?

RIEBER: Looks to me like Bateson's foot.

BATESON: That's one species of description, yes. Some called it a "boot". Any other description?

RIEBER: It seems to have no heel and a flat top over the toes and a point at the very end.

BATESON: About 10% go at it that way and describe it as a boot and then, if pushed, will point out the differences of peculiarity of the boot. The toe is bigger than the heel, etc., etc. But then, there are people who say look it's a hexagon and a rectangle, but there is sort of a gap and they're not quite complete. But in reality, there wasn't any hexagon or rectangle; in fact, there wasn't any boot there either.

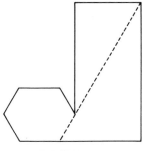

FIGURE 10.3.

Rieber: It's just a bunch of lies, then, I guess. And if it's a boot, it is only a boot because I made it a boot.

Bateson: Yes, because you made it so. But then, there are other people, very ingenious people, who see that there is a line implicitly drawn; that imaginary line completes the hexagon, and that gives them all sorts of internal relations. That enables them to tell the various sizes of the two things, and so forth. These people are the real scientists. This is a demonstration in Maya, the world of illusion in Hinduism. In the final analysis, you make parts in order to make language, in order to understand things so that you can tell what they're like. But while you're making those parts, you should also be knowing that you're making them and that they are not actually real.

Rieber: In what sense do you mean that they are not actually real?

Bateson: They're not like that object, they're on a higher level of abstraction that can't be experienced.

Rieber: What's the purpose of studying differences, as you call it, anyway? What's the ultimate goal?

Bateson: Why study things? Well, partly because they're elegant and partly if you get things wrong it's very dangerous. Study it so that you can know it and therefore not go at it in the wrong way. Why do it? Well, I guess because it's bloody dangerous if you don't.

Rieber: Fine—that's a good note to end on.

The Allan McLane Hamilton Seminars

ERIC T. CARLSON
JACQUES M. QUEN

Body and Mind, edited by Robert W. Rieber, illustrates well the problems and challenges that face those who try to understand the elusive nature of the relationship between the human mind and the body. It is a problem that has vexed humanity throughout written history. To investigate its historical development, however, is no idle exercise of antiquarianism, for most of the issues that have been raised over the years are still alive and pertinent to discussions today; therefore, it is wise to have this book divided into three portions. One section is clearly devoted to historical questions, a second takes a more philosophical view, while a third raises contemporary questions about neurophysiology. At the same time, these three areas overlap and intermingle. What is new to the problem are the biochemical and physiological advances being made in the understanding of the functioning of the central nervous system.

The mind–body problem has been with us since the first human recognized that death removes something, different from the body, that was integral to the living individual. The relationship between the brain and the mind has been a fascinating puzzle for philosophers and psychologists. Psychiatrists have found it an almost insurmountable obstacle in their efforts to study the diseased mind in a manner compatible with a scientific paradigm requiring material that can be weighed, measured, or counted. The mind–body relationship remains the central focus of psychosomatic medicine, which struggles,

253

apparently perpetually, with the question of the transduction of mental phenomena into physical phenomena, and vice versa.

The chapter by Herbert Weiner is a particularly good example of this struggle. He had been chosen to give the first lecture in a series on the mind–body problem because he so ably represented the viewpoint of a modern researcher in psychosomatic medicine, a most useful springboard to a series of historically oriented talks. His chapter and the chapters by Leon Hankoff and Margaret Wilson are presented together here for the first time and are from the Allan McLane Hamilton Seminars on "The Historical Development of the Mind–Body Problems." These lectures were organized by the Section on the History of Psychiatry and the Behavioral Sciences of the Department of Psychiatry of the New York Hospital–Cornell Medical Center.

Although the Section has sponsored informal research seminars for over a decade, it had never launched a cohesive series devoted to one topic, which would be open to all. An opportunity arose when a developmental grant was received from the Josiah Macy, Jr., Foundation, which was intended to strengthen and expand the activities of the Section, enabling it to play an enlarged regional role. In furtherance of this goal, announcements were sent to all psychiatric units in the greater New York area and to all departments of psychology, philosophy, and history. This made an interdisciplinary mixture possible in the list of invited speakers and in the makeup of the audience, a situation that often produced spirited discussions. The seminars were named after Allan McLane Hamilton (1848–1919), the first professor of psychiatry to be appointed at the newly founded Cornell University Medical College (1898) in New York City. Although descended from the distinguished family that included Alexander Hamilton, he was an eminent man in his own right. A famous alienist who often testified in the courtroom, he wrote not only a textbook on jurisprudence, *A Manual of Medical Jurisprudence* (New York: J. R. Bermingham, 1885), but also an informative autobiography, *Recollections of an Alienist, Personal and Professional* (New York: George H. Doran Co., 1916).

The Hamilton Seminars consisted of the following:

Date	Speaker	Topic
10, October 1974	Herbert Weiner, M.D. Professor of Psychiatry Albert Einstein College of Medicine Chairman, Department of Psychiatry Montefiore Hospital New York, New York	Contemporary Research and the Mind–Body Problem
7, November 1974	Leon Hankoff, M.D. Professor of Psychiatry	Body–Mind Concepts in the Ancient Near

	New York Medical College Director of Psychiatry Misericordia Hospital Medical Center New York, New York	East: A Comparison of Egypt and Israel
5, December 1974	Bennett Simon, M.D. Assistant Clinical Professor of Psychiatry Harvard Medical School Boston, Massachusetts	The Discovery of the Mind and the Dis- covery of the Body in Ancient Greece
16, January 1975	George Mora, M.D. Director, Astor Home Rhinebeck, New York Research Associate Yale University New Haven, Connecticut	Mind–Body Concepts in the Middle Ages
27, February 1975	Ivor Leclerc, Ph.D. Professor of Philosophy Emory University Atlanta, Georgia	Renaissance Thought and the Mind-Body Issue
27, March 1975	Margaret Wilson, Ph.D. Professor of Philosophy Princeton University Princeton, New Jersey	Descartes and the Modern Mind–Body Problem
10, April 1975	Lester King, M.D. Book Review Editor *Journal of the American Medical Association* Chicago, Illinois	Mind–Body Problems in the Eighteenth Century
22, May 1975	Otto M. Marx, M.D. Professor of Psychiatry and Socio-Medical Science Boston University School of Medicine Boston, Massachusetts	Body–Mind in Nine- teenth Century Ger- man Psychiatry
12, June 1975	John C. Burnham, Ph.D. Professor of American History Ohio State University Columbus, Ohio	The Mind-Body Problem in the Early Twentieth Century

Subject Index